Cultural Tourism Research Methods

———————————————

FSC
www.fsc.org
MIX
Paper from
responsible sources
FSC® C013604

Cultural Tourism
Research Methods

Edited by

Greg Richards

Department of Leisure Studies
Tilburg University
The Netherlands

and

Wil Munsters

Centre for Cultural Tourism Research
Zuyd University
The Netherlands

www.cabi.org

CABI is a trading name of CAB International

CABI Head Office
Nosworthy Way
Wallingford
Oxfordshire OX10 8DE
UK

Tel: +44 (0)1491 832111
Fax: +44 (0)1491 833508
E-mail: cabi@cabi.org
Website: www.cabi.org

CABI North American Office
875 Massachusetts Avenue
7th Floor
Cambridge, MA 02139
USA

Tel: +1 617 395 4056
Fax: +1 617 354 6875
E-mail: cabi-nao@cabi.org

A catalogue record for this book is available from the British Library,
London, UK

Library of Congress Cataloging-in-Publication Data

Cultural tourism research methods / edited by Greg Richards and
        Wil Munsters. p. cm.
   Includes bibliographical references and index.
   ISBN 978-1-84593-518-4 (alk. paper)
1. Heritage tourism–Research. 2. Tourism–Research. I. Richards,
Greg. II. Munsters, Wil. III. Title.

   G156.5.H47C858 2010
   910.72–dc22

                                                                        2009050370

ISBN: 978 1 84593 518 4

Commissioning editor: Sarah Hulbert
Production editor: Kate Hill

Typeset by AMA Dataset, Preston, UK.
Printed and bound in the UK by Antony Rowe Ltd.

Contents

Contributors

Edit Bárd, PR Manager, Duna Museum, Hungarian Museum of Environmental Protection and Water Administration, Hungary. E-mail: bardedit@mail.dunamus

Esther Binkhorst, Co-creations, C. Angel Vidal 25, 1°, 08870 Sitges, Barcelona, Spain. E-mail: binkhorst.esther@cocreations.es

Francisco Javier Caro-González, Dpto. Administración de Empresas y Marketing, Facultad de CC. Económicas y Empresariales, Av. Ramón y Cajal 1, 41018 Sevilla, Spain. E-mail: fjcaro@us.es

Mario Castellanos-Verdugo, Dpto. Administración de Empresas y Marketing, Facultad de CC. Económicas y Empresariales, Av. Ramón y Cajal 1, 41018 Sevilla, Spain. E-mail: mario@us.es

Miguel Cervantes Blanco, Professor of Marketing, University of Leon, Marketing Area, Business Management and Economy Department, Leon, Spain. E-mail: ddemcb@unileon.es

Jock Collins, Professor, School of Finance and Economics, Faculty of Business, University of Technology, Sydney, 15 Broadway, Ultimo, NSW 2007, Australia. E-mail: jock.collins@uts.edu.au

Simon Darcy, Associate Professor in Events, Sport and Tourism, School of Leisure, Sport and Tourism, Faculty of Business, University of Technology, Sydney, PO Box 222 Lindfield NSW 2070, Australia. E-mail: simon.darcy@uts.edu.au

Teun den Dekker, Co-creations, Bolwaterstraat 23, 5911 GB Venlo (Q4), the Netherlands. E-mail: teun@co-creations.es

Tracey Dickson, Faculty of Business and Government, University of Canberra, Building 6, Room B13, Canberra, Australia. E-mail: tracey.dickson@canberra.edu.au

Deborah Edwards, Faculty of Business, University of Technology, Sydney, PO Box 123, Broadway, NSW 2007, Australia. E-mail: deborah.edwards@uts.edu.au

Jonathan Edwards, Reader, The School of Services Management, Bournemouth University, Fern Barrow, Talbot Campus, Poole, Dorset BH12 5BB, UK. E-mail: jonedwards@bournemouth.ac.uk

Dorothy Fox, Lecturer, Events Management, The School of Services Management, Bournemouth University, Fern Barrow, Talbot Campus, Poole, Dorset BH12 5BB, UK. E-mail: dfox@bournemouth.ac.uk

Júlia Füzi, Xellum Management Consulting, Budapest, 1055 Budapest, Szent István krt. 11. III/30., Hungary. E-mail: jfuzi@xellum.hu

Ana M. González Fernández, University of Leon, Marketing Area, Business Management and Economy Department, Leon, Spain. E-mail: ddeagf@unileon.es

Tony Griffin, Faculty of Business, University of Technology, Sydney, PO Box 123 Broadway, NSW 2007, Australia. E-mail: tony.griffin@uts.edu.au

Bruce Hayllar, Faculty of Business, University of Technology, Sydney, PO Box 123 Broadway, NSW 2007, Australia. E-mail: bruce.hayllar@uts.edu.au

Kirrily Jordan, Research Associate, Faculty of Business, University of Technology, Sydney, 15 Broadway, Ultimo, NSW 2007, Australia. E-mail: kirrily.jordan@student.uts.edu.au

Alison McIntosh, Professor, Department of Tourism Management, Waikato Management School, The University of Waikato, Private Bag 3105, Hamilton, New Zealand. E-mail: info@waikato.ac.nz

Marjan Melkert, Researcher and Consultant, Centre of Expertise for Cultural Tourism, Zuyd University, New Eyckholt 300, PO Box 550, 6400 AN Heerlen, the Netherlands. E-mail: m.melkert@hszuyd.nl

Wil Munsters, Professor of Cultural Tourism, Head of the Centre for Cultural Tourism Research, Zuyd University, Brusselseweg 150, PO Box 634, 6200 AP Maastricht, the Netherlands. E-mail: w.j.munsters@hszuyd.nl

Maria de los Ángeles Oviedo-García, Dpto. Administración de Empresas y Marketing, Facultad de CC. Económicas y Empresariales, Av. Ramón y Cajal 1, 41018 Sevilla, Spain. E-mail: maoviedo@us.es

Xerardo Pereiro, Universidade de Trás-os-Montes e Alto Douro (UTAD), Pólo de Chaves, Avenida Nuno Alvares s/n, Edifício Emperador Flavius, Apartado 61, 5401–909 Chaves, Portugal. E-mail: xperez@utad.pt

László Puczkó, Managing Director and Head of Tourism Section, Xellum Ltd, 1051 Budapest, Október 6. utca 14. V.2., Hungary. E-mail: lpuczko@zellum.hu

Tijana Rakić, Lecturer in Tourism and Events & Deputy Programme Leader for Postgraduate Tourism Programmes, Edinburgh Napier University, School of Marketing, Tourism and Languages, Craiglockhart Campus, Edinburgh, EH14 1DJ, UK. E-mail: t.rakic@napier.ac.uk

Carina Ren, Assistant Professor, Department of Business Communication and Information Science, Centre for Tourism, Innovation and Culture, University of Southern Denmark, Niels Bohrs vej 9, DK-6700 Esbjerg, Denmark. E-mail: ren@sitkom.sdu.dk

Greg Richards, Department of Leisure Studies, Tilburg University, PO Box 90153, 5000 LE Tilburg, the Netherlands. E-mail: g.w.richards@urt.nl

Noel B. Salazar, CuMoRe (Cultural Mobilities Research), Faculty of Social Sciences, University of Leuven, Parkstraat 45, bus 3615, BE-3000 Leuven, Belgium. E-mail: noel.salazar@soc.kuleuven.be

Maria Carmen Rodríguez Santos, Assistant Professor, University of Leon, Marketing Area – Business Management and Economy Department, Leon, Spain. E-mail: ddecrs@unileon.es

Katleen Vos, XIOS Hogeschool Limburg, Campus Hasselt, Vildersstraat 5, 3500 Hasselt, Belgium. E-mail: katleen.vos@xios.be

Keith Wilkes, Acting Dean, The School of Services Management, Bournemouth University, Fern Barrow, Talbot Campus, Poole, Dorset BH12 5BB, UK. E-mail: kwilkes@bournemouth.ac.uk

Gregory Willson, Doctoral Candidate, Department of Tourism Management, Waikato Management School, The University of Waikato, Private Bag 3105, Hamilton, New Zealand. E-mail: gbw2@waikato.ac.nz

Preface

This volume has its roots in the Cultural Tourism Research Project launched in 1991 by the Association for Tourism and Leisure Education (ATLAS). Over the years, this project has involved a large number of researchers from many countries around the globe in undertaking various forms of cultural tourism research. Details of these activities can be found on the website at http://www.tram-research.com/atlas. As outlined in this volume, much of the early research effort was directed at gathering empirical data on the profile of cultural tourists, their motivations and behaviour, mainly through survey research. Although this activity has greatly improved our knowledge of *what* cultural tourists do, recent meetings of the ATLAS Cultural Tourism Research Group have identified a growing dissatisfaction with this more traditional quantitative approach. Critical members, in particular Esther Binkhorst, Marjan Melkert and Katleen Vos, all three of whom are contributors to this volume, therefore began to plead for a qualitative-oriented research philosophy as a breeding ground for methodological innovations which could enrich the field of cultural tourism studies with new insights and perspectives. In 2007 a call for papers was launched among both members of the group and the global cultural tourism research community, resulting in the chapters collected in the current volume. The intention was to focus more attention on the *how* questions relating to cultural tourism research rather than just the *what*. To this end, authors were asked to concentrate on describing the methods used in their research, rather than the findings. They were also asked to reflect on the advantages and disadvantages of the methods used, and the improvements and developments that could be realized by other researchers.

The result is more of a handbook of cultural tourism research methods than a textbook consisting of analysis of case studies. It gives practical illustrations of how specific methods have been applied in the field, rather than explaining the details of specific techniques (which are often described more generally and at greater length elsewhere). The intention is to give (cultural) tourism researchers a clear understanding of the ways in which different methods have been or could be deployed and to help them assess the merits and pitfalls of each. Focusing on the *how*, the index provides an alphabetical overview of the research methods, thus offering a useful aid to discovering parallels and cross-relationships between the applications of methodologies through the different chapters.

We are very grateful to all the researchers for their contributions to the current volume and especially to the members of the ATLAS Cultural Tourism Research Group, either through the chapters published in this collection or through their participation in the research activities of the group in general. The group has always functioned according to open source principles and is constantly seeking to involve new researchers and new initiatives in its projects, with a view to realizing the ideal of a researchers' learning community. We hope that this volume will help to stimulate further discussion about cultural tourism studies and research methods in the years to come.

Greg Richards and Wil Munsters
Tilburg and Maastricht
September 2009

Tables, Boxes, Figures and Appendices

Tables

Boxes

Figures

Appendices

1 Developments and Perspectives in Cultural Tourism Research

Greg Richards and Wil Munsters

Introduction

Cultural tourism is one of the oldest forms of travel and still continues to be a mainstay of the tourism industry in most parts of the world. According to the OECD (2009), cultural tourism accounted for around 40% of all international tourism, or 360 million arrivals in 2007. Although it is often difficult to distinguish these 'culturally motivated tourists' from other travellers because of the growing tendency towards mixed holiday motives, they are particularly desirable for destinations seeking to attract 'high quality' tourism and high value tourists.

As cultural tourists began to arrive in growing numbers and spend relatively large amounts of money, the early research focus was on the economic impact of cultural tourism. In recent years, however, these tourists have increasingly aroused research interest because of the social and cultural dimensions of cultural tourism. Attracting cultural tourists has become a common strategy for countries and regions seeking to conserve traditional cultures, to develop new cultural resources and to create a cultural image (OECD, 2009). Much

cultural tourism research today therefore concentrates on the qualitative nature of the experience and the impact of cultural tourism, both for the tourists themselves and for the places and peoples they visit.

As the interest in cultural tourism research has grown, so has the range of methods and techniques used to explore this phenomenon. As this volume shows, early quantitative, largely survey-based approaches have been increasingly supplemented by more qualitative approaches, drawing on new perspectives on the social, cultural, psychological, anthropological and spatial aspects of cultural tourism. The aim of this book is to review a representative range of innovative approaches to cultural tourism research, illustrating how such methods can help to illuminate different aspects of the complex phenomenon of cultural tourism.

This introductory chapter provides a synopsis of trends in cultural tourism research. In addition to a review of the literature, the chapter refers to the case studies developed in the present volume to illustrate the different paradigms in cultural tourism research and the increasing shift towards qualitative methods.

A Brief Review of Cultural Tourism Research

The fields of cultural tourism research

There has been a dramatic growth in cultural tourism research in recent decades as the search for cultural experiences has become one of the leading motivations for people to travel. The rapid expansion of cultural tourism has attracted the attention of a growing number of researchers and policy makers, vastly increasing the scope of cultural tourism research.

Tourism research in general began to expand rapidly during the 1980s, which saw 'an overall and steady increase in published research on tourism' (Sheldon, 1991: 483). This growth was also reflected in the field of cultural tourism. The cultural tourism bibliography compiled by the Association for Tourism and Leisure Education (ATLAS) Cultural Tourism Research Group indicates that the volume of cultural tourism research has grown considerably in recent decades. The number of sources listed tripled between the early 1990s and the second half of that decade, and in the first 5 years of the new century the level of output remained high (Fig. 1.1).

There are many reasons for this growth in cultural tourism research. The desire of countries and regions to develop cultural tourism and particularly to tap its economic potential has generated more research on cultural tourism markets and the economic impact of cultural tourism. As cultural tourism has grown, so its social and cultural impacts have also become more evident, stimulating an interest in the field from scholars in other disciplines, particularly sociology and anthropology. The desire of regions and cities to distinguish themselves in a globalizing world has produced a raft of studies related to image and identity. The growth of tourism as an area of consumption and experiences has stimulated more research on the consumption patterns of cultural tourists and the psychological mechanisms behind their behaviour. As more cultural tourists start to explore the everyday lives and cultures of the people they visit, there has also been more attention paid to the issue of intercultural communication.

As this analysis of growth factors shows, the field of cultural tourism research has diversified. Many of the early studies of cultural tourism were descriptive, providing demographic and socio-economic profiles of cultural travellers and their behaviour. During the early 1990s there was an explosion in the study of the relationship between tourism and cultural heritage, linked to the discovery of heritage as one of the 'General Motors' of the postmodern economy (Richards, 1996).

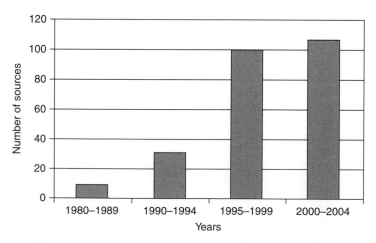

Fig. 1.1. Number of sources listed in the ATLAS Cultural Tourism Bibliography by time period.

In the mid-1990s cultural attractions became major features of the economy of both urban and rural destinations. The 'new cathedrals of consumption' (Ritzer, 1999) depend on being able to attract large numbers of cultural tourists to valorize their cultural content and to maximize economic impacts. The creation of the Guggenheim Museum in Bilbao is perhaps the prime example of such an iconic development strategy (Plaza, 2000), but numerous other locations, including Las Vegas, Abu Dhabi and La Rioja, have also invested in such attractions. This policy of cities and regions to create their own museums as weapons for their economic and marketing arsenal has led to a proliferation of studies on cultural tourism marketing and product development (Munsters, 2007).

Diversification in research topics continued through the 1990s as cultural tourism became linked to contemporary and popular culture (e.g. Hughes, 2000). These new forms of cultural tourism have appeared in both urban and rural environments, because the need to differentiate places and attract inward investment has become more acute (OECD, 2009). In the late 1990s, the link between cultural tourism and cities therefore became even stronger as a wider range of urban cultural and creative resources was utilized for tourism (Bianchini, 1999). Cities such as Amsterdam (Dahles, 1998), Barcelona (Dodd, 1999), Lisbon, Rotterdam, Turin (Russo and van der Borg, 2002) and Sydney (Collins and Kunz, 2007; see also Chapter 8, this volume) all began to deploy a wide range of popular and contemporary cultural resources along with the more traditional heritage product. The diversification of consumption and production into different and more specific forms of culture went on through the early years of the 21st century, as niche markets emerged, including wine tourism (Hall *et al.*, 2000), gastronomic tourism (Hjalager and Richards, 2002), architecture tourism (Lasansky and McLaren, 2004), festival tourism (Robinson *et al.*, 2004) and experiential tourism (Smith, 2006).

Attention was also paid to cultural tourism as performance and how cultural consumption could give symbolic meaning to tourists and tourist sites (Edensor, 1998).

The tourists' experience of different kinds of cultural places was also examined, in terms of the role of both symbolic consumption and production in developing destinations (Herbert, 2001). The development of the 'experience economy' (Pine and Gilmore, 1999) created more interest for the role of visitor experiences in tourism and the way in which destinations could use their cultural resources to develop those experiences (Richards, 2001).

The need to tie culture more closely to the local in the face of global serial reproduction has seen creativity emerge as a major area of cultural tourism research. Creative development strategies can be employed in both urban and rural environments and can use creativity as a direct tourist attraction or as a backdrop to add to the atmosphere of places. That is the reason why the most recent wave of cultural tourism research has been linked to the rise of the creative economy, examining the relationship between tourism, culture and creativity in urban and rural environments (Richards and Wilson, 2007; Wurzburger *et al.*, 2009). The development of creative tourism has also seen research develop into different forms of creativity among tourists, such as language learning (Kennett, 2002) and textile arts (Miettinen, 2007).

The evolution of cultural tourism studies shows obvious parallels to the general development of tourism research as analysed by, amongst others, Xiao and Smith (2006), who note a growing economic and industry orientation in tourism research in the 1980s, followed by an increase of sociocultural studies in the 1990s.

The methods of cultural tourism research

As the concerns of tourism research in general and cultural tourism research in particular have changed, so have the methods employed. In the 1980s cultural tourism research tended towards quantitative work, often in the form of participant surveys submitted to statistical analysis. Examples include Berrol's (1981) work on the motivations of American cultural travellers, the Irish Tourist Board's (1988) development of an inventory of cultural tourism resources in Europe, and Formica and Uysal's (1998) study of the profile of visitors to an Italian festival.

In the early 1990s the discovery of cultural heritage as an economic development tool stimulated many quantitative studies of visitors to heritage sites, again usually based on surveys. Prentice (1993) studied visitors to heritage sites in the UK, and Davies and Prentice (1995) profiled non-consumers of heritage. In the USA, a position paper on cultural tourism was produced by the National Endowment for the Arts (1995), which included a profile of cultural travellers. In Europe, Bywater (1993) drew on a number of quantitative research sources to develop a typology of cultural tourists. In 1991, the ATLAS Cultural Tourism Research Project was launched, with the specific aim of collecting more market information about the profile of cultural tourists and their behaviour. This work is largely based on large-scale surveys of visitors to cultural sites (see Chapter 2, this volume). Another main stream in cultural tourism research concentrated on the economic impact of iconic buildings and mega events (Herrero et al., 2007). These types of cultural tourism studies are usually characterized by a quantitative approach based on economic multiplier methodology and visitor surveys. In recent applications of Pine and Gilmore's (1999) experience economy concept, surveys have still been used to operationalize the different dimensions of the visitor experience (see Chapter 2).

As the 1990s progressed, however, cultural tourism studies became more and more based on qualitative methodology, as research shifted to the social and cultural aspects of cultural tourism production and consumption, particularly as the class-based nature of cultural tourism became evident. Much of this research drew on the work of Bourdieu (1984) relating to the class-based nature of taste and the accumulation of cultural capital. Although Bourdieu's original work was based on large-scale surveys of museum visitors, the later appli-

cations of his ideas in cultural tourism were more often related to qualitative studies, with in-depth interviews as a main research instrument (Richards et al., 2001). Bourdieu's concept of distinction became an important plank in the research on the meaning of cultural tourism consumption and the ways in which this could contribute to building identities for tourists as well as the places they visited (e.g. Richards, 1996).

The multiplication of cultural facilities and events around the globe has stimulated the discussion about the authenticity of different forms of culture used for tourism purposes. Much of this research has been conducted through in-depth interviews with tourists and cultural producers, and increasingly through content analysis of written documents and digital media relating to such features (brochures, websites, etc.). One of the first comprehensive studies was Picard's (1996) work on Bali. Similar analyses of the authenticity of culture have been conducted in Scotland (MacDonald, 1997), New Zealand (McIntosh and Prentice, 1999), North America (Chhabra et al., 2003) and Hong Kong and Macau (McCartney and Osti, 2007).

The volume Tourism, Creativity and Development edited by Richards and Wilson (2007) provides a number of examples of creative development strategies, examined through a range of research methodologies, both quantitative and qualitative, and a range of instruments, including surveys, case studies, in-depth interviews and grounded theory.

The overall trajectory of cultural tourism research therefore describes an arc through different research methodologies and methods. In general, however, the major shift in recent years has been the increasing utilization of qualitative research methods. As cultural tourism has developed, so there has been a desire to understand in greater depth the reasons why people undertake cultural consumption during their holidays and what this behaviour means to them and the attractions and destinations they visit. This has produced a shift towards more qualitative forms of research, often small-scale studies designed to interpret how cultural tourism functions. There has also been a recognition of the importance of intangible factors such as 'atmosphere' and 'liveliness' in attracting tourists, which are difficult to capture using quantitative research methods based on description, measuring and generalization to the whole (statistical) population.

General Aspects of Qualitative Research

Denzin and Lincoln (1994: 2) define qualitative research as:

> multi-method in focus, involving an interpretive, naturalistic approach to its subject matter. This means that qualitative researchers study things in their natural setting, attempting to make sense of, or interpret phenomena in terms of the meanings people bring to them. Qualitative research involves the studied use and collection of a variety of empirical materials, case study, personal experience, introspective, life history, interview, observational, historical, interactional, and visual texts that describe routine and problematic moments and meanings in individuals' life.

Ritchie and Lewis (2003: 5) indicate that 'qualitative methods are used to address research questions that require explanation or understanding of social phenomena and their context'. Riley and Love (2000: 169) argue that the growing use of qualitative methods has effectively represented a paradigm shift in tourism research (Table 1.1).

The emergence of the qualitative research paradigm is evident in the growth of tourism studies based on a qualitative approach (Phillimore and Goodson, 2004). Likewise, Xiao and Smith (2006) indicate that there has been a decline in economically oriented studies and a rise in qualitative studies of socio-cultural issues and community development. Ballantyne *et al.* (2009) confirm that these trends have continued in recent years and interestingly note that there has been a decline in the number of cultural tourism articles in major tourism journals (although this may have much to do with the difficulty of defining 'cultural tourism'). On the other hand, Riley and Love (2000: 180) argue that 'there is little doubt that the "dominant" paradigm is positivism' and Tribe (2006) also states that most tourism research is still economics-based, which favours a quantitative approach.

Table 1.2 indicates that the pace of change in qualitative research has accelerated over time. It is noteworthy that in recent times qualitative researchers have tended to consider their research as 'sites for critical conversations about democracy, race, gender, class, nation, freedom and community' (Denzin and Lincoln, 2005: 14–20) and focus on the analysis of the performative dimension of their research, in order to understand their participation in the macro- and micro-politics of meaning making, serves as a primary consideration in conducting qualitative research.

In the third edition of Denzin and Lincoln (2005), among the new methods added to their review of the field were: indigenous inquiry, critical humanism and queer theory, performance ethnography, focus groups and critical pedagogy, cultural and investigative poetics, qualitative evaluation and social policy, Foucault's methodologies and online ethnography.

Qualitative Research in Tourism Studies

Qualitative tourism research remains fairly basic and does not go beyond the third phase

Table 1.1. Changes in basic beliefs: dominant paradigms versus emergent paradigms.

Dominant paradigm from	Emergent paradigm toward
Simple	Complex
Hierarchy	Heterarchy
Mechanical	Holographic
Determinate	Indeterminate
Linearly causal	Mutually causal
Assembly	Morphogenesis
Objective	Perspective

Table 1.2. The historical development of qualitative research (based on Denzin and Lincoln, 2005).

Period	Methodological shift
Traditional period (early 1900s to WWII)	'Objective' accounts reflecting the positivist paradigm
Modernist phase (post-WWII–1970s)	Formalization of qualitative methods, rigorous qualitative studies of important social processes
Blurred genres (1970–1986)	Employment of a wide range of paradigms, methods and strategies
Crisis of representation (mid-1980s)	Search for new models of truth, method and representation
Postmodern period of experimental ethnographic writing (1990–2004)	Making sense of crisis of representation through new compositions of ethnography, representations of the 'Other' and repressed voices
Post-experimental enquiry (1995–2000)	Experimentation with novel forms of expressing lived experience, including literary, poetic, autobiographical and multivoiced
Methodologically contested period (2000–2004)	Tension, conflict, methodological retrenchment
The future (2005–)	Methodological backlash associated with 'Bush science' and the evidence-based social movement

of the qualitative research evolution model put forward by Denzin and Lincoln (2005). This observation indicates that tourism research in general, and cultural tourism research in particular, have some way to go. In particular, Ateljevic *et al.* (2007) argue the need for critical perspectives in tourism research. In the same volume, Chambers identifies the four principles of critical theory as being interdisciplinary, reflective, dialectical and critical. In her review of tourism research, she concludes that in much work 'there is an absence of any sort of critical reflection on the paradigmatic assumptions on which the research is based' (Chambers, 2007: 115). However, there are now some signs that tourism research is beginning to move ahead. Xiao and Smith (2006: 498), for example, ascertain that more attention has been paid to methodology in tourism journals in recent years:

> Citations of methodology-related headwords have consistently risen over the years. These include cross-references to theory (58 citations), model (57), multiplier (24), ethnography (14), multidisciplinary approach (10), comparative study (7), and case study (5). In addition, several special issues were devoted to methodological topics in sociology, geography, anthropology, social

psychology, methodology, semiotics, and gender/feminist studies. These special issues have helped foster theoretical constructs and the use of methodology in interdisciplinary research.

The breadth of approaches to the study of tourism suggests that the methodological field is not simply divided into qualitative and quantitative research traditions. As Fielding (2003: 526) notes 'The idea of qualitative method as an antidote to positivism both oversimplifies positivism (logical positivism contains idealist and even relativist elements) and ignores the positivist strands in qualitative research'.

The growing range of methods employed and the increasing tendency towards mixed and multiple research methods mean that there is a growing range of tools available to the cultural tourism researcher. The research areas covered by the current volume therefore include a wide range of methods. The different chapters illustrate applications of existing quantitative and qualitative research methods to the cultural tourism fields of study, such as surveys, in-depth interviews and participative observation, but also innovative research approaches and techniques are applied, varying from monitoring, audits and visitor-tracking studies to Internet-based research methods.

Aims and Objectives of the Current Volume

This volume has been compiled to help fill a gap that was identified within the framework of the ATLAS Cultural Tourism Research Project (see Chapter 2). Since 1991, this project has generated a large amount of data and analysis of the behaviour, activities and motivations of cultural tourists around the world (Richards 1996, 2001, 2007). Although our knowledge about the profile of the cultural tourist has grown, it has also, however, become increasingly obvious where the gaps in the research programme currently lie. In particular, there has been a concentration on quantitative methods in order to analyse *what* cultural tourism is and *what* cultural tourists do. At recent ATLAS meetings, members of the group presented an analysis of future research needs, particularly emphasizing the need for qualitative and innovative research techniques to deepen and enhance our knowledge of cultural tourism. In essence, the research questions need to be extended from the *what* towards the *how* of cultural tourism research.

In dealing with the *how* of cultural tourism research, this volume does not seek to engage with detailed debates about research methodologies, nor is it an exhaustive handbook of research methods, substantial coverage of which is available elsewhere. This book seeks to provide a 'taster' of different research approaches, which can stimulate researchers to look at different methods and apply them, broadening the field of cultural tourism research. It provides concrete examples of how a range of methods have been applied and considers their strengths and weaknesses.

In moving from *what* to *how* in cultural tourism, we are also less concerned with defining what cultural tourism is. This issue has been debated at length elsewhere (e.g. Richards, 2001), and as the Australian Bureau of Statistics (2001) argues:

Given the broad range of views on what constitutes cultural tourism, it appears that the feasibility of developing an agreed definition for cultural tourism is not high ... We believe that ideally an agreed definition would be used by all those undertaking research in the area; the existence of such a definition would improve the comparability of results across studies and across time. However, the existence of an agreed definition is not vital. Instead, research that is relevant and fit for purpose that makes use of a valid measure of cultural tourism can still further our understanding of cultural tourism in Australia.

We would tend to agree with the sentiment that defining cultural tourism is not a prerequisite for conducting research. This also seems to hold for the majority of the authors in the current volume, few of whom have specified a definition of cultural tourism. As Richards (Chapter 2) suggests, perhaps the most practical approach is to let the tourists themselves subjectively define the type of tourism they are engaged in while consuming culture.

Review of Chapters in the Current Volume

The chapters in this volume provide a range of examples of how research in cultural tourism has been conducted and the types of methodological approaches which have been used. The chapters are grouped according to the methodological approaches adopted, covering quantitative, qualitative and mixed methods, according to the disciplinary focus chosen by the authors.

In this chapter, an introduction is given to the evolution of methods in the tourism field as a whole and cultural tourism research in particular. In Chapter 2, Greg Richards argues that surveys of visitors to cultural locations have made an important contribution to our knowledge of cultural tourism. He describes the ATLAS Cultural Tourism Research Project, analysing how surveys have been used to investigate a number of key concepts in the field of cultural tourism, including cultural capital of the tourist and the nature of the cultural tourist experience. He illustrates how concepts can be operationalized through questionnaires and highlights the challenges of questionnaire design, sampling and data analysis.

In Chapter 3, Marjan Melkert and Katleen Vos examine the contribution made to cultural tourism research by other disciplines and methodological approaches. In particular they try to sketch a theoretical framework for cultural tourism research, reviewing the many different quantitative and qualitative methodologies that have been adopted in the field. Examining the sources of knowledge relating to cultural tourism, they argue for a multidisciplinary approach and in particular emphasize the need to select the methodological approach best suited to the problem at hand.

Esther Binkhorst, Teun den Dekker and Marjan Melkert extend the argument for a mixed methodological approach further in Chapter 4, by arguing that the starting point for research in tourism should be the human being, placed in relation to a specific time–spatial context. This approach leans on the ethnographic perspective and argues that in a world of blurring boundaries between culture, tourism, work, leisure and other fields of human activity, one has to examine the 'experience environment' of the tourist. This context consists of all the people and phenomena that surround and interact with the tourist. As the very nature of 'cultural tourism' is compromised by the increased blurring of boundaries between tourism and culture, it is more sensible to consider the values attached to such behaviour, their ontological status and the question as to how the value of things is determined. They argue that one should take not just subjective or objective standpoints, but rather accept that there is value in mixing these two standpoints. They examine a range of new methods that can be used to examine the increasingly blurred boundaries of cultural tourism consumption and production.

Part II deals with mixed qualitative–quantitative approaches in cultural tourism studies. In Chapter 5, Wil Munsters shows how the ATLAS surveys have been developed and extended to produce a 'cultural destination experience audit', based primarily on surveys with cultural tourists and observation by means of mystery tourist visits to service providers. The audit makes it possible to measure the visitor's experience in a particular cultural destination by combining different perspectives on visitor experience through triangulation.

László Puczkó, Edit Bárd and Júlia Füzi examine a combination of three different research tools in their study of an open-air museum in Hungary in Chapter 6. Questionnaires served to gather information on visitor profiles and behaviour, while visit time diaries were used to map visitor flows and time spent in different parts of the park and photo diaries analysed how visitors perceive the different elements of the museum as well as the image of the whole.

In Chapter 7, 'grand tour' questions are used by Dorothy Fox, Jonathan Edwards and Keith Wilkes as an aid to understanding garden visiting. Following Spradley's developmental sequence, they illustrate how 'grand tour'-type questions can be used to develop a richer understanding of visitor motivation and behaviour. They trace the different steps of the research process, including informant location, the interview, the ethnographic record and posing descriptive questions. Resident and garden visitor surveys were then combined with ethnographic interviews to examine the basis of decision making in garden visitation.

Jock Collins, Simon Darcy and Kirrily Jordan illustrate the use of mixed methods to study ethnic precincts in Sydney, Melbourne and Perth (Australia) in Chapter 8. Surveys of visitors to ethnic precincts were used to examine the impressions, expectations and activities of cultural tourists. The surveys were supplemented with in-depth key informant interviews, and photos were used to collect images of the ethnic iconography and ethnic façades of the precincts. Data on the public representations of the precincts were collected from annual reports, corporate plans, brochures, advertising and newspaper articles.

In Chapter 9, Deborah Edwards, Tracey Dickson, Tony Griffin and Bruce Hayllar review methods for analysing visitors' spatial behaviour, including large surveys, traffic and people counts, travel or trip diaries and observation. They show how GPS technology now makes it possible to accurately track the paths visitors are taking and to provide greater understanding of their socio-spatial behaviour. A study conducted in two Australian cities, Sydney and Canberra, illustrates the use of a number of methods including GPS tracking, photography, a photo-sharing website, questionnaires and debriefing interviews.

Part III of this volume presents a number of qualitative approaches to cultural tourism research. Grounded theory is used by Mario Castellanos-Verdugo, Francisco J. Caro-González and M. de los Ángeles Oviedo-García in Chapter 10 to analyse the attitudes of residents to tourist activity. Grounded theory enables researchers to integrate information from a wide variety of sources. In this case semi-structured interviews with key informants are combined with the analysis of secondary data and observation at public events. The different data sources were combined using Atlas.ti software. The chapter compares and contrasts the findings produced by the different research tools and illustrates how a combined methodology can yield richer data about the attitudes of different actors towards tourism.

Video is a visual tool that is being more widely used in the social sciences. In Chapter 11, Tijana Rakić argues that video can be used alongside traditional research methods in innovative ways in order to create new visual knowledge in the field of cultural tourism. She draws on examples from a video made at the Athenian Acropolis, showing how this illuminates not only visitor motivations, perceptions and experiences but also facilitates the study of visitor movements and practices. The chapter also discusses the ethical issues of the use of video as well as the 'fit' between video and the methodological underpinnings of different research approaches.

In Chapter 12, Gregory Willson and Alison McIntosh illustrate the use of a hierarchical probing technique based on the laddering theory applied in marketing research, coupled with the use of photographs to facilitate greater emotional responses from tourists. They show how such techniques can help to elicit more information on the multi-layered meanings given to cultural experiences by tourists.

Ana González Fernández, María Carmen Rodríguez Santos and Miguel Cervantes Blanco also use visual materials to research the images of residents and visitors of the city of León in Spain in Chapter 13. Using the qualitative technique of collage, they analyse the cognitive image of the city and atmosphere perceived by residents and tourists. They demonstrate how collage techniques can provide non-verbal information and can be used to overcome communication barriers.

Part IV of the book deals with ethnographic and relational approaches to cultural tourism research. In Chapter 14, Xerardo Pereiro first reviews the epistemological, methodological and technical underpinnings of anthropological research and then considers the integration of anthropological research methods into the field of cultural tourism. In applying these methods to the study of tourism development among the Kuna people of Panama, he illustrates their strengths and weaknesses.

In Chapter 15, Noel B. Salazar shows how a 'glocal ethnography' approach can capture the details of local cultural tourism complexities while at the same time paying attention to global processes and actors. Examining the role of local guides in Indonesia, he draws on a wide range of local and global information sources to relate the lived reality of the guides with supralocal processes. Such holistic approaches can arguably help to uncover many of the important processes taking place at the 'glocal' level of cultural tourism.

Chapter 16 presents an actor–network approach to cultural tourism studies by Carina Ren. It is argued that understanding tourism places as heterogeneous networks or 'tourismscapes' helps to connect

Table 1.3. Overview of the qualitative methods referred to in this volume.

Data collection

Category of method	Type of method	Subtype of method	Chapter(s) in this volume
Textual methods	Diary	Researcher-employed diary	11
		Visitor-employed diary	6
Oral methods	In-depth interview		8, 11, 14, 15
		Semi-structured interview	5, 10, 15
		Unstructured interview	7
		Photo-based interview	12
		Laddering	12
Visual and audio-visual methods	Observation		10
		Participant observation	14, 15
		Participant observation, overt and covert	11
		Tool = researcher-employed video	
		Structured participant observation	5
		Tool = mystery tourist	
		Researcher-employed photography	12
		Visitor-employed photography	6, 9
	Collage technique		13

Data analysis

Content analysis			8, 9, 12
Thematic analysis supported by qualitative data-analysis software			7
Semiotic analysis			9
Qualitative factorial analysis			13
Comparative method			14
Geotagging			9
Descriptive–explorative theories; actor–network theory			16

Simultaneous data collection and analysis

Theory generation by induction: grounded theory • theoretical sampling • constant comparison method supported by qualitative data analysis software			10

global and local perspectives. The chapter illustrates the analysis of tourism through socio-material methods that attempt to capture the complexity of relationships between actors and networks. It shows how such complexities can be traced through the example of a local Polish cheese and its relations to cultural tourism systems.

Table 1.3 provides an overview of the different qualitative methods covered in the different chapters in this volume.

In Chapter 17, Wil Munsters and Greg Richards analyse, synthesize and evaluate the principal elements of the methodological approaches presented in the volume.

References

Ateljevic, I., Pritchard, A. and Morgan, N. (eds) (2007) *The Critical Turn in Tourism Studies: Innovative Research Methodologies*. Elsevier, London.

Australian Bureau of Statistics (2001) Cultural tourism statistics. Available at: /www.culturaldata.gov.au/publications/statistics_working_group/cultural_tourism/cultural_tourism_statistics (accessed 25 June 2009).

Ballantyne, R., Packera, J. and Axelsena, M. (2009) Trends in tourism research. *Annals of Tourism Research* 36, 149–152.

Berrol, E. (1981) Culture and the arts as motives for American travel. *Proceedings 12th Annual Travel and Tourism Research and Marketing Conference*, Salt Lake City, Utah, pp. 199–200.

Bianchini, F. (1999) The relationship between cultural resources and tourism policies for cities and regions. In: Dodd, D. and van Hemel, A.-M. (eds) *Planning Cultural Tourism in Europe*. Boekman Foundation, Amsterdam, pp. 78–90.

Bourdieu, P. (1984) *Distinction: a Social Critique of the Judgement of Taste*. Routledge, London.

Bywater, M. (1993) The market for cultural tourism in Europe. *Travel and Tourism Analyst* 6, 30–46.

Chambers, D. (2007) Interrogating the 'critical' in critical approaches to tourism research. In: Ateljevic, I., Pritchard, A. and Morgan, N. (eds) *The Critical Turn in Tourism Studies: Innovative Research Methodologies*. Elsevier, London, pp. 105–119.

Chhabra, D., Healy, R. and Sills, E. (2003) Staged authenticity and heritage tourism. *Annals of Tourism Research* 30, 702–719.

Collins, J. and Kunz, P. (2007) Ethnic entrepreneurs, ethnic precincts and tourism: the case of Sydney, Australia. In: Richards, G. and Wilson, J. (eds) *Tourism, Creativity and Development*. Routledge, London, pp. 201–214.

Dahles, H. (1998) Redefining Amsterdam as a tourist destination. *Annals of Tourism Research* 25, 55–69.

Davies, A. and Prentice, R. (1995) Conceptualizing the latent visitor to heritage attractions. *Tourism Management* 16, 491–500.

Denzin, N.K. and Lincoln Y.S. (eds) (1994) *Handbook of Qualitative Research*, 1st edn. Sage, London.

Denzin, N.K. and Lincoln Y.S. (eds) (2005) *Handbook of Qualitative Research*, 3rd edn. Sage, London.

Dodd, D. (1999) Barcelona the cultural city: changing perceptions. In Dodd, D. and van Hemel, A.M. (eds) *Planning European Cultural Tourism*. Boekman Foundation, Amsterdam, pp. 53–64.

Edensor, T. (1998) *Tourists at the Taj: Performance and Meaning at a Symbolic Site*. Routledge, London.

Fielding, N.G. (2003) The norm and the text: Denzin and Lincoln's handbooks of qualitative method. *British Journal of Sociology* 50, 525–534.

Formica, S. and Uysal, M. (1998) Market segmentation of an international cultural–historical event in Italy. *Journal of Travel Research* 36, 16–24.

Hall, C.M., Sharples, L., Cambourne, B. and Macionis, N. (eds) (2000) *Wine Tourism Around the World: Development, Management and Markets*. Butterworth–Heinemann, London.

Herbert, D. (2001) Literary places, tourism and the heritage experience. *Annals of Tourism Research* 28, 312–333.

Herrero, L.C., Sanz, A., Devesa, M., Bedate, A. and del Barrio, M.J. (2007) Economic impact and social performance of cultural macrofestivals. In: Richards, G. (ed.) *Cultural Tourism: Global and Local Perspectives*. Haworth Press, Binghamton, New York, pp. 303–328.

Hjalager, A.-M. and Richards, G. (eds) (2002) *Tourism and Gastronomy*. Routledge, London.

Hughes, H. (2000) *Arts, Entertainment and Tourism*. Butterworth–Heinemann, London.

Irish Tourist Board (1988) Inventory of cultural tourism resources in the member states and assessment of methods used to promote them. DG VII, European Commission, Brussels.

Kennett, B. (2002) Language learners as cultural tourists. *Annals of Tourism Research* 29, 557–559.

Lasansky, D.M. and McLaren, B. (2004) *Architecture and Tourism: Perception, Performance and Place*. Berg Publishers, Oxford, UK.

Macdonald, S. (1997) A people's story: heritage, identity and authenticity. In: Rojek, C. and Urry, J. (eds) *Touring Cultures: Transformations of Travel and Theory*. Routledge, London, pp. 154–175.

McCartney, G. and Osti, L. (2007) From cultural events to sport events: a case study of cultural authenticity in the dragon boat races. *Journal of Sport & Tourism* 12, 25–40.

McIntosh, A.J. and Prentice, R.C. (1999) Affirming authenticity – consuming cultural heritage. *Annals of Tourism Research* 26, 589–612.

Miettinen, S. (2007) *Designing the Creative Tourism Experience*. University of Art and Design, Helsinki.

Munsters, W. (2007) *Cultuurtoerisme*, 4th edn. Garant, Antwerp–Apeldoorn, Belgium.

National Endowment for the Arts (1995) *Cultural Tourism in the United States*. A position paper for the White House Conference on Travel and Tourism. Washington, DC.

OECD (2009) *The Impact of Culture on Tourism*. OECD, Paris.

Phillimore, J. and Goodson, L. (2004) *Qualitative Research in Tourism: Ontologies, Epistemologies and Methodologies*. Routledge. London.

Picard, M. (1996) *Bali: Cultural Tourism and Touristic Culture*. Archipelago Press, Singapore.

Pine, B.J. and Gilmore, J.H. (1999) *The Experience Economy*. Harvard University Press, Boston, Massachusetts.

Plaza, B. (2000) Evaluating the influence of a large cultural artifact in the attraction of tourism: the Guggenheim Museum Bilbao case. *Urban Affairs Review* 36, 264–274.

Prentice, R. (1993) *Tourism and Heritage Attractions*. Routledge, London.

Richards, G. (1996) *Cultural Tourism in Europe*. CAB International, Wallingford, UK.

Richards, G. (2001) *Cultural Attractions and European Tourism*. CAB International, Wallingford, UK.

Richards, G. (2007) *Cultural Tourism: Global and Local Perspectives*. Haworth Press, Binghamton, New York.

Richards, G. and Wilson, J. (2007) *Tourism, Creativity and Development*. Routledge, London.

Richards, G., Goedhart, S. and Herrijgers, C. (2001) The cultural attraction distribution system. In: Richards, G. (ed.) *Cultural Attractions and European Tourism*. CAB International, Wallingford, UK, pp. 71–89.

Riley, R. and Love, L. (2000) The state of qualitative tourism research. *Annals of Tourism Research* 27, 164–187.

Ritchie, J. and Lewis, J. (2003) *Qualitative Research Practice. A Guide for Social Science Students and Researchers*. Sage, London.

Ritzer, G. (1999) *Enchanting the Disenchanted World: Revolutionizing the Means of Consumption*. Pine Forge Press, Thousand Oaks, California.

Robinson, M., Picard, D. and Long, P. (2004) Festival tourism: producing, translating and consuming expression of culture(s). *Event Management* 8, 187–190.

Russo, A.P. and van der Borg, J. (2002) Planning considerations for cultural tourism: a case study of four European cities. *Tourism Management* 23, 631–637.

Sheldon, P. (1991) An authorship analysis of tourism research. *Annals of Tourism Research* 18, 473–484.

Smith, W.L. (2006) Experiential tourism around the world and at home: definitions and standards. *International Journal of Services and Standards* 2, 1–14.

Tribe, J. (2006) The truth about tourism. *Annals of Tourism Research* 33(2), 360–381.

Wurzburger, R., Aageson, T., Pattakos, A. and Pratt, S. (2009) *Creative Tourism: a Global Conversation*. Sunstone Press, Santa Fe, New Mexico.

Xiao, H. and Smith, S.L.J. (2006) The making of tourism research: insights from a social sciences journal. *Annals of Tourism Research* 33, 490–507.

2 The Traditional Quantitative Approach. Surveying Cultural Tourists: Lessons from the ATLAS Cultural Tourism Research Project

Greg Richards

Introduction

The practice of conducting surveys of cultural tourists is well established in tourist destinations around the world. Surveys can provide a useful means of studying visitor activities, motivations, behaviour and expenditure. Although surveys and other quantitative methods of research are often regarded with disdain by proponents of qualitative approaches, surveys are often the only way to gauge the relative role of cultural tourism in a destination or the prevalence of cultural tourism consumption in the population as a whole. Surveys also provide a useful means of monitoring trends over time – a vital concern in a fast-moving consumer marketplace.

This chapter reviews some of the key issues in doing survey research in cultural tourism through the lens of the Association for Tourism and Leisure Education (ATLAS) Cultural Tourism Research Project, probably the largest and longest-running global research project in cultural tourism. The aim of this analysis is to illustrate the advantages and disadvantages of survey methods in cultural tourism, to highlight some common problems of these methods, to illustrate the influence of questionnaire design on responses and to demonstrate the way in which questions can be used to operationalize specific theoretical concepts related to cultural tourism.

The ATLAS Cultural Tourism Research Project

ATLAS is an international network of institutes in the field of education and research in tourism, leisure and culture. ATLAS grew from an initial group of 18 European member universities to a network of around 300 organizations in over 70 countries worldwide by 2009 (http://www.atlas-euro.org). The Cultural Tourism Research Project was launched in 1991, with the support of the Tourism Unit of the European Commission. The research focused originally on visitors to cultural attractions in the European Union (EU), but the scope of the research has increased to cover first Central and Eastern Europe and more recently Africa, Asia, Australasia and Latin America as well. The original aims of the research programme were to:

1. Devise definitions of the nature and scope of cultural tourism.
2. Collect data on cultural tourism visits to European attractions.
3. Assess the profile and motivations of cultural tourists.

4.   Develop case studies of cultural tourism management.

Many of these aims were at least partially fulfilled in the first phase of the research programme, which was undertaken in 1991–1993, and the results of which were published in Richards (1996). The initial visitor surveys covered 6300 interviews with visitors to 26 cultural attractions in 9 countries.

The visitor research was repeated in 1997, with over 8000 surveys at 50 sites in 9 European countries. Some initial results of these surveys have been published in Richards (1998, 1999, 2001). The 1997 research was expanded in scope to include countries then outside the EU (Hungary, Poland) and to include more 'popular culture' attractions and events. The notion of 'culture' covered by the 1997 research is therefore somewhat broader than in the 1992 research (Richards, 2001).

A third survey wave was carried out between 1999 and 2001 and the scope of the research was again expanded to include more information on marketing issues and to include countries outside Europe for the first time. The fourth major wave of surveys was conducted in 2004–2005, extending the research to Latin America for the first time. Since then, the research instrument has been redesigned to be used over a longer period of time, and a smaller number of surveys were completed each year in the period 2006–2008. In total, over 40,000 surveys are now in the ATLAS database, and a project is underway to compare the different data sets longitudinally (Table 2.1).

The survey programme was originally designed to answer the basic question: 'who are the cultural tourists?'. The research programme has progressively addressed different aspects of cultural visitor behaviour. In 1997 the focus was on motivations and the position of cultural visitation within overall leisure and tourism consumption. Statements relating to cultural motivations were added, which were developed through the study of 'new producers' by Saskia Goedhart (1997). The theoretical perspectives that were introduced into the research included Bourdieu's (1984) notion of cultural capital. Different aspects of Bourdieu's analysis of cultural consumption were operationalized in the motivational statements included in the questionnaire, including the effect of socialization and the link between occupation, cultural capital and cultural tourism.

For the research undertaken in 1999–2000, it was decided to concentrate more on the marketing aspects of cultural visitation. Questions were added on sources of information about the attractions visited and the point at which the decision to visit the attraction was taken. This last question was also added to examine the type of 'markers' being used by tourists in visiting cultural sites (Leiper, 1990).

Since 1994 the cultural visitor surveys have been supplemented by a series of specific studies on different aspects of cultural tourism, mainly conducted by students at Tilburg University or participating in the Programme in European Leisure Studies (PELS). These studies have covered the motivation of cultural visitors (Roetman, 1994; van 't Riet, 1994), the role of new cultural intermediaries or new producers in the production of cultural attractions (Goedhart, 1997), the policies of European cities regarding cultural

Table 2.1. Surveys completed in the ATLAS Cultural Tourism Research Project 1992–2008.

Date	Surveys	Sites/events	World regions
1992	6,300	26	Western Europe
1997	8,268	58	Western and Eastern Europe
1999–2001	12,197	120	Asia, Africa, Australasia, Europe
2004–2005	5,569	35	Asia, Africa, Australasia, Europe, Latin America
2006	3,769	26	Europe, Australasia
2007	4,666	20	Asia, Europe, Latin America
2008	3,003	17	Europe, Latin America
Total	*43,772*	*302*	

and heritage tourism (Green, 2001) and the role of tour operators in developing cultural destinations (Herrijgers, 1998).

Many other members of the ATLAS research programme have also contributed to the development of the survey and its application in different situations. Öter and Özdoğan (2005) employed the ATLAS questionnaire to analyse the destination image of cultural tourists visiting the Selçuk–Ephesus area, which houses a famous archaeological site. Pereiro (2005) examined the profile and behaviour of tourists in the rural areas of north-east Portugal, paying particular attention to visitors to ecomuseums and other rural cultural sites. Kastenholz *et al.* (2005) analysed the different segments of cultural tourists visiting the historic city of Coimbra in central Portugal. Richards and Wilson (2004) used the ATLAS data to examine the impact of the European Cultural Capital event on the image of Rotterdam and other cities. Binkhorst (2007) used the surveys to analyse the development of 'creative tourism' in the Spanish resort of Sitges. Isaac (2008) also used the ATLAS questionnaire in his study of the behaviour of cultural tourists in the Netherlands. All of these studies extended or enriched our understanding of cultural tourists in some way, achieving a range of different research goals by utilizing the same basic research instrument.

Because of the many different research perspectives involved, the definition of cultural tourism also evolved during the research programme, in line with the expanding horizons of our knowledge of cultural tourism consumption. Originally we began with a technical definition, which facilitated the fieldwork. A conceptual definition was devised to describe the nature of cultural tourism itself, which we viewed as being focused on the motivations of tourists (Richards, 1996). This conceptual definition was also more suited to the types of qualitative research approaches that evolved as the programme developed.

Technical definition of cultural tourism: all movements of persons to specific cultural attractions, such as heritage sites, artistic and cultural manifestations, arts and drama outside their normal place of residence.

Conceptual definition of cultural tourism: the movement of persons to cultural attractions away from their normal place of residence, with the intention to gather new information and experiences to satisfy their cultural needs.

Since these definitions were published there has been some comment made on them by other researchers. For example, Alzua *et al.* (1998: 3) have argued that because 'intention is a complex concept to measure' it would be better to use a scale of tourist motivations, such as that incorporated in Silberberg's (1995) definition of 'visits by persons from outside the host community motivated wholly or in part by interest in the historical artistic, scientific or lifestyle/heritage offerings of a community, region, group or institution'. Our research has shown that it is hard to find a tourist who is not interested at least in part in some aspect of the culture of the destination they are visiting. The point about using intent as a distinguishing feature is to differentiate between the 'culturally motivated' visitor, who makes a conscious, mindful decision to consume culture on holiday, and the 'culturally interested' visitor, who may be almost an accidental cultural tourist (Bywater, 1993). This is a dimension of cultural tourism behaviour later developed further by McKercher and Du Cros (2002).

Marciszewska (2001) also suggested that the definition of cultural tourism should include a consideration of wants and desires as well as cultural needs. As Leiper (1990: 373) has pointed out, needs are the underlying factors influencing tourist motivations to visit attractions, 'but a single need might be expressed in dozens of different motivations and wants and, conversely, a single want might reflect any of several different needs'. An analysis of wants and desires may be useful for a practical discussion about the consumption of individual attractions, but this does not provide a sound basis for the definition of the phenomenon of cultural tourism. The use of needs as the basis of motivations also relates more closely to the findings of tourism motivation studies, which have consistently identified the need for learning and new experiences as one of the core tourist motivations.

Research methodology

It is clear that the basic methodology adopted in the early phases of the ATLAS Project was positivist and quantitative. Although more qualitative approaches have developed over the life of the programme, the bulk of the research effort remains focused in this direction. In addition to the need for a comparative approach, and other issues outlined in the following section, the methodological focus was also determined to some extent by the way in which the data were collected. Most of the research partners use students to undertake face-to-face interviews, often as part of a research methods course. The quantitative approach makes it relatively easy to work with large groups of students to collect, process and analyse the data. The ATLAS surveys also have the benefit of allowing students to compare their results with those of other locations in their own or in other countries.

Research instrument

The transnational nature of the original survey meant that the development of a standard research instrument was crucial. The basic survey questionnaire was developed for the 1992 survey and has subsequently been revised in the light of experience and as new aspects have been added to the research programme. The same basic questionnaire was used by all the survey participants. The English language version of the questionnaire used in the period 2007–2009 is shown in Appendix 2.1. The English language questionnaire was used by the survey team to produce versions of the questionnaire in different languages. In 1997 the questionnaire was translated into Dutch, Finnish, French, German, Hungarian, Italian, Polish, Spanish and Swedish. The translations were made by native speakers who were also familiar with the research programme. In each case the wording and the order of the questions was left as close to the original English text as possible.

Although there are obviously problems involved with conducting transnational research on this scale and without structural funding, there is no doubt that the project has generated important research data that are not available from other sources. The following sections go on to look at the process of actually implementing the research, looking both at issues of a general nature and at specific problems encountered in the ATLAS research.

The Process of Survey Research

In any survey research project there are a number of basic steps that have to be undertaken:

- developing research questions;
- operationalizing concepts;
- questionnaire design;
- sampling;
- implementation of the questionnaire; and
- analysis.

Defining the research question

The essential first step in any piece of research is to define the problem being addressed. In most cases, this will be related to a gap in our knowledge, which leads the researcher to ask questions about the phenomenon being investigated. In cultural tourism, for example, we can usually observe that many tourists visit cultural attractions and events, but we often know very little about their motivations for doing so, why they visit particular sites or what factors influenced their decision to travel. These are important questions from a social science point of view (finding out more about human behaviour) as well as from an economic perspective (how can we manage and market cultural facilities more effectively to increase tourist satisfaction, repeat visitation and spending?).

In the case of the ATLAS research, the basic research questions stemmed from a very simple piece of curiosity. A call for proposals for projects in the field of cultural tourism was launched by the European Commission in 1990. This document indicated that cultural tourism was one of the most important forms of tourism in Europe and that it was growing rapidly. One of the strange things, however, was that nowhere in this document was there a definition of cultural tourism. So apparently projects were being sought for an important area of tourism activity that had not been defined. This simple omission led to the basic question: 'what is cultural tourism?'. In posing this basic question, a range of others began to emerge, including:

- What kinds of people engage in cultural tourism?
- Are these people different from other tourists?
- What kinds of culture do they consume?
- What role does culture play in their decision to visit a particular place?

These basic research questions could be addressed using quantitative or qualitative methods. Although surveys are often used to ask people about their background, their behaviour on holiday and their motivations, more detailed information on many of these issues might be gained from qualitative research methods, such as in-depth interviews.

In the case of the ATLAS research, however, there were a number of factors that determined the choice of surveys as the main research instrument. The fact that we were trying to develop a 'European' perspective on cultural tourism meant that we had to compare between countries and compare tourists of different nationalities. We also wanted to compare the role of different types of attractions in cultural tourism as well as say something about the scale of cultural tourism in Europe.

These considerations implied that a comparative research instrument would need to be developed which could be deployed in different countries at different sites and deal with tourists speaking different languages. The solution was therefore to design a standard questionnaire, through which the same questions could be posed in different locations. By translating the questionnaire into a number of different languages the instrument could also be deployed in situations where the interviewer did not speak the same language as the tourist, greatly increasing the potential coverage of the research.

Having identified the research problem, we need to make sure that it can be researched. The trick is to ensure that your question can be answered in the timeframe and with the resources available. As Peter Medawar (1967) pointed out, research is 'the art of the soluble', so it makes no sense to pose questions which cannot be answered. In many cases this may mean adjusting or changing our research questions to fit the reality of research environment.

In the case of the ATLAS research this meant adopting a more focused approach. In particular, the questionnaires tended to avoid the 'why' questions about cultural tourism behaviour, concentrating more on the 'who', 'what' and 'where' questions, which were easier to compare between research locations. The why questions tended to be posed in the qualitative studies carried in more detail in specific locations.

Operationalizing concepts

Once we know what research questions we want to ask, we have to translate them into questions which can actually be posed to the research subjects in order to yield the answers we are looking for. This essentially means that the concepts which are built into our research questions or models have to be made operational.

In the case of the ATLAS surveys, there were a number of basic concepts which had to be operationalized in the questionnaire, including:

- culture;
- tourist;
- social class; and
- cultural capital.

As discussed in more detail by Richards (1996), many of the basic concepts bound up in the notion of cultural tourism are difficult to operationalize. Culture is a concept that has been endlessly discussed, and there are hundreds of different definitions that could be used. Similarly, tourism is a phenomenon which has definitional problems, including questions such as 'how far does one have to travel to be a tourist?'. As far as possible, we tried to overcome these problems by adopting existing operationalizations of such concepts, such as the World Tourism Organization (1993) definition of tourism.

Operationalizaton is a basic part of empirical research, which translates basic concepts into operational questions. If, for example, we wanted to pose the question: 'Does cultural capital influence cultural attraction visitation?', both cultural capital and cultural attraction visitation need to be measured. The process of moving from concepts such as cultural capital or cultural visitation to a set of questionnaire items, such as a scale to measure cultural capital, is the process of operationalization.

If we take the example of cultural capital, this is a theoretical concept taken from the work of Bourdieu (1984). He argued that the propensity to consume different forms of culture was dependent on the amount of cultural capital or cultural competence possessed. Without sufficient cultural capital it is difficult for consumers to interpret or enjoy museums, artworks or other cultural experiences. Bourdieu argued that cultural capital was developed through the habitus (or home environment) and through education. This means that in order to fully operationalize cultural capital we need to know something about the home background and educational level of tourists. To examine the habitus we could ask questions such as 'did you go with your family to museums as a child?'. These questions were posed in some of the more detailed studies related to cultural capital and cultural tourism (e.g. Goedhart, 1997), but for the international version of the questionnaire, simpler solutions were sought, for example by asking about the highest level of educational attainment. Because educational attainment is also often strongly correlated with habitus

(because of the strong influence of parental background on education), we were able to use education as a surrogate measure for cultural capital in the questionnaires.

One strategy that we applied to deal with the complexity of 'culture' was to use the visitor's self-definition of 'cultural holiday' in order to identify 'cultural tourists'. The decision to adopt this subjective approach (see Chapter 3) was based on the complexity of developing a coherent, consistent external definition of culture that could be operationalized in the questionnaire. However, a problem with the self-definition approach is that many visitors to cultural attractions and events do not see themselves as 'cultural tourists', even though they would normally be considered as such in tourism statistics in many countries.

Questionnaire design

Once we have determined our research questions and operationalized the key concepts we want to research, we can then start designing the questionnaire. Although it may seem simple to produce a list of questions, there are a number of issues that have to be addressed in order to ensure that the questions are clear, that they measure what we want to measure and that the questions flow logically. We also need to think about how the data collected through the questionnaire will be analysed, so that we can ensure that the data collected are usable and will yield the desired information.

There are therefore a number of important issues to consider in designing the questionnaire.

Logical flow of the questions

A logical flow of questions is more likely to stimulate respondents to give clear answers than a series of questions that jumps about from one subject or time period to another. In the ATLAS questionnaire, for example, questions relating to the current holiday, to general opinions on culture or demographic background are all grouped together. In the latest version of the ATLAS questionnaire, questions about a single subject have also been grouped into a series of modules arranged in a logical sequence, allowing participants to add their own questions without interfering with the general flow of the basic questionnaire (see Appendix 2.1).

Questionnaire length

Because it is often important to maximize response rates, there is also a careful balance to be struck between the need to ask lots of questions in order to generate detailed data and the need to keep the questionnaire short so that respondents do not terminate the survey early.

Questions must be capable of being answered by respondents

It is not just the number of questions that can be problematic, but also their complexity. If a respondent is asked to do too much work in answering a questions, for example by providing a large number of examples or by being asked to recall events that happened a long time ago, this can also add to the time needed to respond (see also Chapter 12). In the ATLAS questionnaire we asked tourists which types of cultural attractions they had visited on the current trip (including those they intended to visit, if they were not at the end of the trip). It might also have been useful to ask people what they had done on previous holidays (to see whether particular types of attractions are regularly visited, for example), but it is unlikely that people could recall in any detail the attractions visited on a holiday taken 12 months ago or even longer.

Clear and simple language must be used

Particularly where tourists from different countries and different cultures are being surveyed, it is important to ensure that respondents understand the questions. The ATLAS questionnaire therefore uses simple but clear language, which also facilitates the task of translation.

What type of questions should be asked?

An important question often asked in survey design is whether certain questions should be open or closed. The use of open questions is often indicated where a more 'qualitative' or 'mixed method' approach is desired (see Parts II and III), giving respondents the opportunity to respond more flexibly to questions. Often there is a tendency to ask open questions in the hope that these will yield useful additional information or throw light on the responses to closed questions. In the case of the ATLAS research, however, a deliberate decision was made to keep open questions to a minimum. Because tourists speak different languages, it would have been very difficult to translate the answers in order to compare the responses to the open questions. However, such comparisons may now be a little easier to make using web-based translation tools, and some other suggestions for dealing with open question responses are made in Chapter 8.

Use of scales

Scales can be a very useful tool for operationalizing concepts such as quality of service or experience, or for measuring attitudes to statements about the phenomenon being investigated.

In the ATLAS research, scales have been used to measure different aspects of visitor motivation and experience. Discussions about how to implement these scales reflect a number of common problems in the use of scales in questionnaires. For example, there has been discussion about the number of points in each scale. Some ATLAS participants were in favour of a four- or six-point scale, in which the lack of a natural mid-point forces respondents to choose a positive or negative position. Others urged that a five- or seven-point scale should be used, to allow respondents to adopt a neutral position in the middle of the scale. In statistical terms at least, there is no real difference between these two options (van der Ark, personal communication, 2005), although if a neutral position is included this needs to be made clear to the respondents (Ryan, 1995).

The survey sample

In terms of the consumption of culture and tourism, there are two basic sampling strategies that can be adopted. A sample of the general population generated through a household survey would cover all potential cultural tourists, including people who did not participate in tourism or who did not undertake cultural activities on holiday. Such a sample is useful from the point of view of estimating the proportion of total participants in the population as a whole and therefore being able to establish the significance of cultural tourism relative to other types of tourism. On the other hand, a participant survey only covers those people who visit cultural attractions or events. This does not allow us to estimate the proportion of cultural tourists in the population as a whole, but it is much more likely that it will generate a substantial number of responses from cultural tourists. As cultural tourism is an activity undertaken by a minority of the total population, one would need a far larger sample from a household survey to study cultural tourism behaviour. By undertaking a participant survey it is much easier to examine the activities of a large number of cultural tourists and to make comparisons between different groups of visitors and different sites or types of events. Household surveys can be used to generate other types of information on cultural tourism consumption. For example, the UK Tourism Survey, the Continu Vakantie Onderzoek in the Netherlands or the Reiseanalyse in Germany all collect data on holidays with a cultural motivation or activity. These surveys can give a far more accurate picture of the prevalence of cultural tourism behaviour in the population as a whole and can show if culturally motivated travel is increasing or decreasing.

The problem with such population surveys is that it is often very difficult to track specific holiday behaviour, i.e. what an individual did during a specific trip to a specific destination. Because it is very difficult to ask lots of details about all the trips taken by people during a period of time (usually a quarter or whole year), population surveys generally ask about general patterns of behaviour (e.g. 'have you visited a cultural site or event in the last 12 months?') or they have to rely on respondents having extremely good memories about what they did when and where. Isaac (2008) suggests that this may be one of the main reasons for the differences in estimates of cultural tourism consumption between population surveys and visitor surveys. Visitor surveys can provide much more detailed information on a single trip and allow the different aspects of that trip (motivation, attraction, travel and accommodation choices, spending) to be directly linked to one another, rather than relying on general correlations.

For the ATLAS surveys it was therefore decided to undertake a participant survey, as it was more important to uncover information about the detailed behaviour of cultural tourists than to be able to say something about the propensity to undertake cultural tourism in the population as a whole. However, in order to provide comparisons between 'cultural tourists' and other types of tourists, the ATLAS questionnaires were designed to cover all visitors to a site or event, including local residents, and domestic and international tourists. Surveying all visitors enables an analysis to be made of the relationship between different visitor groups and to contrast motivations, behaviour and background of local residents and tourists.

Sometimes the sampling strategy adopted may have a large impact on the data analysis. For many destinations, for example, foreign tourists are often of more interest than domestic visitors (usually because the former spend more). The problem is that foreign visitors often make up a small proportion of the total, which means that a stratified sample must be adopted to make sure a significant number of the target group is interviewed. Such a sampling strategy has implications for the data analysis, however, as the data for each visitor group will also need to be analysed separately. No overall averages can be produced for the visitor sample as a whole unless the proportions of the different visitor segments in the visitor population are known.

The total visitor population in principle consisted of all visitors to the attraction or event being surveyed who were 16 years or older. In some cases, however, a few visitors younger than 16 were also interviewed, as it was difficult to judge the lower age limit visually. The sample obtained at each attraction depended to a large extent on local circumstances. Usually exit interviews were conducted, and visitors were sampled on a random basis, with the sampling interval being adjusted to the visitor stream. For groups of visitors the 'next birthday' principle was used to select respondents (Veal, 1992). Wherever possible, interviews were held over different days and time periods, to ensure that all visitor groups were sampled. The questionnaire was deliberately kept as short as possible, to minimize problems of refusal. Visitors who could not speak the language of the country concerned or where the interviewer was unable to speak their language could often be offered a self-completion questionnaire in their own language. In the early survey rounds there is a likelihood, however, that Japanese and other Asian visitors will have been under-represented in the sample because of the lack of questionnaires in non-European languages. This problem was later at least partially addressed by translating the questionnaire into Japanese, Chinese and Korean.

For each survey site, information was also gathered on a number of background variables, including the date and times of interviews, details of sampling methods used and the number of face-to-face interviews and self-completion questionnaires gathered. A standard form was circulated to all survey participants for this purpose.

Implementation

In order to facilitate comparison, standard classifications were used wherever possible. The employment question, for example, is based on the International Standard Classification of Occupations. This made the job of translation easier, since EU documents, such as the European Labour Force Survey, provide translations of the categories in different languages. The Euro was also used as the basic monetary unit, with conversion scales being provided for the different language versions. Terms that might cause some differences of interpretation were also clarified in order to facilitate comparison. For example, there was considerable discussion over the meaning of the term 'heritage' in different languages.

Survey procedures

The questionnaire was designed to be used either by an interviewer or through self-completion. In most cases, however, the questionnaires were interviewer-completed, as this tended to give a higher degree of accuracy and generated a higher response rate.

Research location

The locations at which surveys are undertaken can have an important impact on the results. Ideally one should try and capture a random sample in which all visitors have an equal chance of being surveyed. However, there are a number of factors that can influence visitor flows, including the time of day, day of the week and the weather. The ATLAS surveys are in principle designed to be spread out across different time periods, but often factors such as the availability of interviewers would prevent a perfectly even spread of surveys. Data were collected on weather conditions during the fieldwork, because these might influence not only sampling but potentially also visitor responses. At open-air attractions, for example, the visitor experience is likely to be different when the weather is poor than when the sun is shining.

In the case of the ATLAS research, surveyors also had to make a choice of location between a specific cultural site (which would tend to maximize the number of cultural visitors interviewed) or a location in the vicinity of a cultural attraction (which would tend to indicate the proportion of tourists visiting those sites).

The need to facilitate completion of the surveys can also influence the location where these are conducted. Ideally, surveying should be completed in a location where visitors have the time and also facilities (e.g. chairs, tables) to complete the survey form in comfort, protected from the vagaries of the weather. The desirability of sampling visitors at or near the end of their visit to a cultural attraction in order to capture as much information as possible also led to many surveys being undertaken in the café or shop of an attraction (often found at the exit to attractions). However, the use of such facilities requires a relatively high degree of cooperation from attraction or event managers, which may not always be forthcoming.

Scope of the destination

When undertaking surveys in a specific location, one question that inevitably arises is the physical area that constitutes the 'destination'. This is important to distinguish tourists from other visitors, since the World Tourism Organization definition of tourism requires tourists to have travelled outside their 'normal area of residence'.

The questions in the ATLAS survey that refer to the area in which the survey is being conducted are designed to refer to the local area, site or region. For example, for a cultural attraction or event within a city, the local area would usually mean the city itself, whereas for a rural attraction the question would usually refer to the municipality or province in which it is located. The extent of the 'area' is therefore reasonably flexible in order to accommodate the wide differences in survey locations.

Operationalizing Concepts through Surveys

The basic ATLAS survey provides a simple but flexible tool to gather standardized quantitative information from visitors to specific sites. In spite of (or perhaps because

of) its simplicity, the ATLAS survey also provides the opportunity to address a wide range of theoretical issues related to cultural tourism. Because the survey provides a wide range of basic background data on the profile of tourists and their behaviour, it is relatively easy to add questions to the basic survey to operationalize specific theories relating to cultural tourism. The examples described here include Leiper's (1990) attraction systems model and the dimensions of experience developed by Pine and Gilmore (1999). However, the ATLAS questionnaire has been used to investigate other concepts in cultural tourism, including omnivorous patterns of cultural consumption (Toivonen, 2005), compensation theories of leisure consumption (Thrane, 2000) and ethnic identity (see Chapter 8).

One of the basic discussions about tourist attractions is whether they really 'attract' people like some kind of 'magnet' (Gunn, 1988). MacCannell (1976) argued that tourist attractions give meaning to modern existence for a new leisure class, which is drawn to them as representations of the differentiations of modernity. The consumption of tourist attractions for MacCannell is therefore a form of pilgrimage, where certain 'must see' sites are marked out from other potential destinations through the use of markers that set them apart as special places to visit. In his reformulation of MacCannell's concepts into 'attraction systems', Leiper (1990) defined an attraction as 'an empirical relationship between a tourist, a sight, and a marker – a piece of information about a sight' (p. 370).

Rather than attractions pulling tourists towards them as a form of pilgrimage, Leiper's system-based model suggests that tourists can make the decision to visit an attraction at any point in their journey. Some attractions will obviously have a bigger influence on travel decisions than others, and these might be considered as 'generating markers'. Leiper argues that 'at least one generating marker is necessary, referring to some kind of phenomenon that acts as a primary nucleus, before an individual can become motivated to set off on a touristic trip' (p. 379).

The visitor is motivated to visit a destination by information received from a generating marker that matches their needs and wants. En route the visitor can encounter transit markers that lead to other attractions, or in the destination they can find contiguous markers of yet more nuclei. In contrast to Gunn's (1988) concept of attraction magnetism, Leiper tourists are not 'attracted' or 'pulled' towards an attraction but 'are pushed ... by their own motivation towards the places and/or events where they expect their needs will be satisfied' (p. 380).

This is an interesting conceptual model of the attraction system, which relates to a number of key concepts in cultural tourism and in particular MacCannell's influential ideas about the semiotic role of attractions. However, in order to establish the operation of this model in real tourism systems, some form of empirical testing is required.

In order to test the Leiper model, the ATLAS surveys carried out in 1999–2000 included a specific operationalization of the type of 'markers' being used by tourists in visiting cultural sites. Over 6000 visitor surveys were conducted at cultural sites, including museums, monuments, art galleries, historic properties, heritage centres, performing arts venues and festivals. Respondents were asked at what point they had made the decision to visit the interview location. The three options available were 'before leaving home', 'during the trip here' and 'when I arrived in the area'. The concept of the 'nucleus' was therefore operationalized as the attraction being visited by the tourist. Because tourists were also asked about the extent to which they had been motivated to travel by the attraction they were visiting, the extent to which the attraction functioned as a nucleus could be established. The role of the visitors in attraction systems could be analysed by asking them about their motivations, trip characteristics, use of information and socio-economic background. In this way, all three elements of attraction systems could be studied.

The ATLAS surveys indicated that almost half of those interviewed had decided to visit a specific cultural attraction before departure. These generating markers were by far the most important for cultural tourists in their travel behaviour, with less than a quarter of respondents visiting an attraction en route to the destination and less than 30% deciding which attractions to visit after arrival. The indications are that visitors are 'pushed' towards attractions by their motivations rather than being pulled by some magnetic force within the attraction (Richards, 2002). This seems to be confirmed by the strong relationship between motivation, the geographical origin of visitors, their socio-demographic characteristics, travel form, marker use and attraction visitation. The use of markers is also likely to be dependent on cultural capital and consumption skills. These patterns tend to suggest that motivations, which are also linked to the personal and social characteristics of visitors, tend to determine who will visit which type of attraction and when. These relationships provide strong empirical support for the attraction system as proposed by Leiper.

Another example of how the ATLAS questionnaires have been used to operationalize concepts in cultural tourism is in the analysis of the 'experience economy' (Pine and Gilmore, 1999). Pine and Gilmore argue that the economy has gone through a transition from extracting commodities to making goods, delivering services and currently staging experiences as the primary arena of value creation. They argue that experiences are an economic offer distinct from services. Whereas services are delivered, experiences must be staged in a way that engages the customer to create a memorable event. Experiences are personal, and therefore no two individuals can have the same experience.

The idea that experiences are overtaking services as the major realm of competition between producers to attract consumers is highly applicable in the field of cultural tourism, where the development of attractions and events is increasingly about the creation of experiences. But what does a cultural tourism experience consist of? According to Pine and Gilmore, there are four major 'realms' of experience: entertainment, education, aesthetic and escapist. According to them, an ideal experience should balance these different realms.

In order to measure the extent to which cultural visits incorporate these different experience realms, questions were devised to operationalize them. The questions were developed by studying the concept as described by Pine and Gilmore, and also through discussion within the ATLAS Cultural Tourism Research Group.

The final statements devised for the 'experience scale' were:

- This experience has increased my knowledge (education).
- This experience has stimulated my curiosity (education).
- It was very pleasant being here (aesthetic).
- This is an attractive place (aesthetic).
- There are lots of interesting things to see (entertainment).
- The people here are fun to be with (entertainment).
- This place feels very different (escapist).
- I completely escaped from reality here (escapist).

Each experience realm was therefore operationalized through two separate questions. The degree of correlation between the pairs of questions for each realm was high. The scale as a whole had a high degree of reliability, with a Cronbach's alpha of 0.84. The coherence of the scale was also confirmed by the high correlation scores between the individual items. However, as is the case in many scales, the high alpha score is partly a product of the large number of items in the scale. For subsequent versions of the survey, therefore, the number of experience questions was lowered to four, one for each experience dimension. This still produced a scale with an alpha of more than 0.7, which is acceptable.

The analysis of over 3000 surveys from different parts of the world indicated that there were significant differences in the experiences of visitors according to their background and the type of cultural attraction. When people with different educational attainment levels are compared, for example, it is clear that those with higher education levels have a more 'educational' experience, whereas those with lower attainment are more likely to experience escapism. For both groups, however, the educational aspect remains the most important dimension of a cultural attraction (Fig. 2.1).

Those visitors who saw themselves as 'cultural tourists' were also more likely than other visitors to have high scores across all the experience dimensions, indicating that the cultural tourist is seeking a more intense, holistic cultural experience. Comparing different types of cultural attraction also indicates that different facilities provide different types of experience. Visitors interviewed in cities, for example, consistently gave a lower experience score than those visiting individually managed attractions. This does tend to indicate that the ability of

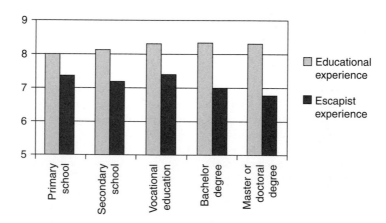

Fig. 2.1. Educational and escapist experience realms by highest education level.

enclosed attractions to manage different aspects of the visitor experience will provide a more satisfying experience. Even for different types of managed attractions, however, there were also notable differences in the experience scale. For example, the following three attractions were compared.

Admiraliteitshuis, Friesland, the Netherlands

The former Admiralty building of Friesland and Groningen has been a regional museum since 1963. Built in 1618, this former 'sea office' was responsible for the protection of trade. The museum exhibits popular regional art, children's toys of yesteryear, ceramics, a prestigious textile collection and a collection of silverware. There is also an exhibition about St Boniface, the English bishop who came to Dokkum and was murdered in 754 AD.

Whaka Village, Rotorua, New Zealand

At Whaka Village visitors can experience a day in the life of a living Maori village. There are steaming mineral springs and natural bathing areas used daily by the villagers, bubbling mud pools and hot steam vents (a hangi), where food is slowly cooked in its own juices. Cultural performances and meals are also provided.

Auckland War Memorial Museum, New Zealand

Auckland War Memorial Museum tells the story of New Zealand, its place in the Pacific and its people. The museum is a war memorial for the province of Auckland and holds one of New Zealand's top three heritage libraries. It has pre-eminent Maori and Pacific collections, significant natural history resources and major social and military history collections, as well as decorative arts and pictorial collections.

All three of these attractions provide different types of experiences for the visitor. Whaka Village had the highest overall score on the experience scale, indicating that it was more successful in providing a holistic cultural experience. This was probably linked to the 'living culture' elements of the village, with escapism scoring particularly highly compared with the other two attractions. The Admiraliteitshuis scored highest for the aesthetic and entertainment aspects of experience, whereas, perhaps not surprisingly, the Auckland War Memorial Museum scored lowest on entertainment (although not by much) (Fig. 2.2).

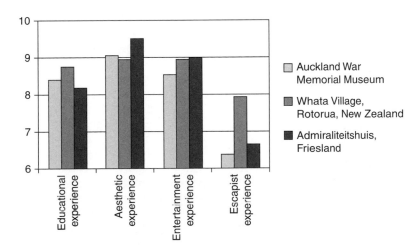

Fig. 2.2. Experience scores at different types of attractions.

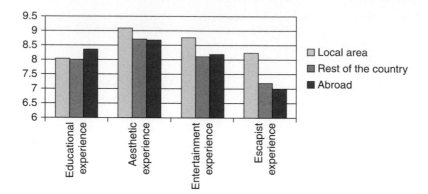

Fig. 2.3.   Experience scores by visitor origin.

In terms of visitor origin we can also observe differences in experience. In general, local residents will tend to emphasize the aesthetic and entertainment aspects of attractions above education. For foreign visitors, however, the educational dimension of the visit was seen as being more important (Fig. 2.3).

The experience of a cultural attraction or event therefore depends not just on the activities of experience producers but also on the interaction of different visitor groups with the cultural experience. This underlines the role of the consumer in producing their own experiences in a system of 'co-creation' (Binkhorst, 2007).

Conclusions

Quantitative surveys clearly have their limitations, as many other authors in this volume argue. In spite of this, it is also clear that surveys can have a very important role to play in the collection of empirical data in cultural tourism research. Not only can surveys produce a profile of cultural tourists and their behaviour, but they can also be used to operationalize a wide range of theoretical concepts. A major advantage of such surveys is that they can be used in a variety of locations and contexts, allowing comparisons to be made between different countries, regions and attractions. This can be particularly important in cases where the context of cultural tourism consumption plays an important role in the experience of tourists. By studying the experiences and behaviour of cultural tourists in these different contexts, we can identify those elements of cultural tourism experience that are common to a wide range of situations and those that are more site or event specific. In doing so, we can perhaps also contribute to the analysis of the relationships between the global and local dimensions of cultural tourism, or as Salazar (Chapter 15) terms it the 'glocal' element of cultural tourism.

A further advantage of such surveys is the ability to analyse changes in cultural tourism over time. This is an aspect of the ATLAS research programme that has so far remained relatively undeveloped, but the few longitudinal comparisons that have been made have already suggested that significant changes are taking place in the nature of 'cultural tourism' in many places around the world and that the experience of cultural tourism is also changing. The growing significance of 'atmosphere' and other intangible elements of cultural tourism is clearly traceable in the ATLAS surveys, but much remains to done in collecting empirical data on cultural tourism and providing some justification for some of the many claims made for this 'good' form of tourism.

References

Alzua, A., O'Leary, J.T. and Morrison, A.M. (1998) Cultural and heritage tourism: identifying niches for international travelers. *Journal of Tourism Studies* 9, 2–13.

Binkhorst, E. (2007) Creativity in tourism experiences: the case of Sitges. In: Richards, G. and Wilson, J. (eds) *Tourism, Creativity and Development*. Routledge, London, pp. 125–144.

Bourdieu, P. (1984) *Distinction: a Social Critique of the Judgement of Taste*. Routledge, London.

Bywater, M. (1993) The market for cultural tourism in Europe. *Travel and Tourism Analyst* 6, 30–46.

Goedhart, S. (1997) 'New producers' in cultuurtoerisme. MA thesis, Tilburg University, the Netherlands.

Green, M. (2001) Urban heritage tourism: globalization and localization. In: Richards, G. (ed.) *Cultural Attractions and European Tourism*. CAB International, Wallingford, UK, pp. 173–197.

Gunn, C.A. (1988) *Vacationscape: Designing Tourist Regions*. Van Nostrand Reinhold, New York.

Herrijgers, C. (1998) De culturele stedenreis. MA thesis, Tilburg University, the Netherlands.

Isaac, R. (2008) *Understanding the Behaviour of Cultural Tourists: Towards a Classification of Dutch Cultural Tourists*. NHTV Expertise Series No. 5, NHTV, Breda, the Netherlands.

Kastenholz, E., Carneiro, M.J. and Eusébio, C. (2005) The impact of socio-demographics on tourist behavior – analyzing segments of cultural tourists visiting Coimbra. ATLAS, Arnhem. http://www.tram-research.com/atlas/Aveiro.pdf (accessed 5 August 2009).

Leiper, N. (1990) Tourist attraction systems. *Annals of Tourism Research* 17, 367–384.

MacCannell, D. (1976) *The Tourist: a New Theory of the Leisure Class*. Macmillan, London.

Marciszewska, B. (2001) The consumption of cultural tourism in Poland. In: Richards, G. (ed.) *Cultural Attractions and European Tourism*. CAB International, Wallingford, UK, pp. 215–226.

McKercher, B. and Du Cros, H. (2002) *Cultural Tourism: the Partnership between Tourism and Cultural Heritage Management*. Haworth Press, Binghamton, New York

Medawar, P.B. (1967) *The Art of the Soluble*. Methuen, London.

Öter, Z. and Özdoğan, N. (2005) Destination image of cultural tourists: the case of Selçuk–Ephesus. *Anatolia* 16, 127–138 [in Turkish with English abstract].

Pereiro, X. (2005) Informe de Investigação Sobre O Perfil Do 'Turista Cultural' No Nordeste Transmontano. ATLAS, Arnhem. http://www.tram-research.com/atlas/Altodouro.PDF (accessed 5 August 2009).

Pine, B.J. and Gilmore, J.H. (1999) *The Experience Economy*. Harvard University Press, Cambridge, Massachusetts.

Richards, G. (ed.) (1996) *Cultural Tourism in Europe*. CAB International, Wallingford, UK.

Richards, G. (1998) Cultural tourism in Europe: recent developments. In: Grande Ibarra, J. (ed.) *Actas del Congreso Europeo sobre Itinereos y Rutas Temáticas*. Fundación Caja Rioja, Logroño, Spain, pp. 105–113.

Richards, G. (1999) European cultural tourism: patterns and prospects. In: Dodd, D. and van Hemel, A.-M. (eds) *Planning European Cultural Tourism*. Boekman Foundation, Amsterdam, pp. 16–32.

Richards, G. (ed.) (2001) *Cultural Attractions and European Tourism*. CAB International, Wallingford, UK.

Richards, G. (2002) Tourism attraction systems: exploring cultural behavior. *Annals of Tourism Research* 29(4), 1048–1064.

Richards, G. and Wilson, J. (2004) The impact of cultural events on city image: Rotterdam Cultural Capital of Europe 2001. *Urban Studies* 41(10), 1931–1951.

Roetman, E.E. (1994) Motivatie in retrospectief: een onderzoek naar motivatie voor cultuurtoerisme tijdens de Mondriaantentoonstelling te Amsterdam. MA dissertation, Tilburg University, the Netherlands.

Ryan, C. (1995) *Researching Tourist Satisfaction: Issues, Concepts, Problems*. Routledge, London.

Silberberg, T. (1995) Cultural tourism and business opportunity for museum and heritage sites. *Tourism Management* 16, 361–365.

Thrane, C. (2000) Everyday life and cultural tourism in Scandinavia: examining the spillover hypothesis. *Loisir et Société* 23, 215–234.

Toivonen, T. (2005) Omnivorousness in cultural tourism: an international comparison. http://www.tram-research.com/atlas/timotoivonen.PDF (accessed 5 August 2009).

van 't Riet, S. (1994) Back to basics: an analysis of tourist motivations for visiting cultural attractions. MA thesis, Programme in European Leisure Studies, Tilburg University, the Netherlands.

Veal, A.J. (1992) *Research Methods for Leisure and Tourism: a Practical Guide*. Longman, London.

World Tourism Organization (1993) *Recommendation on Tourism Statistics*. WTO, Madrid.

Appendix 2.1. ATLAS Cultural Tourism Research Project standard visitor questionnaire (English version, European sites, 2007–2009).

ATLAS Cultural Tourism Research Project

English Questionnaire Modules (European Version)

Module A: Motivation

A1) Have you ever been to this area/site before?

☐ Yes   ☐ No

A2) To what extent do you agree or disagree with the following statements?

(Please circle a number from 1 to 5)

This experience has increased my knowledge
     Disagree 1 2 3 4 5 Agree
It was very relaxing being here
     Disagree 1 2 3 4 5 Agree
There are lots of interesting things to see
     Disagree 1 2 3 4 5 Agree
I like the atmosphere of this place
     Disagree 1 2 3 4 5 Agree

A3) What is the primary purpose of your current trip?

☐ Holiday
☐ Visit a cultural attraction
☐ Attend a cultural event
☐ Visiting relatives and friends
☐ Business
☐ Conference
☐ Sports event
☐ Shopping
☐ Other

(continued)

Appendix 2.1. *Continued.*

A4) If you are on HOLIDAY, what type of holiday are you taking?

☐ Sun/beach holiday

☐ Health/wellness

☐ Cultural holiday

☐ Ecotourism/nature holiday

☐ Creative/educational holiday

☐ Rural holiday

☐ Touring holiday

☐ City trip

☐ Sports holiday

Module B: City Comparisons

B1) Please tick from the following list the FIVE cities which you think are most suitable for a cultural holiday

☐ Amsterdam

☐ Athens

☐ Barcelona

☐ Belgrade

☐ Berlin

☐ Brussels

☐ Budapest

☐ Copenhagen

☐ Dublin

☐ Edinburgh

☐ Florence

☐ Glasgow

☐ Helsinki

☐ Istanbul

☐ Linz

☐ Lisbon

☐ Liverpool

☐ London

☐ Luxemburg

☐ Madrid

☐ Moscow

☐ Oporto

☐ Paris

☐ Pécs

☐ Prague

☐ Riga

☐ Rome

☐ Rotterdam

☐ Sibiu/Hermanstad

☐ Stockholm

☐ Venice

☐ Vienna

☐ Warsaw

Module C: Stay and Activities (Visitors Only)

C1) In what type of accommodation are you staying?

☐ Own home

☐ Second residence

☐ Hotel

☐ Self catering accommodation

☐ Bed & breakfast/room in private house

☐ Caravan/ tent

☐ With family & friends

☐ Youth hostel

☐ Not sure yet

C2) How many nights will you be staying in this area?

Write in number _____

(continued)

Appendix 2.1.   *Continued.*

C3) Have you visited or are you planning to visit any of the following cultural attractions or cultural events in this area?

☐ Museums   ☐ Cinema
☐ Monuments   ☐ Pop concerts
☐ Art galleries   ☐ World music events
☐ Religious sites   ☐ Classical music events
☐ Historic sites   ☐ Dance events
☐ Theatres   ☐ Traditional festivals
☐ Heritage/crafts centres

C4) How satisfied are you with your visit to this area/site, on a scale from 1–10?

Very Unsatisfied   Very Satisfied

       1   2   3   4   5   6   7   8   9   10

Module D: Expenditure (Visitors Only)

D1) Can you indicate approximately how much you have spent (or will spend) during your stay in this area?

                                        Currency_____

Travel   _____
Accommodation   _____
Food, drink, shopping   _____

Total   _____

Module E: Information Sources (Visitors Only)

E1) How did you arrange the travel and/or accommodation for your trip?

☐ All-inclusive package
☐ Travel and accommodation booked separately
☐ Nothing booked in advance

E2) If you made a travel or accommodation booking, did you

☐ Book in person at travel agency
☐ Book via internet
☐ Book directly (by phone, fax or email)

(continued)

Appendix 2.1. *Continued.*

E3) What sources of information did you consult about this area BEFORE YOU ARRIVED here?

☐ Family/friends   ☐ TV/Radio

☐ Previous visit   ☐ Newspapers/Magazines

☐ Internet   ☐ Tour operator brochure

☐ Tourist board   ☐ Guide books

☐ Travel agency

E4) What sources of information have you consulted AFTER YOU ARRIVED in this area?

☐ Family/friends   ☐ Local brochures

☐ Tourist information centre   ☐ Guidebooks

☐ Internet   ☐ TV/radio

☐ Tour operator information   ☐ Tour guide

☐ Newspapers/magazines

Module F: Profile

F1) Where is your current place of residence?

☐ Local area   ☐ Abroad (country)

☐ Rest of the country   _____

F2) Please indicate your gender

☐ Male   ☐ Female

F3) Please indicate your age group

☐ 15 or younger   ☐ 20–29   ☐ 40–49   ☐ 60 or over

☐ 16–19   ☐ 30–39   ☐ 50–59

F4) What is your highest level of educational qualification?

☐ Primary school   ☐ Bachelor degree

☐ Secondary school   ☐ Master or doctoral degree

☐ Vocational education

F5) Which of the following categories best describes your current position?

☐ Employee   ☐ Housewife/man or carer

☐ Self-employed   ☐ Student (go to F7)

☐ Retired   ☐ Unemployed

(continued)

Appendix 2.1. *Continued.*

F6) Please indicate your current (or former) occupational group

☐ Director or manager
☐ Professional (doctor, lawyer, teacher, etc.)
☐ Technical professions (technicians, nursing)
☐ Clerical/administration
☐ Service and sales personnel
☐ Manual or crafts worker

F7) Is your current occupation (or former occupation) connected with culture?

☐ Yes   ☐ No

F8) Which category best describes your annual household gross income group?

☐ 5,000 Euro or less   ☐ 30,001–40,000 Euro
☐ 5,001–10,000 Euro   ☐ 40,001–50,000 Euro
☐ 10,001–20,000 Euro   ☐ 50,001–60,000 Euro
☐ 20,001–30,000 Euro   ☐ More than 60,000 Euro

3 A Comparison of Quantitative and Qualitative Approaches: Complementarities and Trade-offs

Marjan Melkert and Katleen Vos

Introduction

There is a wealth of studies that have been undertaken on cultural tourism in recent years, most of which take their justification from the increasing importance of cultural tourism in global and local markets. However, much of this discussion is based on conjecture rather than on empirical data.
(Richards and Queirós, 2005: 4).

As noted in the previous chapter, the ATLAS Cultural Tourism Research Project has been generating quantitative empirical data on cultural tourism worldwide since 1991. So, in fact, current research needs may lie more in the field of qualitative research, which can arguably produce a more detailed understanding of cultural tourists and their behaviour and provide more answers to the *how* questions regarding cultural tourism. At the end of the day, however, a combination of quantitative and qualitative approaches may develop a more complete understanding of cultural tourism.

This chapter discusses how quantitative and qualitative approaches might be brought together in a multidisciplinary context. It is not simply the difference between the quantitative and the qualitative approaches that matters. Both approaches are valuable, and in many cases will go hand in hand in analyses of cultural tourism, as many other contributions to this volume show. Cultural tourism studies should be multidisciplinary in nature in order to do justice to the subject matter. This chapter aims to provide a conceptual framework for this methodological discussion.

Quantitative and Qualitative Research

The qualitative approach and the quantitative approach usually involve different research methods. However, the use of both approaches may be complementary, with each adding insights to the overall picture (see Part II of this volume). In this section the differences as well as the complementarities between the two will be highlighted.

In cultural tourism research, as in most other social research, two contrasting paradigms can be distinguished: positivism and phenomenology. The first tries to explain human behaviour through cause and effect, whereas the second aims to understand and interpret human actions through the individual's own reality (Finn *et al.*, 2000; see also Chapter 14, this volume). These different paradigms generally lead to distinct approaches to data collection: the quantitative and the qualitative. This distinction is not clear cut: methods are not exclusively part of one research tradition or paradigm,

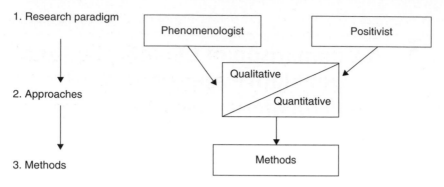

Fig. 3.1.   Research paradigms and methodologies.

for example the positivist as well as the phenomenologist can use survey methods to collect data. Figure 3.1 shows the links between research paradigm, approaches and methods (Finn *et al.*, 2000).

A large number of quantitative research methods are used in the field of tourism studies, and it is beyond the scope of this chapter to describe all of them. Quantitative research is mainly based on the collection of data, which are then analysed through a variety of statistical techniques. It usually tends to obtain a relatively small amount of information on a large number of respondents or observations. These results are often extrapolated to a larger population (Weaver and Lawton, 2002). Quantitative research is often considered as the model for all scientific research, as it involves a precise process of hypothesis formulation, detached observation, data collection, data analysis and the acceptance or rejection of the hypothesis.

Qualitative research can be defined as research that aims to obtain in-depth insight into the social reality on the basis of a relatively small number of respondents or observations. The methodology does not usually rely on sampling or employing statistical analysis. Qualitative research is suited for situations where little is known about the subject matter to be analysed. Sometimes qualitative research methods are referred to as 'data enhancers' (Ragin, 1994: 92). Miles and Huberman (1994: 6) state:

> Qualitative research is conducted through an intense and/or prolonged contact with

the field or life situation. These situations are typically 'banal' or normal ones, reflective of the everyday life of individuals, groups, societies, organizations. The researcher's role is to gain a 'holistic' overview of the context under study: its logic, its arrangements, and its explicit and implicit rules.

Some representative examples of qualitative research methods are:

- *Case studies*: defined by Yin (1994: 13) as 'an empirical inquiry that investigates a contemporary phenomenon within its real-life context, when the boundaries between phenomenon and context are not clearly evident, and in which multiple sources of evidence are used'. Most of the chapters in this book include case studies.
- *Grounded theory*: a research strategy that aims at generating theory inductively from data (Punch, 2005). See Chapter 10 of this volume for an example.
- *Ethnography*: consisting of 'describing a culture and understanding a way of life from the point of view of its participants; it is the art and science of describing a group or culture' (Punch, 2005: 149). A favoured method in ethnographic research is *participant observation*: the group or case is studied in its natural setting and the researcher becomes part of that setting (Fielding, 1996). In countries such as Australia and New Zealand, where the cultural

tourism product is often based on visits to indigenous communities, much of the cultural tourism research has been ethnographic (Smith, 2003). See Part IV of this volume for examples.

• *Action research*: focused on solving problems, a cyclical and iterative method that brings together the acting and the researching (Punch, 2005). It is generally thought to involve a 'spiral of self reflective cycles of planning a change, acting and observing the consequences of the change, reflecting on these processes and consequences, and then replanning, acting and observing, reflecting, and so on.' (Kemmis and McTaggart, 2000: 595–596; see also Chapter 5, this volume).

To sum up, the quantitative approach is usually strictly structured, collects statistical data and tests hypothesis, whereas the qualitative approach is more flexible, explores meanings by analysing texts and words, and develops new theoretical insights. The difference between qualitative and quantitative research is mainly related to the method of data collection or the amount of data analysed. Table 3.1 presents a synopsis of the differences between quantitative and qualitative research approaches (see also Chapter 14).

Complementarities

The positivist paradigm has always dominated the natural sciences but has also become common in social and tourism studies. Some tourism researchers claim that the quantitative approach is more reliable than the qualitative approach, since the former is supposed to reflect better the 'real world', as it is founded on rigorous procedures and has the ability to extrapolate the results to a wider population. These researchers even adopt a dismissive attitude towards the 'soft' and 'subjective' qualitative research approaches (Weaver and Lawton, 2002). Since the two research approaches are in fact complementary, this attitude is rather inopportune.

It is true that qualitative research is inductive and can be considered as intuitive, but it also allows us to generate models and hypotheses that can then be tested by means of quantitative (or qualitative) research methods (Weaver and Lawton, 2002). In both quantitative and qualitative research, good reasoning is of paramount importance. Proposition logic can reinforce the researcher's ability to set up valid and sound arguments and to learn to recognize fallacy in scientific studies. In proposition logic, one or more statements are offered as support, justification, grounds, reason or evidence for another statement. What in proposition logic is called 'argument' is the way in which claims to truth are supported. However, they do not establish the truth of the conclusions. Logicians only study the correctness of reasoning, the validity of the inference and not the truth of statements themselves. So statements can be true or false and arguments can be valid or invalid. Suber (1997) states: 'Validity pertains to reasoning, not propositions, while truth pertains to propositions, not reasoning. The

Table 3.1. Quantitative and qualitative research styles. Source: Neuman (1997, in Weaver and Lawton, 2002: 389).

Quantitative	Qualitative
Measure objective facts	Construct social reality, cultural meaning
Focus on variables	Focus on interactive processes, events
Reliability is the key	Authenticity is the key
Value free	Values are present and explicit
Independent of context	Situationally constrained
Many cases or subjects	Thematic analysis
Statistical analysis	Thematic analysis
Researcher is detached from subject	Researcher is involved in subject

first fundamental principle of logic is the independence of truth and validity'. Nevertheless, it is possible to see different relations between the validity of reasoning and the truthfulness of propositions. 'When the reasoning in an argument is valid and all its premises are true, then it is called sound. Otherwise the argument is unsound. If an argument is sound, then its conclusion must be true and we would be illogical to disbelieve it' (Suber, 1997).

Arguments can be divided into two categories: deductive and inductive. In the case of deductive arguments, the premises claim to give firm grounds for the truth of their conclusion or they claim to support the conclusion with necessity. In the case of inductive arguments, the premises support but do not guarantee the conclusion:

> The black and white categories of validity and invalidity apply only to deductive arguments; inductive arguments are strong or weak. In a valid deductive argument with all true premises, the truth of the conclusion is necessary and its falsehood is impossible. In a strong inductive argument with all true premises, the truth of the conclusion is merely probable and its falsehood merely improbable.
>
> (Suber, 1997)

The conclusions of valid deductions are not a matter of degree but of the 'all or nothing' kind. The conclusions of inductions are a matter of degree: they have a 'more or less' nature. Inductions are not bad deductions: 'The difference between deduction and induction is not the difference between good and bad reasoning, but between two ways to support the truth of conclusions. Deduction is the subject of a rigorous exact science; induction is not' (Suber, 1997).

Deductive arguments go hand in hand with the positivist paradigm and quantitative research, whereas inductive arguments belong to the phenomenological paradigm and qualitative research. Nevertheless, more important is the difference between sound arguments and unsound arguments.

> A fallacy is a bad method of argument, whether deductive or inductive. Arguments can be 'bad' (or unsound) for several

reasons: one or more of their premises may be false, or irrelevant, or the reasoning from them may be invalid, or the language expressing them may be ambiguous or vague. There is certainly an infinity of bad arguments; there may even be an infinity of ways of arguing badly. The name fallacy is usually reserved for typical faults in arguments that we nevertheless find persuasive. Studying them is therefore a good defence against deception.

> (Suber, 1997)

Trade-offs

Walle (1997) underlines the need for tourism scholars to develop an adequate framework for determining why specific research strategies are useful in certain situations, while at the same time being aware of the 'trade-offs' involved in adopting a certain strategy. He started with the tentative adoption of the emic/etic (art/science: see also Chapter 15, this volume) dichotomy and applied it to the strategies of tourism research. The matrix Walle created as an overview of this perspective draws the attention to three of the more relevant implications of the art/science dichotomy (Table 3.2).

Both methods have their strengths and weaknesses. Therefore some researchers choose to combine them in order to minimize the weaknesses of each method and to maximize its strengths. The combination of methods can also improve the validity of the research. Often the technique of triangulation is used, whereby the results from one method can be checked with the findings of the other method (see Chapter 5 and Chapter 14, this volume). Triangulation implies the use of multiple methods, diverse data sources, multidisciplinary investigators and various theories in a research process (Finn *et al.*, 2000). In this context, a distinction should be made between multiple methods and mixed methods. Multiple methods are used to examine different perspectives of the same research question (Philip, 1998), whereas the use of mixed methods implies the use of different methods at the same time in the research process. According to Henderson (1990: 181) 'the

Table 3.2. Implications of the dichotomy between the scientific and qualitative research approaches. Source: Walle (1997).

Tourism term	Scientific method	Qualitative research
Anthropology term:	Etic (science)	Emic (art)
Characteristics:	Formality/rigour emphasized	Insight/intuition employed
	Mathematical tools prominent	Qualitative data employed
Especially useful when:	Appropriate data can be gathered	Formal/scientific methods will not result in needed data
	Questions can be attacked via the scientific method	Formal models are not useful
	Many informants needed	Few informants are available
	Adequate time for research available	Time pressures do not permit formal research
Net result of trade-offs:	A sacrifice of possible important data and/or abandoning certain research topics is accepted in order that research is placed upon a firm scientific foundation	Rigour is sacrificed for the sake of attacking questions that formal methods cannot easily pursue. Insights/intuition of skilled researchers are allowed a free hand. Possible time savings

value of multiple methods is that they lead to multiple realities'. It can even happen that strategies that combine different methods deliver inconsistent results. Therefore, one needs to know which method is most appropriate for a given circumstance. As Veal (2006) states, 'cultural tourism researchers should rather opt for a "horses for courses" approach'. He argues that techniques are not intrinsically good or bad, but are considered to be appropriate or inappropriate for the task in hand. Furthermore, he maintains that it is not a question of good or bad techniques that should be considered, but good or bad use of techniques.

From a Monodisciplinary to a Multidisciplinary Approach

Cultural tourism: a multidisciplinary field of study

As Smith (2003) observes:

Cultural tourism studies is a relatively new and little known academic discipline, and one which may be described as a composite discipline, since it draws on a number of different academic areas for its theoretical underpinning. This includes areas such as

anthropology, cultural studies, sociology, urban planning, arts management, heritage and museum studies, to name but a few.

Cultural tourism is hence a multidisciplinary and, in the ideal case, an interdisciplinary field of study. As tourism researchers with different academic backgrounds work more and more together, Weaver and Lawton (2002) argue that the multidisciplinary approach in tourism research is gradually evolving into an interdisciplinary approach, in which the perspectives of various disciplines are combined and synthesized. An interdisciplinary approach means that subfields of research that do not fit neatly into one particular discipline are involved (Melkert, 2007). Smith (2003) also states that it is no longer wise to remain rooted firmly in one discipline or to specialize in one sector alone.

The contribution of the historic–critical method to cultural tourism research

In order to conduct research on cultural tourism in a sensible way, one has to seek a methodological framework that fits the subject matter. This framework will, in most cases, be multidisciplinary and interdisciplinary, as has been explained above. In many cases, history will be an important element in the disciplinary mix, either history in a broad sense or specific fields such as history of art, architecture, literature, music, theatre or opera. Therefore this section proceeds with an explanation of the empirical approach within historic research.

How can we study events that have already passed? This question is at the heart of historical research and it becomes more pregnant if one wishes to research the past in an empirical manner. The 19th century German historian Von Ranke (1824) argued in his book _Geschichte der Romanischen und Germanischen Völker von 1494 bis 1514_ (History of the Latin and Teutonic Peoples from 1494 to 1514) that the historian has to have a pure love for truth and therefore should be concerned only with the thorough study of facts about the past. For Von Ranke, only written historic documents can provide the solid base for history as a science. From the 19th century onwards this methodology of history has been further developed, and one of the things that historians of cultural tourism have to learn is how to deal with historic sources in order to be able to establish the facts about the past.

Knowledge of the past is based on primary and secondary sources. Primary sources are the written material from the past. For cultural tourism research, useful primary sources can be travel journals, autobiographies, letters and postcards. The historic works for which primary sources are used are called secondary sources or literature. Examples of relevant secondary literature for cultural tourism studies are the biographies of the great travelling women of the Victorian age (e.g. Kikkert's 1980 biography on the Dutch traveller Alexandrine Tinne).

Besides written sources, people from the past have also left other material traces: artefacts, buildings, pictures and changes in the landscape. Vedute di Roma, the etchings from Giovanni Battista Piranesi, were made to be sold to the young noblemen on the Grand Tour. The black-and-white views were cherished at home either as a souvenir or as an appetizer for future travellers.

These material traces will also be referred to as sources if they provide the historian with useful knowledge of the past. In order to retrieve significant information from these sources, the historian has to pose the right questions. What the right questions are is derived from the best practices in history as science, so it depends on the experiences gathered through the process of historic research and history writing. Historians have to check if they can ask specific questions of the sources, if the sources can provide the right answers to their questions, and how these answers can be derived. This approach is called the historic–critical method and was also developed during the 19th century. The core activity of this method is to try to place the source as precisely as possible into its historic context and try to understand how the source was understood in its own time. This also establishes how representative a source is for developments in the historical period it dates from. A good example of this for cultural tourism is the exhibition and catalogue 'Piranesi as a designer' (Lawrence _et al._, 2007), which places the Vedute di Roma in the much larger context of the whole lifespan of Piranesi as architect, interior and furniture designer, draughtsman and antiquarian. In addition to official publications such as the Vedute, there were also intimate contributions to the Album Amicorum of the Dutchman Aernout Vosmaer by Piranesi and his two sons Francesco and Angelo. The latter was only 12 years old when he made a little drawing of the marbles of the Villa Albany in 1776. Vosmaer had enjoyed the company of Piranesi, who on occasions acted as a _cicerone_ (guide) for the travelling _milordi_ (gentlemen), who received something special to bring home from their Grand Tour.

Tradition and Überreste

The 19th-century scientist Johann Gustav Droysen distinguished between tradition and Überreste when typifying sources. Sources that are labelled tradition are written with the goal of giving a personal interpretation of the subject matter. Examples are memoirs, chronicles, travel records, biographies, autobiographies and essays. Since tradition gives a distorted picture, it is important to try to ascertain the position the author holds with regard to what is described when looking back at things. As the historian is aware of this when using these sources, he or she can approach them in a way that they may still provide objective information. Überreste are the direct record of actions that took place in the past and which are written without an interpretation of the historical period when they took place. Examples include bills, minutes, notes, diaries, letters, memoranda, charters, contracts, etc. Überreste are fragmentary and intertwined with historical developments. Like the tradition, they may give a distorted view and they may also avoid taboo matters and be a product of hidden agendas themselves. The historian must also be well aware of these pitfalls when using these sources, as they seem to be very objective in nature. Sources that from one perspective are labelled tradition, such as the memoirs of Churchill, could also be called Überreste when seen as a vision of the Second World War in post-war times.

How can a source be placed within its historic context? First, the researcher has to ascertain the authenticity of a source with the aid of three questions about its nature:

1. Is it an original or a fake? Is it the original, a copy or a rendering?
2. Is it complete?
3. What sort of source is it: tradition or Überreste?

After answering these basic questions the researcher must try to establish the identity of the author and try to gain certainty as to when and where the source was written or produced. We also need to know: why the source was written or made and to what end? The role of the author of the source has to be investigated too. Did the author witness the event or collect information from others? How reliable is the author? Another question is to what contemporary matter the source refers. All the answers to these questions relate to the reliability of the historic information. Such questions are important in researching cultural tourism, particularly given the importance of history, heritage and authenticity in the production and consumption of culture by tourists.

But as the chapters in this volume show, such questions are also important in relation to contemporary culture as well. For example, the grounded theory analysis of tourism development in Santiponce (Chapter 10) shows how important it is to uncover the origin and context of different sources. Are particular statements being made from a certain political position, for example? Are the interpretations of 'culture' and 'heritage' being used by different commentators always the same? A quick comparison of the different usages of terms such as 'culture' or 'authenticity' in the present volume would suggest that knowing about the origin and context of the different sources being examined is vital in cultural tourism research.

Conclusion

We have argued here for the integration of quantitative and qualitative approaches to the study of cultural tourism. A review of the approach taken to evidence by historians reveals much about potential means of integrating different forms of data into a holistic analysis. In the first place we need to be aware of the importance of asking the right questions and we then need to seek the appropriate types of data to answer those questions. The quantitative approach has the virtue of traditional scientific method, but as the example of historic analysis shows, qualitative information can also be tested and interpreted in a rigorous way.

Our argument here is that what is required is a more holistic approach which combines the virtues of both qualitative and quantitative research, and which is better able to place the different data sources in an appropriate historical and/or contemporary context.

References

Fielding, N. (1996) Qualitative interviewing. In: Gilbert, N. (ed.) *Researching Social Life*. Sage Publications, London, pp. 35–53.

Finn, M., Elliot-White, M. and Walton, M. (2000) *Tourism and Leisure Research Methods: Data Collection, Analysis and Interpretation*. Pearson Education, London.

Henderson, K.A. (1990) Reality comes through a prism: method choices in leisure research. *Society and Leisure* 13, 169–188.

Kemmis, S. and McTaggart, R. (2000) Participatory action research. In: Denzin, N. and Lincoln, Y. (eds) *Handbook of Qualitative Research*, 2nd edn. Sage Publications, Beverley Hills, California, pp. 567–605.

Kikkert, J.G. (1980) *Een Haagsche Dame in de Sahara. Het Avontuurlijke Leven van Alexandrine Tinne 1835–1869*. Maarten Muntinga, Amsterdam (reprinted in 2005).

Lawrence, S.E., Wilton-Ely, J., Eisenman, P., Gonzáles-Palacios, A., Graves, M., Jarrard, A., Miller, P.N., de Leeuw, R., Rosand, D. and Sørensen, B. (eds) (2007) *Piranesi as a Designer*. Cooper-Hewitt National Design Museum, Smithsonian Institute, New York.

Melkert, M. (2007) Maastricht: a cultural & historical treasure trove! Reflections on the development of a 'cultural biography' of Maastricht in relation to its role as cultural tourist city in the Euregion Meuse-Rhine. In: Richards, G. and Pereiro, X. (eds) *Cultural Tourism: Negotiating Identities*. Sector Editorial dos SDE serviços Gráficos da UTAD, Villa Real, Portugal, pp. 171–187.

Miles, M.B. and Huberman, A.M. (1994) *Qualitative Data Analysis: a Sourcebook of New Methods*, 2nd edn. Sage Publications, Thousand Oaks, California.

Philip, L.J. (1998) Combining quantitative and qualitative approaches to social research in human geography – an impossible mixture? *Environment and Planning* 30, 261–276.

Punch, K.F. (2005) *Introduction to Social Research: Quantitative and Qualitative Approaches*. Sage Publications, London.

Ragin, C.C. (1994) *Constructing Social Research: the Unity and Diversity of Method*. Pine Forge Press, Thousand Oaks, California.

Richards, G. and Queirós, C. (2005) *ATLAS Cultural Tourism Survey 2004*. ATLAS, Arnhem, the Netherlands.

Smith, M.K. (2003) *Issues in Cultural Tourism Studies*. Routledge, London.

Suber, P. (1997) *Basic Terms of Logic*. Available at: www.earlham.edu/~peters/courses/log/terms1.htm (accessed 28 May 2009).

Veal, A.J. (2006) *Research Methods for Leisure and Tourism: a Practical Guide*, 3rd edn. Prentice-Hall, Harlow, UK.

Von Ranke, L. (1824) *Geschichte der Romanischen und Germanischen Völker von 1494 bis 1514*. Phaidon-Vollmer, Essen, Germany.

Walle, A.H. (1997) Quantitative versus qualitative tourism research. *Annals of Tourism Research* 21, 524–536.

Weaver, D. and Lawton, L. (2002) *Tourism Management*. Wiley and Sons, Milton Keynes, UK.

Yin, R.K. (1994) *Case Study Research. Design and Methods*, 2nd edn. Sage Publications, London.

4 Blurring Boundaries in Cultural Tourism Research

Esther Binkhorst, Teun den Dekker and Marjan Melkert

Introduction

Tourism development is often hindered by the way tourism is claimed and framed. Driven by an economic growth perspective, tourism developers and policy makers allow tourism to increase, laying claim to natural, social, cultural, historical and other resources. We argue here that the starting point for tourism development should be human beings and their time-spatial context. This humanistic vision is very much inspired by the ethnographic perspective (see also Part IV of this volume). For tourism this implies an innovative approach. It means doing away with distinctions between supply and demand, company and customer, tourist and host, tourism and non-tourism spaces. Instead we should view tourism as a holistic network of actors connected in experience environments and operating within different time-spatial contexts (Binkhorst and Den Dekker, 2009).

A central role for the human being and thinking in experience networks are needed all the more so because of the blurring of boundaries between tourism, art, culture, sport, hobbies and learning, which are hard to deal with using traditional research approaches. When is someone actually a tourist? When is someone a cultural tourist? What hobbies, activities and experiences are considered to be (cultural) tourism experiences? Is it possible to distinguish between someone's cultural (tourism) activities and other (tourism) activities? How can tourists as human beings best be studied in an era of blurring boundaries? The aim of this chapter is to explore potential new ways of researching cultural tourism.

The Tourist as Human Being

Tourism experience networks

The essential information necessary to understand tourism phenomena and to be able to develop tourism is hidden in each human being who becomes a tourist or who, in one of his or her experience environments, comes into contact with tourism. A tourism network approach allows us to understand the interaction between individual tourists and other actors as well, in other words anyone and anything involved in the tourism network.

In tourism, the 'experience environment' is made up of all the people and things that surround the tourist. This not only includes the time when people are actually travelling but also the period in which the decision to travel is taken and the post-travel period after returning home. Consequently each person is surrounded by a unique 'tourism experience network' of all the stakeholders involved in his or her tourism experiences, whether they are real, virtual or even imaginary. The argument made here is that we should define tourism as an experience network in which various actors co-create as they engage in tourism experiences. This relates very much to what van der Duim (2007) called 'tourismscapes', or the complex processes of ordering of people and things. Such tourism experience networks are immense and connect the human being with: the people they travel with (friends, partner, family, special-interest group, colleagues), the Internet, virtual travel communities, travel agencies, tour operators, suppliers of transport, hoteliers, guides, local entrepreneurs offering activities at the destination, local residents, sights and activities at the destination such as attractions, typical landmarks, museums, heritage sites, events, natural landscapes, technology and so on.

Tourismscapes also include the governmental and non-governmental agencies that shape the conditions of travel (see also Chapter 16). Figure 4.1 provides a simple representation of such a tourism experience network.

The tourism experience network approach forces us to put the human being at the centre, not as a tourist but as a human being. In the first place, any tourist is a person or actor in his or her home environment (see Fig. 4.2). This is where he or she will usually spend most of the time and where lots of memorable social experiences will be undergone. In the home environment, people also spend much time on obligations such as work and school. The network in which the person acts basically guides him or her through life and will also respond to life's changes. The need for a tourism experience might evolve at a certain moment, which consequently changes the person's network. New actors will be sought or links

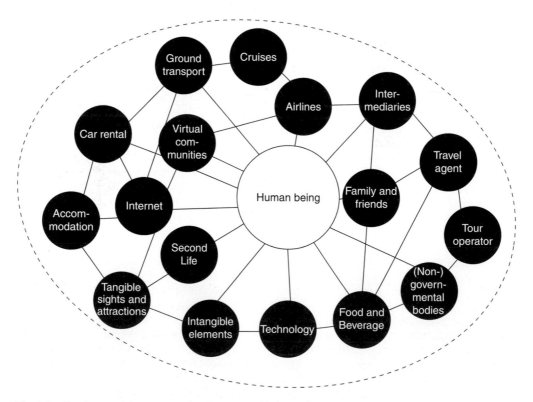

Fig. 4.1. Tourism experience networks. (Source: Binkhorst and Den Dekker, 2009.)

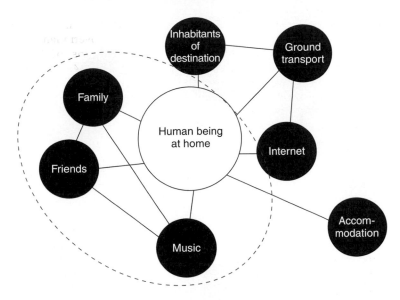

Fig. 4.2. Experience network of the home environment. (Source: Binkhorst and Den Dekker, 2009.)

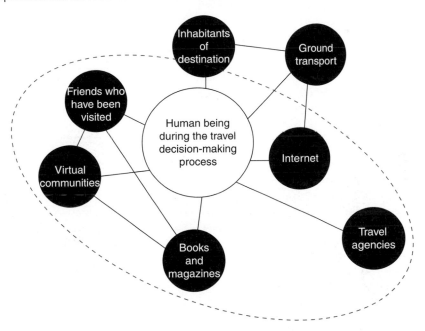

Fig. 4.3. Experience environment during the travel decision-making process. (Source: Binkhorst and Den Dekker, 2009.)

with existing actors will be strengthened to achieve one's objectives to fulfil the need to travel (see Fig. 4.3).

Once the person has been through the travel decision-making process he or she will leave the daily experience environment for a holiday or a break (see Fig. 4.4) and will return again to the home environment after travel (see Fig. 4.2). The first two experience environments, the home environment and the work and/or learning environment, are often neglected in tourism studies. When

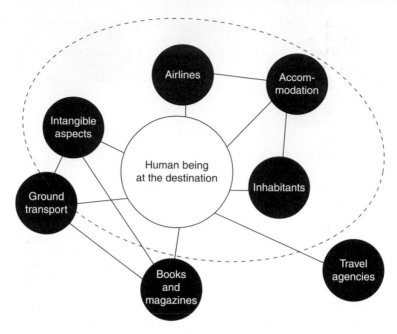

Fig. 4.4.   Experience network at the destination. (Source: Binkhorst and Den Dekker, 2009.)

picturing a tourist, researchers routinely begin with an image of someone in the third experience environment, that of free time, characterized by the freedom, time and money to travel to other areas outside the daily living environment. Moreover, they tend to imagine the tourist either when travelling to or being at the destination. We do not usually consider persons as a 'tourist' while they are still in their own daily context. But the daily context is exactly where a 'tourist' spends most of the time and where decisions are taken about future trips and where a lifestyle might influence a travel style. Certain newspapers and magazines drop regularly into the 'tourist's' mailbox; certain TV channels are watched; donations to certain organizations are made; certain souvenirs in the home environment and clothes in the wardrobe remind us of previous trips; books, CDs and DVDs on the shelves tell us about art, culture, music, painting, pottery, history, travel destinations; favourite bars, restaurants or clubs are visited; certain websites connect the 'tourist' through the Internet with the rest of the world; stories and experiences are exchanged with family members, colleagues and friends; and a certain type of work or education shapes 'the tourist's' life. By studying the various experience environments in their daily context, researchers could get to know the tourist better, or, more accurately, the human being behind the tourist. The following sections examine how the study of tourism is complicated by questions of subjectivity and objectivity. We then examine the case for striking a balance between these two extremes (see also Chapter 3) and finally we provide some examples of potentially innovative approaches to researching the increasingly blurred world of the tourist.

The Cultural Tourism Product: the Subjectivist versus the Objectivist Approach

How can we define culture?

If blurring of boundaries leads us to regard and research the cultural tourist as a human being, then what will this process mean for the object or the cultural experience? Well, nothing new to start with. As Richards (1996: 42) remarks: 'One of the few areas of certainty in cultural tourism is the difficulty of defining it. Few studies are agreed about what the cultural element of cultural tourism should encompass'. The best way to proceed is therefore to try to find out what is meant by the term 'culture' itself in different contexts. Richards (1996) explains that culture can refer to a process or a product. The idea of culture as a process stems from anthropology and sociology. Codes of conduct that are embedded in a specific group define what culture is for that group. Culture is therefore the process through which people make sense of themselves and their lives. An example of this is the music CD that a tourist may bring home having attended a dance performance on holiday. Hearing it at home will probably not evoke the same kind of experience, because of the change in context.

The idea of culture as a product was developed within art criticism. The cultural product is the result of individual or group activities to which certain meanings are attached. These meanings can define something as 'high' or 'low' culture. The definitions of high and low culture evolve continuously, as is noted and described within postmodern discourse. An illustrative example is offered by the new policy of the British Museum welcoming back its anthropological collections and even staging special events connected with them, such as modelling and worshipping a clay Hindu goddess in the museum. Several decennia ago, the same collections would have been removed from this temple of high culture and such events would have been labelled as popular culture.

Because of all these uncertainties, it may be more sensible, as an aid to understanding why what is being said where, to consider the matter from the point of view of the philosophy of values. The ontological status of values depends on the question if values exist in their own right or if they exist only if there is an evaluating entity. Therefore the status of values depends on the context in which they are seen – the

general outlook on life – and whether this is subjective or objective. In other words: is it an entity – a human being – that evaluates the world or are there immanent values to be found in the world itself?

Subjectivism

Radical subjectivity implies that the point of reference is the subject, in this case the cultural tourist. The subject attaches values to things. Since this is a human act, it is the behaviour of the human being which has to be studied in order to understand personal preferences relating to specific – in this case cultural – objects and experiences.

In the subjective picture of the world, again, values do not exist independently in themselves. Objects that are evaluated positively are those that are desirable for the subject. The subject constructs the values and these do not depend on a correspondence with reality. Subjectivists argue that if there were no evaluating subjects, there would be no values. The seven different subsets or niche components that Smith (2003) identifies with the term 'cultural tourism' can be related to the subjective preferences or profile of the cultural tourist.

1. The tourist who likes heritage visits castles, palaces, country houses, archaeological sites, monuments, architecture, museums and religious sites.
2. The tourist who likes arts visits the theatre, concerts, galleries, festivals, carnivals, events and literary sites.
3. The tourist who likes to be creatively engaged will undertake photography, painting, pottery, cookery, crafts and language learning.
4. The tourist who likes urban culture will visit historic cities, regenerated industrial cities, waterfront developments, arts and heritage attractions.
5. The tourist who likes rural culture will visit villages, farms and agro-tourism objects, eco-museums, national parks and follow wine trails.
6. The tourist who likes indigenous culture will visit hill tribes and participate

in desert or mountain trekking. They will also visit cultural centres and be interested in arts and crafts products, cultural performances and festivals.

7.   The tourist who likes popular culture will visit theme parks and theme attractions, shopping malls, pop concerts, sporting events, media and film sets, industrial heritage sites and fashion and design museums.

Once the tourist has been identified as the subject who 'makes' the cultural tourism product, the boundaries between these different types of products blur. Because the cultural tourist is a human being with various preferences, he or she will choose, combine and mix the components of the cultural tourism product in accordance with his or her needs and wants. So a wide range of different tourist experiences may be sought by the same individual: swimming in a river in the morning, visiting a temple in the afternoon and dancing at a beach party at night. This goes especially for the postmodern tourist consumer belonging to the 'zap' generation, whose behaviour is as eclectic as it is unpredictable.

According to Schouten (2003), what the visitor wants (to experience) should be interesting, unique and meaningful. That is why interpretation and imagination play an important role in presenting the cultural tourism product. But what about the authenticity of the cultural object or event? By stating that authenticity is determined by the visitors themselves, Gilmore and Pine (2007) take an extreme subjectivist position in the debate on this issue. The danger of this subjectivist point of view is that the focus on personal preferences of the tourist may lead to the commodification of culture on the one hand and cultural relativism on the other.

The value that the subject attaches to an object or the intrinsic value of an object is not the same as its moral value. Moral implications can only be found within a theory of moral obligations, where objects become moral objects. The way in which a moral object is treated can be judged as good or bad. In eco-philosophy, ecosystems are regarded as moral objects. Cultural objects

too are often regarded as moral objects, as indicated by all the measures taken to prevent cultural heritage from crumbling under the pressure of too many tourists and the use of the money these visitors bring in for restoration. So dealing morally with cultural objects can be described in terms of preservation and development, two processes that are frequently analysed in cultural tourism studies. A good example is the cultural tourism sustainability mix developed by Munsters (2005): preservation (of the cultural object), population (the interests of the host community), public (the experience of the cultural tourist) and profit (for the tourism industry) should be in balance, in order to guarantee the sound development of cultural tourism.

Objectivism

The opposite philosophical stream to subjectivism is objectivism. For this school of thought everything begins with the object. From an objective perspective the point of reference is the set of characteristics of the object observed. The object is valued because of its intrinsic values. Values here are not a function of human desire, but they exist in their own right as the characteristics of the object and independent of the presence of an evaluating entity, because reality contains much more than we can consciously conceive. In this outlook on reality, the (tourist) subject does not attach value to an object but rather discovers it. The cultural tourist visits cultural objects or events in order to enjoy their immanent qualities. The characteristics are the things that enable us to evaluate an object.

Munsters (2007) makes it very clear that a cultural object, event or spectacle has to be open for the public in order to be able to become a cultural tourism product (see also Chapter 5). The attractive value is primarily being defined in terms of the measure of accessibility. The characteristics the cultural offer possesses *sui generis* are secondary. Munsters' (1996, 2007) general typology of cultural tourism resources, categorized

Box 4.1. General typology of cultural tourism resources. (Source: Richards, 1996: 110.)

1. Attractions

(a) Monuments
   Religious buildings
   Public buildings
   Historic houses
   Castles and palaces
   Parks and gardens
   Defences
   Archaeological sites
   Industrial–archaeological buildings

(b) Museums
   Folklore museums
   Art museums

(c) Routes
   Cultural–historic routes
   Art routes

(d) Theme parks
   Cultural–historic parks
   Archaeological parks
   Architecture parks

2. Events

(a) Cultural–historic events
   Religious festivals
   Secular festivals
   Folk festivals

(b) Art events
   Art exhibitions
   Art festivals

(c) Events and attractions
   Open monument days

into attractions (permanent by definition) and events (temporary by definition), may be qualified as objectivist or ideographic, as it is based on the attributes of the cultural resources (Richards, 2001) (Box 4.1).

From the objectivistic point of view, knowledge of an object and taking the time to get to know it are of paramount importance for an adequate evaluation. Lack of knowledge makes the judgment of value unreliable. In the objectivistic perspective on reality, taste becomes something that can be disputed while education is considered as crucial for the improvement of the ability to evaluate things. This point of view risks attracting the reproach of elitism. Schouten (2005) calls it the 'what the expert says' aspect of cultural tourism: the conservator and the restorer of cultural heritage qualify their activities in terms such as 'important', 'significant', 'relevant', 'content', 'facts' and 'history'. Experts prefer a public of connoisseurs of art and history and they have a negative opinion of tourists. The gap that may result from this line of thought is also felt by the general public when art and heritage presentations do not match with their interests.

In the discussion on authenticity, objectivists hold totally opposite views to subjectivists. With regard to the authenticity of historic buildings, Denslagen (2004) feels it is confusing that different meanings become attached to the term 'authentic'. This Tower of Babel evaporates the content of the term and leads to a practice of 'anything goes'. His advice is to make a clear distinction between 'authenticity' and 'originality'. The authentic is the historic object itself, regardless of wear, tear and change. The original is the state in which the object was first presented. Only the substance of an object, work of art or building can be authentic and nothing else. At the 1994 conference of the International Council of Monuments and Sites in Japan, it was decided that besides the material authenticity of the (historic) substance it should be possible to label other things as authentic too. Denslagen mentions the continuity of local definitions of cultural heritage and local restoration traditions as examples. This theory may well apply to historic buildings and artefacts, but it falls short for the performing arts. Before the pianola and the wax roll were developed, it was difficult to tell what a piece of music sounded like. Until then, music notation systems put on paper what should reverberate within the ear of the listener. Therefore one of the great artistic experiences has been the study and performance of the 'Alte Musik Tradition', (i.e. medieval, Renaissance and Baroque music). Since Vivaldi (in 1958) and Bach (in 1964) have been played on historical instruments, musicologists have been working hard to find out how music originally was performed, on what instruments, in what sort of architectural environment, for what sort of audience(s) and trying to relive those experiences. The authenticity of the performance remains a point of discussion, but the advice of the singer Marco Beasley (2005) to take the heart as one's guide may be the best direction to follow here, even if this seems 'unscientific'.

Virtus in medio

Subjectivism and objectivism are radically different approaches to reality. However, as Melkert and Vos argue in Chapter 3, they do not necessarily exclude each other. It is possible to give a place to evaluating subjects within a world where objects have intrinsic values and to realize an exchange between subjects and objects according to Horace's words: *virtus est medium vitiorum et utrimque reductum* (virtue is the middle between two vices, and is equally removed from either extreme).

It is clearly beneficial for the study of cultural tourism products if researchers are well aware of their position and that of their fellow researchers within the field of tension between subjectivism and objectivism. This awareness would enable them to understand who says what with regard to the cultural tourism product. The approach of sociologists, anthropologists and art critics, who see culture either as a process or as a product, puts them on the subjective side of the spectrum. Nevertheless, within their field of study, an objective approach could also be possible and might even help to change interpretations. The place in the middle may also be the place where experts meet exploiters and where cooperation is possible between these two sides in the process of cultural tourism product development.

The question of what is authentic 'in the middle' may create, as in the case of the 'Alte Musik Tradition', a true 'battlefield' of expectations, new discoveries and incessantly growing insights. The conclusion might even be that it is impossible to define what is authentic at all. The quest for a definition of authenticity may even be destructive, as Hildesheimer (1985) claims in *Der ferne Bach*, because it stands in the way of new interpretations. Nevertheless, the performers of ancient music present the world with a breathtaking series of rehearsals, concerts and audio recordings that either enchant or provoke disgust and that set hearts and minds at work. A case of fertile, even procreative, misunderstanding? Admirers of ancient music become cultural tourists as they travel to the historic castles, convents and churches and other places where the concerts take place. Films like Corneau's *Tous les matins du monde* and Corbiau's *Farinelli – il castrato* and *Le Roi danse* have made the results of the quest accessible for a larger audience. These films may even be an incentive to visit the remains of the architectural decor they evoke (such as Versailles) and can so produce a spin-off in the form of cultural tourism.

Claiming this middle ground requires us to put ourselves in the position of the tourist, and to place the tourist as human being at the centre of the tourism experience. The problem with this new positioning is the difficulty of capturing the new insights generated using traditional tourism research methods. We would argue, therefore, that what is needed is a new range of research tools capable of traversing the middle ground and seeking out the innovative behaviours and experiences of the tourist. In the following section we outline some innovative new ways of approaching the tourist, which may provide a means to capture new dimensions of their experience.

Developments in Methodological Innovation

If we want to acknowledge the tourist as human being in an experience environment, new research methods are needed to be able to understand tourist behaviour better. Conventional research methods can be sufficient to describe and register tourism behaviour, but when researchers really want to understand the tourist as a human being, innovative methods are required to explore the experience environments and how these are used by the tourist. Two main developments can be distinguished in innovative methods. First, a shift from top-down to bottom-up approaches, with dialogues between equal partners taking the place of traditional top-down methods. Second, a shift can be observed from real to virtual methods. The use of virtual worlds such as Second Life is becoming common in tourism, as it is in other areas of social life. These tools provide numerous innovative ways of doing both qualitative and quantitative research.

Figure 4.5 shows a wide range of research methods, from the more conventional methods at the bottom to the more innovative at the top. The most innovative of these methods will be explained with the

help of illustrative cases from tourism and other fields.

The use of websites as a research tool: the case of IKEA in the Netherlands

The central theme of a Dutch website initiated by IKEA is 'Design Your Own Life'. The website aims at getting insight into the way people shape their own lives and enjoy living. Consumer research by the market research company TNS-NIPO forms the basis of the website. Visitors can discuss topics on a forum, do tests, read advice and in the process learn more about themselves. IKEA as a company can learn a lot from the input visitors provide. As an example of an instrument used to gather visitor information by means of a bottom-up approach, this tool is also perfectly applicable

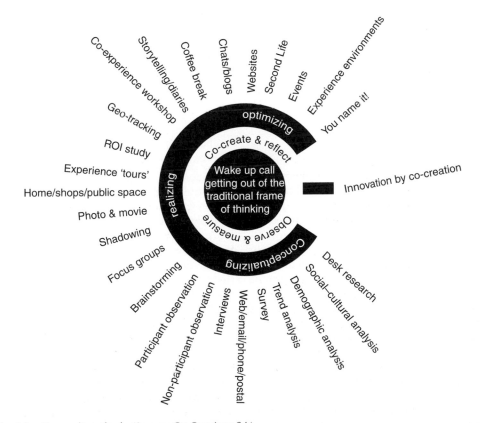

Fig. 4.5. Research methods. (Source: Co-Creations S.I.)

within the framework of tourism destination management.

The use of geo-tracking: the case of Ipoki, Spain

Geo-tracking takes the investigation of human spatial behaviour to a more sophisticated level. New technologies provide researchers with other possibilities to track tourists during their journey. Today there are two main tracking technologies available: satellite navigation systems and land-based navigations systems (Shoval and Isaacson, 2007). Through the Spanish social network Ipoki (http://www.ipoki.es), geo-tracking is available for everyone (see also Chapter 9). Ipoki members can trace the movements of their friends through GPS software downloaded to their mobile phones. By creating an Ipoki group among tourists, it should also be possible to monitor tourist movements without the need for sophisticated hardware. Recent developments and new models in the mobile phone industry make geo-tracking via GPS even more easy and accessible.

The use of experience environments: the case of the Co-lab in Sitges, Spain

The Co-lab is an apartment-cum-office in the Spanish coastal village of Sitges, where tourism practice and research go hand in hand. A type of tourism based on the principle of co-creation has been developed there to showcase the possibilities for innovation in tourism development (Binkhorst, 2007). This means, on the one hand, that locals participate in enhancing the experience of the tourist and, on the other hand, the tourists themselves can play an active role in the co-creation of their tourism experiences. At present, real-life experiences are being developed, and the next step will be to create an experience environment in which both tourists and locals can also virtually shape and share their experiences. At the same time a data collection tool will be developed. In addition to the traditional

questionnaire and (in-depth) interview, one of the research methods used in the Co-lab to gain insight into how tourists experience the destination and their holiday in general is to have them picture their holiday through their own eyes during the 'do it yourself tour'. The data will be used to create a (virtual) book written or, better said, pictured by tourists about their holiday and the destination (see also Chapter 13). These data will be shared with anyone whose experience environments they come across.

The use of public space: the case of the New Zealand Travel Café, Tokyo, Japan

The New Zealand Travel Café in Tokyo, Japan, is a public space used to teach Japanese people in an informal way about New Zealand as a tourism destination. Their visit to the Travel Café, which is part of their home environment, has an influence on their travel decision-making process. The Travel Café is an interesting opportunity for the tourism industry and governmental tourism bodies in New Zealand to get in contact with potential visitors before they actually visit the country.

The use of storytelling: the case of Audio Snacks/N8 geluiden in the USA and the Netherlands

Audio Snacks and N8 geluiden (Sounds of the Night) are similar initiatives from the USA and the Netherlands. The basic concept is that anybody with a sound recording device (such as an MP3 player) can make their own audio guide of a certain destination and can share it through the Web. By tracking download and upload behaviour, researchers can learn a lot about what people tend to seek in a certain destination.

All the examples mentioned above show a similar tendency: the blurring of boundaries between the different experience environments of the tourist. When we acknowledge those blurring boundaries and keep in mind the evolution from top-down to bottom-up and from real to virtual approaches, abundant possibilities are at hand in order to generate a more profound understanding of the behaviour of the tourist as a human being.

Conclusions

As the boundaries between different types of consumption become blurred, so it becomes increasingly important to place the tourist at the centre of the tourism system. In this way, the complex connections between different forms of consumption in different types of environments can be traced and interlinked. Collecting data on these new forms of tourist consumption requires new methods that are able to cross the boundaries between home and tourist environments and quantitative and qualitative information. Advances in technology are making such innovative approaches increasingly viable and should open up exciting new avenues for research in the future.

References

Beasley, M. (2005) A voice, a way. In: Beasley, M. and Morini, G. (eds) *Recitar Cantando/Accordone*. Cypres Records, Brussels (CD).

Binkhorst, E. (2007) Creativity in tourism experiences, a closer look at Sitges. In: Richards, G. and Wilson, J. (eds) *Tourism, Creativity and Development*. Routledge, London, pp. 125–145.

Binkhorst, E. and Den Dekker, T. (2009) Agenda for co-creation tourism experience research. *Journal of Hospitality Marketing and Management* 18, 311–327.

Denslagen, W. (2004) *Romantisch Modernisme, Nostalgie in de Monumentenzorg*. SUN, Amsterdam.

Gilmore, J.H. and Pine, J. (2007) *Authenticity: What Consumers Really Want*. Harvard Business School Press, Boston, Massachusetts.

Hildesheimer, W. (1985) *Der ferne Bach*, 2nd edn. Insel Verlag, Frankfurt am Main, Germany.

Melkert, M. (1995) Within you without you: over objectivistische waardentheorieën en Milieu-filosofie. MA thesis. University of Limburg, Maastricht, the Netherlands.

Munsters, W. (1996) Cultural tourism in Belgium. In: Richards, G. (ed.) *Cultural Tourism in Europe*. CAB International, Wallingford, UK, pp. 109–126.

Munsters, W. (2005) Culture and tourism: from antagonism to synergism. *ATLAS Reflections 2005*, 41–50.

Munsters, W. (2007) *Cultuurtoerisme*, 4th edn. Garant, Antwerpen–Apeldoorn, Belgium.

Prahalad, C.K. and Ramaswamy, V. (2003) The new frontier of experience innovation. *MIT Sloan Management Review* 44, 12–18.

Prahalad, C.K. and Ramaswamy, V. (2004) *The Future of Competition: Co-creating Unique Value with Customers*. Harvard Business School Press, Boston, Massachusetts.

Richards, G (1996) The scope and significance of cultural tourism. In: Richards, G. (ed.) *Cultural Tourism in Europe*. CAB International, Wallingford, UK, pp. 19–45.

Richards, G. (2001) The development of cultural tourism in Europe. In: Richards G. (ed.) *Cultural Attractions and European Tourism*. CAB International, Wallingford, UK, pp. 3–29.

Schouten, F. (2003) About the quality of life, and nothing less. In: *Creating a Fascinating World*. Breda University of Professional Education (NHTV), Breda, the Netherlands pp. 9–14.

Schouten, F. (2005) Productontwikkeling voor erfgoedtoerisme (weer) in het verdomhoekje. *Vrijetijdsstudies* 23, 47–50.

Shoval, N. and Isaacson, M. (2007) Tracking tourists in the digital age. *Annals of Tourism Research* 34, 141–159.

Smith, M.K. (2003) *Issues in Cultural Tourism Studies*. Routledge, London,

Van der Duim, V.R. (2007) Tourismscapes. An actor–network perspective. *Annals of Tourism Research* 34(4), 961–976.

5 The Cultural Destination Experience Audit Applied to the Tourist-historic City

Wil Munsters

Introduction

In studies on destination management, little attention has been paid to the measuring of the tourist experience. In particular the hospitality experience of the guests in their contacts with both professional tourist service providers and the local population has been neglected. One of the major reasons for this lacuna in visitor survey research is to be found in the methodological problems connected to the measuring of visit experiences (Page and Connel, 2006; see also Chapter 12, this volume). Yet it is a fact that the visitor's experience is one of the key factors for the quality of the stay and for possible repeat visits.

The purpose of this study is to contribute to the methodological discourse on the evaluation of the tourist experience in cultural destinations. Being the most complex and interesting case of a cultural tourist destination, the tourist-historic city has been chosen as a case study. Not only the material core product of tourist-historic cities, consisting of monuments, ancient street patterns, museums and cultural events (the 'hardware'), but also the immaterial attraction elements (the 'software'), of which hospitality is often one of the most important, run the risk of suffering from tourism pressure, given the growing popularity of old monumental towns as tourist destinations. Moreover, the level of hospitality is closely related to the social carrying capacity of the local community: the stronger/weaker the social carrying capacity, the higher/lower the level of hospitality (Munsters, 2007).

The Tourist-historic City as a Cultural Tourism Product

The attractiveness of a historic city for tourists depends not only on the cultural offer it possesses but also on the supply of additional urban services and transport facilities, together with which it forms a complete tourism product.

On the basis of the elementary definition of the tourism product as an addition of attractions plus accommodations plus transportation, the cultural tourism product offered by the tourist-historic city can be defined as a composition of:

- the core product, being the cultural tourism supply (monuments, street patterns, museums, art galleries, theatres, cinemas, routes, cultural events, local culture) and the related specific cultural tourist services, such as information and education; and

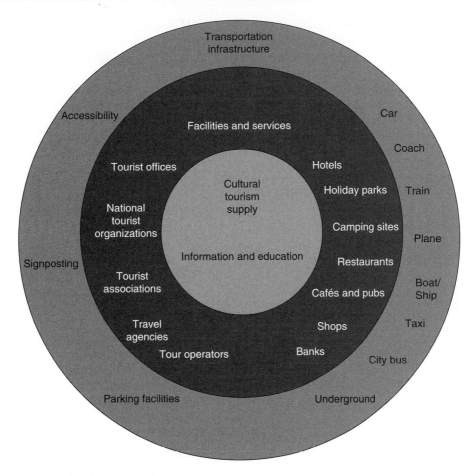

Fig. 5.1.   The cultural tourism product.

- the additional product, being the general tourism product elements and the related tourist services consisting of:
  - general tourist facilities and services;
    - tourist organizations and travel intermediaries: tourist information offices, tourist associations, travel agencies, tour operators;
    - accommodation suppliers: hotels, holiday parks, camping sites;
    - catering industry: restaurants, cafés and pubs;
    - retail business: (souvenir) shops, outdoor markets, banks;
  - transportation infrastructure:
    - accessibility, signposting, parking facilities;

  - private and public inner-city transporters: taxi companies, city bus service, underground (Munsters, 2005) (Fig. 5.1).

Within the three major components of the cultural tourism product, all kinds of urban service providers assure the delivery of the product or service elements to the consumer, i.e. the cultural tourist. The area of the cultural tourism product in which the provider is active determines the type of service provider. So we can distinguish between:

- the core product: the specific cultural tourist services related to the cultural attractions and rendered by, for example, city guides, museum guides or museum custodians; and

- the additional product: the general tourist services related to the general tourist facilities and the transportation infrastructure and rendered by, for example, tourist office employees, hotel receptionists, waiters, shop assistants, bus drivers or police officers.

The Cultural Destination Experience Audit of the Tourist-historic City: General Methodology

Genesis and structure of the research model

Originally, the cultural destination experience audit was an extended version of an earlier research model, the so-called *hospitality audit*. This model has been applied to the city of Maastricht. Being by far the most-visited tourist city in the southern Netherlands, Maastricht is confronted with the problem of overcrowding of the historical centre, which might become a threat to its well-known hospitality. That is why in 1999 the parties concerned (local authorities, tourist office and tourism industry) commissioned a field research on the hospitable image of Maastricht with tourists, tourist service providers and local inhabitants. The findings provided a basis for developing a visitor management policy focused on the immaterial tourist-historic product. The main conclusions of the final report were that tourists find themselves welcome in the city but that at the same time the locals were concerned about the identity of Maastricht because of the growing number of visitors. Preventive measures were proposed to guarantee a hospitable attitude towards tourists from both the inhabitants and the service providers in the future (Van den Braak *et al.*, 2000).

One of the recommendations of the report was to repeat the first survey, employing it as a baseline for future monitoring. This research project was carried out in Maastricht in the autumn of 2001. It has given the opportunity to elaborate and test an integral hospitality audit, a systematic assessment of the hospitality of the tourist-historic city with the help of specific measurement instruments. To that end, hospitality meters have been developed by improving the quantitative-statistical and qualitative tools to measure hospitality proposed in the 2000 report (Casier *et al.*, 2002).

Subsequently, the hospitality audit has served as a basis for the development of the cultural destination experience audit, which takes into account all the elements of the cultural tourism product. The cultural destination experience audit has been applied in two small tourist-historic cities near to Maastricht in the region South-Limburg: Valkenburg and Vaals (Alves de Oliveira *et al.*, 2005; Berbers *et al.*, 2005; Bijnagte *et al.*, 2008).

The cultural destination experience audit is based on the combination of quantitative and qualitative research methods. Three instruments, all of them appropriate data-collecting methods for field research, have been selected to measure the visitor's experience in tourist-historic cities (Table 5.1).

Thus the audit makes it possible to measure the visitor's experience by combining three different but complementary perspectives according to the principle of methodical triangulation, which helps to compensate for the shortcomings of one method through the strengths of the other and conversely by means of trade-offs (see Chapters 3 and 10, this volume). The personal surveys, the mystery tourist visits and the in-depth interviews have to meet the

Table 5.1. Methodology of the cultural destination experience audit.

Research type	Research method	Research instrument	Population
Quantitative	Interrogation	Personal survey	Cultural tourists
Qualitative	Observation	Mystery tourist visit	Service providers
Qualitative	Interrogation	In-depth interview	Service providers

basic research requirements of representativeness, validity and reliability. The repeating of the measurements as well as the complementariness of the methods enhances the reliability. The comparison of the results of the three research methods can be used as an extra validity test. If the scores match, one can speak of converging validity.

The cultural tourist survey

From expectation to experience

The survey consists of the basic questionnaire of the ATLAS Cultural Tourism Research Project with additional questions comparing the subjective experiences of the cultural tourist with their expectations. These additional questions are inspired by the principles of the SERVQUAL model, applied in the service industry, which measures the quality of a service, characterized by five basic features (called *dimensions*), on the basis of the differences (called *gaps*) between the expectation and the experience of the guest. The experience is examined in such a way that it can be compared with the expectation (Kotler *et al.*, 1999; Page and Connel, 2006). One string of the additional questions focuses on the expectations and the experiences concerning the hospitality of the tourist-historic city in general, including the attitude of the local inhabitants, and on the hospitality of the urban service providers working within the core cultural tourism product or within the additional cultural tourism product. After having indicated their expectations before the visit, the respondents are asked how they have experienced the hospitality of the urban service providers during their stay. For each question the respondent has to make a comparison between the expected and the experienced hospitality in order to find out to what extent the experience meets the expectation.

The definition of hospitality applied to the tourist-historic city

Since hospitality is a multi-interpretable concept, the validity of the survey is a point

meriting particular attention. That is why one of the first questions of this part of the questionnaire to be submitted to the respondent is to define their conception of hospitality with five previously selected basic features of hospitality and, according to the SERVQUAL method, to indicate the weight of each feature by putting them in order of importance. By doing so, it is possible to establish a general ranking of the five features on the basis of the answers of the respondents.

The guest (the cultural tourist) experiences hospitality at each interaction they go through with one of the hosts (the urban service providers or the local residents). In simple terms, *hospitality* can be defined as the experience of being received as a guest. Comparative analysis of different definitions of hospitality shows that five features return in most of them:

- satisfaction of needs of the guest;
- unselfishness towards the guest;
- sincere friendly approach towards the guest;
- gaining trust of the guest; and
- giving a feeling of safety to the guest (Vijver, 1996; Casier *et al.*, 2002).

The experiences with the survey in Maastricht indicated that no respondent missed any element in the definition of hospitality.

As hospitality is also an intangible concept, it has to be operationalized in terms of measurable behaviour if one wants to develop instruments that are suited to evaluating objectively the hospitality experience. The five selected features can be operationalized as follows:

- Satisfaction of needs of the guest: offering products and services that are part of the core business to the guest. Example: museum personnel are willing to answer questions about the museum.
- Unselfishness towards the guest: offering products and services that are *not* part of the core business to the guest; a non-commercial attitude without any expected compensation. Example: the bus driver is willing to change money.
- Sincere, friendly approach towards the guest: giving the guest the feeling of being

Table 5.2. Visitor questionnaire (excerpt).

How do you experience the hospitality of city X with regard to the following aspects?	Expected Level				Real Level			
	Low			High	Low			High
General impression	1	2	3	4	1	2	3	4
Commercial urban service providers								
Cultural attractions	1	2	3	4	1	2	3	4
	not applicable				not applicable			
Hotels, holiday parks, camping sites	1	2	3	4	1	2	3	4
	not applicable				not applicable			
Restaurants, cafés and pubs	1	2	3	4	1	2	3	4
	not applicable				not applicable			
Shops and banks	1	2	3	4	1	2	3	4
	not applicable				not applicable			
Non-commercial urban service providers								
Public inner-city transporters	1	2	3	4	1	2	3	4
	not applicable				not applicable			

a special, individual person instead of giving the idea of only approaching the guest correctly because this is the right thing to do. Example: local residents are willing to show the way.

- Gaining trust of the guest: the guest can rely on the host to receive what he expects to receive; the guest feels comfortable because the host is taking care of them, also in the case of questions and incidents. Example: the waiter serves the guest within an acceptable time.

- Giving a feeling of safety to the guest: in the light of social trends and political events such as growing criminality, pointless violence in public places and terrorist attacks, safety is not self-evident any more; for this reason, guests are stricter on this matter (see Chapter 8). Example: the standard illuminated green sign shows the emergency exit.

A division in various branches has been made in order to make the concept of the 'urban service provider' more tangible for the respondent and to be able to draw specific conclusions per type of service provider. The urban service providers are divided into commercial and non-commercial, i.e. not subsidized versus partly or totally subsidized by the government. This distinction has been made as it is essential for the nature of the hospitable behaviour of the service provider if they are focused on service for profit or on service not for profit (Vijver, 1996) (Table 5.2). Next, the respondent is interrogated about the attitude of the local inhabitants towards tourist guests, which is also part of the hospitality experience.

Since the interviewers are previously provided with a manual, own interpretation of the questions by the interviewers is excluded and vagueness is prevented with the interviewees, because the interviewers are able to explain the questionnaire. In addition, the interviewer can further operationalize the features with concrete examples of hospitable behaviour per feature in order to ensure a univocal interpretation of the concept. All this in order to increase the validity of the survey.

The second category of the additional questions deals with the expectations and the experiences of the tourist concerning the tangible and intangible – other than hospitality – cultural tourism product elements such as:

- variety of the supply of attractions and accommodations;
- price–quality relation within the catering industry; and
- general atmosphere of the tourist-historic city.

Representativeness of the survey

Since it is impossible to interrogate all the cultural tourists, a representative sample has to be taken. In order to ensure that all visitor categories are sampled, the respondents are selected on a random basis and are interviewed over different days and time periods. The cultural tourists are selected from the total population of tourist visitors by undertaking the survey at the cultural attractions. The sample is determined by means of the following formula fit for an infinite population:

$$n > z^2 \bullet p(1-p)/a^2$$

- z = required reliability. The survey is reliable if the same results are obtained under different circumstances. That is why, for example, the surveys have to be carried out under different weather conditions. A reliability level of 95% is necessary to be sure that the result of the sample is not based on coincidences. This leads to a z-value of 1.96.
- $p(1-p)$ = indication for the spread in the elements of the population, where $p(1-p) \leq 0.25$.
- a = accuracy of the confidence interval. The a-value is 0.05.
- n – sample. The result of this formula is the minimum response rate required for a representative sample of visitors that meets the fixed quality standards of reliability and accuracy.

If the sample is set up so as to be statistically representative of the total population of cultural tourists, the interpretation of hospitality by the respondents, for example, can be generalized for all cultural tourists visiting the tourist-historic city. In the case of Maastricht, the survey provided the following interpretation of hospitality (Table 5.3).

Table 5.3. Hospitality conception (%) of the cultural tourists visiting Maastricht (2002).

Sincere, friendly approach	27.9
Satisfaction of needs	21.0
Giving a feeling of safety	19.6
Gaining trust	18.5
Unselfishness	13.0
Hospitality	100.0

The mystery tourist visits to urban service providers

The hospitality of the urban service providers was also examined by means of mystery guest visits. The mystery guest visit is a measurement tool extensively used in the hotel and catering industry, which borrowed it from the service industry, where it is commonly termed *mystery shopping* (Hudson *et al.*, 2001). The instrument consists of structured participant observation of service providers by an anonymous professional visitor, followed by the evaluation of the service quality. The advantage of this qualitative research method is that actual behaviour can be analysed more objectively, as the observed company or employee does not (need to) know that they or their surroundings are the subject of examination. Since in this study the mystery guest or shopper plays the role of a tourist visitor, this anonymous observer will be referred to as a *mystery tourist*.

The mystery tourist observation forms have been drawn up per category of urban service provider. On the basis of the method used in the SERVQUAL model, the same five main features of hospitality that were used for the tourist survey were operationalized in detailed questions allowing a thorough investigation of the hospitality practice, as an excerpt of the mystery tourist form for cultural attractions shows (Table 5.4).

The mystery tourist visits have to be reliable, valid and representative. In order to ensure interobserver reliability, two to four visits by couples of observers have to be made to the same type of service provider. There has to be an average consensus percentage of at least 80% per hospitality feature between the visits to have a reliable mystery tourist research. The consensus percentage can be calculated with the following formula, based on the Cohen's kappa test, a statistical measure of inter-rater agreement for qualitative items:

$$(x_1/x_2) \bullet 100\% \geq 80\%$$

- x_1 = visit with lowest score
- x_2 = visit with highest score

Table 5.4. Mystery tourist form for cultural attractions (excerpt).

Features of hospitality	Yes	No	Not applicable
Satisfaction of needs Is the visitor served within an acceptable time?			
Unselfishness Are the personnel willing to answer the questions of visitors that are not related to the interests of the service provider?			
Sincere friendly approach Is the visitor greeted when entering?			
Gaining trust Are the personnel sincerely willing to resolve complaints?			
Safety Is the exit free of obstacles?			

The Cohen's kappa test requires a consensus percentage of at least 50%. For the mystery tourist visits, the score has been put up to a minimum of 80%, in order to guarantee substantial or even, in the best case, complete agreement between the mystery tourists as judges. The reason why this high percentage has been chosen is that the mystery visits are not made to one and the same service provider, but to the same type of service provider. If the final percentage is below 80%, other mystery tourist visits have to be undertaken until the consensus percentage has been reached.

Before the visits are undertaken, it is necessary to write a clear manual for the interpretation of the questions. This avoids subjective interpretation of the questions by the interviewer and ensures the validity of the research. In order to enhance the validity, the mystery tourists should have an educational and/or a professional background in hospitality management and preferably receive special training, including role plays. Finally, the concealment of the observation also strongly contributes to the validity of the visit outcomes.

In order to be representative of the cultural tourist visitor population, the mystery tourist visits are undertaken at all types of urban service providers. Per type of provider a selection is made on the basis of the consumer behaviour of the average cultural tourist. Furthermore, the visits are spread over one weekday so as to reflect a day of a cultural tourist. The visiting moments are concentrated during peak times because that is when most visits are paid, while in those periods in particular the hospitality can be under pressure and has to be maintained at an acceptable level.

The in-depth interviews with urban service providers

The in-depth interview is set up as a half-structured/half-open conversation focusing on the elements of the cultural tourism product and the visitor's experience considered from the subjective viewpoint of the urban service providers and in particular the commercial service providers. Whereas the other two measurement instruments deal with the demand side, this instrument analyses the supply side. Since the local service providers form a relatively small group, it is feasible to apply this time-consuming (a disadvantage inherent in most qualitative research techniques) method to explore the subject matter in depth. The interviewer brings up the topics and stimulates his interlocutor to give his opinion and to express his needs by continuing to ask questions.

In order to be representative, the in-depth interviews have to cover the different sectors of cultural tourist services within the core cultural tourism product and the additional cultural tourism product (see Fig. 5.1). Within each sector, the service providers selected to be interviewed are key informers as they are strongly involved in the tourism policy development, for example as a member of the council, of the board of the tourist information office or of the entrepreneur's organization (see Chapter 10). This selection criterion enhances the representativeness and reliability (in the non-statistical sense of trustworthiness) of the in-depth interviews because the interviewed service providers will voice not only their personal opinion but also the ideas of the stakeholders they represent (see Chapter 7).

The validity of the interviews is guaranteed by the fact that the questions cover, on the one hand, all the different elements of the cultural tourism product and their quality level according to the service providers. On the other hand, the respondents are asked to give their opinion on the quality of the tourist experience, especially with respect to the hospitality offered by the service providers. As the same topics are put to all of the respondents, the results can be compared afterwards so as to draw general conclusions about the point of view of the local service providers.

Evaluation and Future Research Orientations

The audit has been set up in such a way as to be universally applicable and usable in any given cultural destination as an empirical instrument for marketing and visitor management. The outcomes of the audit provide valuable information for local tourism policy. For example, if the experience of the tourist-historic city turns out to be below expectation and consequently expectations are not fulfilled, it would be interesting to know the causes, in order to be able to improve the marketing and the visitor management of the city. If, for example, the cause of the tourist dissatisfaction appears to be the lack of hospitality, the mystery tourist visits produce a lot of useful information

about the reasons why urban service providers are not hospitable.

To gather this kind of information, the results of the three researches have to be combined and compared. From a methodological point of view, it is essential to select first the results that match, because this means that there is converging validity. In other words, one can be sure that the measures of hospitality are based upon the shared opinions of the key stakeholders both on the demand side and on the supply side.

Thanks to the combined use of different quantitative and qualitative research methods and the study of both the demand and the supply side, the cultural destination experience audit offers a broader scope than measurement instruments that focus in essence on the quantitative analysis of consumer behaviour, like the HOLSAT model developed by Tribe and Smith (1998) and improved by Truong and Foster (2006). This model addresses the multidimensional character of consumer satisfaction with a destination by comparing the performance of holiday attributes of the destination against tourists' expectations. The basic research instrument is a questionnaire asking respondents to rate their expectation of each holiday attribute and to rate the performance of the same attribute according to their experience as a tourist. The collected data are submitted to a quantitative analysis.

In the cultural destination experience audit, the questions on the expectations and the experiences of the cultural tourist have been integrated into the questionnaire of the ATLAS Cultural Tourism Research Project. Thus it is possible to establish cross-relations – if statistically significant – between expectations and experiences of the visitor, on the one hand, and variables shaping expectations and experiences like origin, age, education, information sources, previous visits, motivations, attractions visited, etc., on the other hand. These comparisons provide relevant input for the marketing and visitor policy in the framework of destination management.

The audits carried out in South-Limburg have led to recommendations that can give an idea of possible policy measures. For example, in the field of service development, in order to prevent unsatisfactory information requests by tourists, the tourist offices can standardize their customer service. These standardizations can be applied by using standard operating procedures (SOPs). The SOPs can be developed for handling telephone calls, reservations, demands for information and face-to-face visits. Staff training is necessary for professional application of these SOPs. With regard to visitor management, culture appears to be an adequate instrument for spreading the tourist flows, as older cultural tourists plan their visits on weekdays while cultural tourists in the 40–49 age group prefer weekends and holiday periods. It is useful to keep in mind these visit patterns while developing promotional plans and measures.

The tourist survey in its current set-up simply identifies the symptoms. So it could be extended with open-ended questions concerning the causes of guest dissatisfaction, not only for each type of service provider but also for local residents, because the interactions of these hosts with the tourist visitors are not covered by the mystery tourist observations. Thanks to these additional questions, the audit will lead to an even more complete diagnosis as a basis for remedial and preventive measures in the planning and development of local visitor management policy.

Acknowledgements

The author wishes to thank the students of the management project groups of the Maastricht Hotel Management School, who assisted by working out and testing the hospitality audit and the cultural destination experience audit.

References

Alves de Oliveira, T. *et al.* (2005) *Gemeente Vaals. Verrassend Veelzijdig Veelkleurig. Destination Experience Audit.* Management project report, Maastricht Hotel Management School, Maastricht, the Netherlands.

Berbers, D. *et al.* (2005) *Destination Experience Audit Valkenburg. Beleef het bestaande!* Management project report, Maastricht Hotel Management School, Maastricht, the Netherlands.

Bijnagte, R. *et al.* (2008) *Kwaliteitsimago-onderzoek naar het toerisme in de Gemeente Vaals.* Management project report, Maastricht Hotel Management School, Maastricht, the Netherlands.

Casier, R. *et al.* (2002) *Hospitality Audit Maastricht.* Management project report, Maastricht Hotel Management School, Maastricht, the Netherlands.

Hudson, S., Snaith, T., Miller, G.A. and Hudson, P. (2001) Distribution channels in the travel industry: using mystery shoppers to understand the influence of travel agency recommendations. *Journal of Travel Research* 40, 148–154.

Kotler, P., Bowen, J. and Makens, J. (1999) *Marketing for Hospitality and Tourism*, 2nd edn. Prentice Hall, Upper Saddle River, New Jersey.

Munsters, W. (2005) Culture and tourism: from antagonism to synergism. *ATLAS Reflections 2005: Tourism, Creativity and Development*, 41–50.

Munsters, W. (2007) *Cultuurtoerisme*, 4th edn. Garant, Antwerp–Apeldoorn, Belgium.

Page, S.J. and Connell, J. (2006) *Tourism: a Modern Synthesis*, 2nd edn. Thomson Learning, London.

Tribe, J. and Smith, T. (1998) From SERVQUAL to HOLSAT: holiday satisfaction in Varadero, Cuba. *Tourism Management* 19, 25–34.

Truong, Th. and Foster, D. (2006) Using HOLSAT to evaluate tourist satisfaction at destinations: the case of Australian holidaymakers in Vietnam. *Tourism Management* 27, 842–855.

Van den Braak, J. *et al.* (2000) *Visitor Management in Maastricht.* Management project report, Maastricht Hotel Management School, Maastricht, the Netherlands.

Vijver, H. (1996) *Ethiek van de Gastvrijheid. Een Bedrijfsethiek voor de Dienstverlening.* Van Gorcum, Assen, the Netherlands.

6 Methodological Triangulation: the Study of Visitor Behaviour at the Hungarian Open Air Museum

László Puczkó, Edit Bárd and Júlia Füzi

Introduction

Visitor studies are hardly new, nor are studies of visitor behaviour in museums. However, in the new European Union member countries, one might see a different picture. Certainly this is the case in Hungary, where visitor studies in the museum environment have been so rare that the Ministry of Education and Culture initiated a year-long nationwide study of museum visitors in 2007. Considering the lack of information and limited research orientation, one can say that the management of the Hungarian Open Air Museum (HOAM) has been playing a pioneer role in the approach to museum management and to visitor studies in Hungary. They have been carrying out visitor studies for many years, and in 2007 they assigned a professional advisor to develop a new data collection system. The most important elements of this project are presented in this chapter.

The Hungarian Open Air Museum

An interest in village dwellings arose in the second half of the 18th century, initially in northern and western parts of Europe. This was a period when growing interest in ethnography coincided with the emergence of national cultures. Researchers studied dwelling houses and other areas of rural life, established house types, described their regional versions and looked for archetypes to define national architecture. The appearance of peasant houses at world exhibitions in the latter half of the 19th century, albeit mainly out of socio-political considerations, indicated widening interest. Vernacular architecture and sacred buildings were shown at the World Exhibitions in Paris (1867) and in Vienna (1873). Authenticity of materials or structures was not expected, however. Despite their inauthentic character, they increased the interest of both researchers and the general public. They also enabled the comparison of village houses in different countries.

The open air museum concept can be traced back to the founding of Skansen in Sweden in 1891 by Arthur Haselius. He decided that buildings typical of different areas of Sweden and various ethnic groups should be collected and preserved in one place in the form of a permanent exhibition. As a result of his efforts, research and collecting work, including the continuous transplantation of selected structures, Skansen became the first open air museum. Following this example, many open air museums were established, first in

Scandinavia and then in other European countries.

The Hungarian Open Air Museum close to Szentendre (some 20 km from Budapest) was founded in 1967, originally operating as the Village Museum Department of the Budapest Ethnographical Museum. In 1972 it became an independent institution and opened its first exhibition as a national museum in 1974.

The aim of the establishment of the Hungarian Open Air Museum (HOAM) was to present folk architecture, interior decoration, farming and way of life. The collection represents how people lived in areas where Hungarian was the dominant language (including the territories that now belong to neighbouring countries but which were part of Hungary before World War II).

The curators looked for original artefacts, furniture, farmyard tools, clothing, etc., representing the period between the second half of the 18th century and the first half of the 20th century. One of the most important and critical parts of the selection procedure was to find and to relocate houses and other buildings. These properties were, like a puzzle, disassembled, every piece carefully numbered and then reassembled and arranged as they had been located in their original villages.

The ever-expanding museum houses more than 400 buildings, arranged into village-like units that are based on unique ethnographical qualities. Today HOAM has seven units spread over 60 ha. Within the units, buildings are fitted into the traditional arrangement of peasant households, supplemented by sacred buildings, communal buildings and outbuildings that used to be integral parts of traditional village life. Dwellings and farm buildings represent the typical homes and outbuildings that evolved through the years in each region (Cseri *et al.*, 2007) (Fig. 6.1).

Since the early 1970s, the HOAM has become one of the most successful museums in the country. This success is illustrated by various indicators, such as the popularity of the exhibition grounds and special programmes and events, the level of infrastructure development, and professional and scientific results. During the 7-month opening season, from Easter until the end of October, HOAM receives almost 250,000 visitors per year.

The achievements and the approach of the museum have attracted awards on many occasions too. It obtained the Museum of the Year title in 2000, the Visitor-friendly Museum of the Year in 2004, and the Prima Primissima Award in 2005. This latter award is perhaps the most valued by the management, since this award is presented to those organizations and persons, regardless of their field, that achieved something remarkable and deserve acknowledgement at a national scale.

Visitor Orientation and Past Research Activity

The Visitor-friendly Museum of the Year award did not come easily to HOAM. Since the mid-1990s the museum has been applying many interpretation tools and practices, such as demonstrations, in-situ presentations, moving objects, enactments, etc., most of which still seem to be new to many museums in Hungary. To encourage visitors to spend their free time in HOAM, even 'just' for a picnic, the museum has developed different kinds of activities as well as rest and refreshment areas and venues for eating and drinking.

In the first period of the museum's history, when it had only one exhibition unit, it already started to organize some visitor studies. During a guided tour or a bread-baking demonstration, for example, staff applied mainly unobtrusive research methods, especially unstructured observation by watching the ways guests used the museum. In addition, members of staff talked to the participants and tried to collect opinions about the visit and the museum. These attempts were not based on a systematic research strategy or objectives, but still could give some valuable information and could direct further developments. In line with the expansion of the museum's exhibitions, the information, orientation

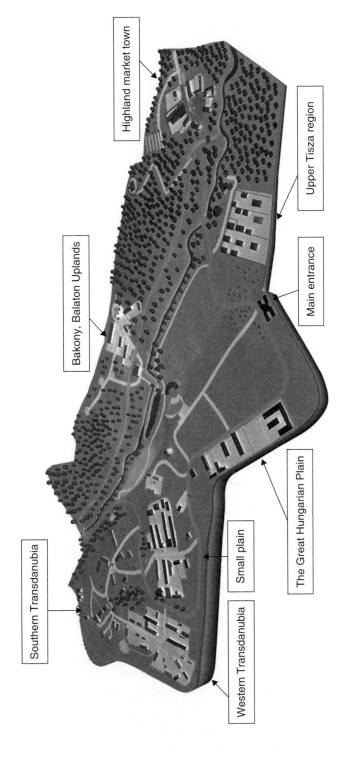

Fig. 6.1. Bird's eye view of HOAM.

and way-finding services and the visitor-friendly infrastructure (entrance building, shop, restaurant, resting areas, playground) have also been further developed.

The management of HOAM understood that to become even more visitor-friendly, they needed to know more about the visitors. So they started using mainly questionnaire-based data collection aimed at gathering information about:

- the motivations of visitors;
- their activities during their stay; and
- their opinions about the demonstrations and family activities.

During the next phase of visitor research in 2000–2001, the museum launched a survey, which applied the questionnaire developed by the Westfälisches Freilichtmuseum (Detmold, Germany). They asked visitors upon arrival about their museum-visiting habits and collected demographic data. At the end of the visit, visitors were asked to fill in the second part of the questionnaire, giving information about the experiences they gained. Unfortunately, HOAM was dissatisfied with both the method and the results. The research method did not fit the visitors' characteristics, and the competence of HOAM staff was not sufficient to implement the survey.

Learning from these difficulties of data collection, HOAM tried to narrow the range of the research so as to get more useful results. The new approach concentrated the limited research resources on festivals, since 30% of visitors come to the museum for events such as Easter, the Pentecostal games and the wine festival. These events require special attention and efforts from the staff; therefore it seemed to be good idea to limit the survey period to these days (altogether some 12 days a year). The shortened questionnaire (of 15 questions) focused on three main topics:

- part 1: the motivation for the visit, including questions about the number of previous visits to the museum, decision making for the visit and the main visit motive;
- part 2: the ways in which visitors collected information prior to the event; and

- part 3: level of satisfaction with the event and more specifically about orientation, the natural environment, the activities and the catering and shopping facilities.

The visitors were interviewed upon departure with a self-administered questionnaire. Although it was not representative research, the management found the information more useful than had been expected. These data helped the management to make improvements to the public relations strategy. Furthermore, the research also highlighted some elements of the events that needed further attention and development (Paálné Patkó, 2003).

In the last few years the Ministry of Education and Culture (the governing body of the HOAM) has required a more structured planning procedure from all museums governed by the state. This new policy had an influence on the way in which museums approach data collection, because the analysis of statistical data and research results has become more important. Museums now have to discuss their performance based on various indicators such as interpretation and visitor satisfaction, as well as care of the collection.

The management of the HOAM itself recognized that all the income-generation activities (grants, sponsors, renting out the museum's facilities) strongly depend on the high reputation of the museum. Even the work of the scientific staff (i.e. expanding the collection, publishing research papers and building exhibitions) has to correspond with the visitors', as well as social and educational, expectations. The staff of the Marketing and Communication Department plays a significant role in the collection and analysis of information about visitors to HOAM. The public relations manager is responsible for the visitor surveys, since it is seen as a means of communication between the institution and its different visitor groups.

Following a government decision in July 2007, the HOAM was selected as one of the key development projects enjoying significant funds from the Regional Operative

Programme of the European Union. Besides a new exhibition unit (a village from northern Hungary), a new entrance building will be built and a train will ease transportation within the museum and will serve as added attraction. To become more prepared for the new era, the management understood that a new approach to visitor studies should also be applied. This resulted in a 3-year visitor research plan. In the following sections the methods and findings of the pilot survey are presented.

Research Plan Formulation

Anyone organizing a comprehensive research project can and should consider all possible options. There are many ways in which data can be collected, applying either quantitative or qualitative methods. When formulating the research questions, 'the what' should come first, the selection of the methods ('the how') that fit the questions, second. This approach, of course, is a rule of thumb in any (market) research activity, but doing quite the opposite is also common. Cultural tourist attractions often make the mistake of selecting the research method(s) first. This is due either to tradition ('we always use this or that method') or to financial constraints. When announcing a call for tender, it is much easier to make the prospective research agencies submit proposals based on a given methodology. This highlights the problems between the clients, in this case a museum, and (field) research agencies. When any organization assigns an agency to carry out field research, it often assumes that the in-house staff are able to design, manage and monitor the field surveys. Considering the organizational structure and overall management style of museums in Eastern Europe, the reality is often the contrary. It is rare to see institutes having the necessary knowledge and experience onboard.

A more fruitful approach would be to assign a professional consultant who can collaborate with a research company. This 'consortium' can formulate all the necessary questions before the research and can make the organization answer them. On the basis of these answers, they can come up with applicable methods, from which the organizations can make a selection. The participation of a professional consultant can assure the organization that the results will be analysed according to the given cultural–historical context and not presented just as numbers and averages. The latter draws attention to another challenge cultural organizations have to face: how to translate these data into useful information. Marketing language, for example, can be very difficult to understand, especially for those whose language, like curators, is quite different. Therefore, marketing techniques and terms often have to be interpreted for museum staff.

The management of HOAM decided to formulate their research questions first. Learning from earlier studies and considering the data needs of the planned extensions, the management articulated research objectives, which were then translated into research questions. The management wanted to find out more about visitors in order to:

1. Make a more focused segmentation and communication strategy and plan.
2. Understand what visitors actually do and for how long during their visits.
3. Find out what visitors thought was important and memorable from the visit.

Based on the information needs the following research questions were formulated for the pilot study:

1. What is the basic demographic profile of visitors?
2. How long does an average visit take?
3. Which parts of the museum do visitors visit?
4. How would visitors describe their own experiences after they left the museum?

The representatives of HOAM and the consultants discussed various options and they considered the available time, and human and financial resources. Their decision followed the approach of triangulation by using more than one method in order to develop a more detailed understanding. Combining different methods is a way of validating qualitative data (James, 2005). It was expected that triangulation would help to make connections between different sets of data and to enable appropriate conclusions to be drawn (see Chapter 5).

Selecting Applicable Research Methods

The selection procedure

Visitor (or consumer) research methodologies can vary, depending on considerations (after Puczkó and Rátz, 2000) including:

- How unobtrusive or obtrusive should or could the method be?
- How much involvement does any method need from the visitor?
- Does the researcher want to carry out the research on site or not?
- Does the researcher want to capture opinions, activities or memories in real time or retrospectively?

There are a large number of methods that can fit the above-mentioned research questions, but several other parameters had to be taken into consideration, such as:

- This was to be a pilot study, i.e. it was supposed to test research methods as well as providing basic information useful to perfecting the whole research strategy.
- The available time allocated for the test was no more than 2 months (since the museum was to be closed for winter).
- Human and financial resources were very limited and the museum had only one member of staff who could be partially involved in the field research, with the consequence that any method was to be outsourced.

Based on the consultants' recommendation and the above-mentioned circumstances, the management of HOAM selected three very different methods for the pilot data collection. These were: (i) visitor interviews with a standard questionnaire; (ii) visitor-employed diaries (VED); and (iii) visitor-employed photography (VEP). Triangulation needs various methods to be used at the same time, and these methods should be harmonized too. This means that special attention was given to all research questions in the three different methods. The findings of the three methods were to support and complement, but not repeat, data and information resulting from any of the three methods. Also, every method had to focus on only one or two of the four main research questions (Table 6.1). This allowed the consultants to limit the total number of questions and to sharpen the focus of the research.

Standard questionnaire

There were many reasons for choosing the selected methods. The standard questionnaire method was selected because of the need for quantitative results. The 15 questions had 59 items altogether, including:

- the primary motivation for the visit;
- decision making about the visit;
- activities during the visit;
- the most memorable visitor experiences (described in words);

Table 6.1. Triangulation methodology.

Method	Research object		
	Segmentation	Activities during the stay	Memories
Questionnaire	XX	X	X
VED	X	XX	X
VEP	X	X	XX

XX, primary data source; X, secondary data source.

- channels of information used; and
- basic demographic parameters.

Since the questionnaire had items that might have been difficult for visitors to understand, the data collection was facilitated by interviewers. The interviewers were given a guide from which they could become familiarized with the content, the sometimes very site-specific vocabulary and, of course, the whole museum. The selection of respondents was based on random sampling. This meant that every fifth visitor leaving the museum was requested to participate.

Visitor-employed diaries

It was assumed by the management of HOAM that the average visiting time was about 2 to 3 h. This assumption, however, was not supported by any rigorous research data. The management also did not have any information about the activities during the stay. Finding out what visitors actually did during the visit was seen as particularly important. The reason being the fact that, theoretically, just to walk all around the museum should take approximately 2 h – without visiting any of the buildings.

That is why the consultants suggested the application of visitor-employed diaries (VED). Diaries, as a data collection method, can be seen as a very detailed and informative method that needs very strong involvement from the participants. To participate in a diary-based data collection, visitors should write down every activity they do and indicate the starting and finishing times of these activities. This structured data collection can actually make the visit an unpleasant experience, since during the whole stay participants hold a diary form and look at their watches many times. This can be very disturbing, to the experience itself and/or to the visitor and his/her party. Every participant, therefore, after they returned the diary, received a gift (or incentive), a copy of the museum guide and an invitation for two persons to the Saint Márton New Wine and Goose Days Festivities.

The diary had two parts. The first contained a few general questions about demographic parameters. The second part was composed of the diary questions, including the description of weather conditions upon arrival and departure, a map of the whole museum indicating every area, and area maps with all the buildings, houses and other features. Participants were asked to indicate in every area they visited the time of entering and leaving, plus the buildings they visited in the museum unit.

There can be several pitfalls of diaries or self-reported routes. One of the most important is related to the time the method requires. Participants can find the expected involvement too taxing and therefore may leave the diary incomplete or skip certain parts of it. Also, rounding the time up can result in biased information and visitors may not recognize the site or location that they should mark. GPS-based surveys could offer a solution to these problems (Hallo *et al.*, 2004; see also Chapter 9, this volume).

Visitor-employed photography

The VEP method has been extensively used in landscape studies and research on perceptions of the landscape. As Jacobsen (2007) summarized in his overview of the available photo-based data collection methods, the main advantage of this method is to provide researchers with the observers' responses to the actual landscape, site or area while they are experiencing it. As an experience-recording technique, the photographs resulting from the VEP research can be seen as cultural documents showing evidence of how participants see the world (Richard *et al.*, 2004).

The research team was aware of the fact that the VEP results and their translation very much depend on how the initial research question was formulated. To reduce complexity, visitors were asked to do only one thing: make pictures of anything (e.g. places, memories, experiences, people, sites) they would like to show to their friends and family when they got back home again.

Every participant received a disposable camera (of 24 pictures) upon arrival. The researcher registered the main demographic data, the parts of the museum visited, age and profession. The participants returned the camera upon departure and afterwards HOAM sent the CD-ROMs back to them.

The tabulation and the analysis of the vast number of pictures taken was not an easy task. To structure the analysis the following variables were applied:

- location: seven units and the entrance area;
- captured main content: food and beverage, interpreter, event location, indoor, outdoor, building, nature, animal, the visitors themselves, capturing landscapes, events, interpretation or plays and games;
- elements of landscape, events, interpretation, plays and games; and
- people: family, kids, friends, group, interpreters or other members of staff in focus, people not in focus or no people at all.

For both VEP and VED, the selection of respondents was based on stratified random sampling. This meant that according to visitor statistics from the previous 3 years, a target number of respondents was set by considering the days of the week (weekday, weekend, a day with festival/event) and the types of visitors (family, student, adult and concessions).

Main Findings

All three methods were applied during the same time period during the autumn months of 2007. Altogether:

- 171 visitors completed the questionnaires;
- 135 guests participated in the VEP (with 1880 photos made); and
- a further 50 visitors filled in the diaries.

The three methods met expectations and provided HOAM management with very complex results. Each method had some added value for the study and could highlight certain issues the management was not yet aware of. Also, the application of these very different methods assured the management that it is really useful to apply non-mainstream methodology.

Duration and frequency of visits

A large number of visitors were in the 30–59 age group. They tended to have at least a General Certificate of Education (CSI) or an even higher (college or university) qualification. Respondents in this group were mostly white-collar workers or managers. Seventy per cent of this age group arrived at the museum as a part of a trip of a few hours; the other 30% spent a whole day in the attraction. During this time half of the 30–59 age group visited all the units of the museum, while the others sought out only areas that they had not visited before, or just walked around the buildings using the museum simply as a venue for spending free time. The oldest age group are regular visitors to the museum as well. Over 40% of visitors over the age of 60 have visited the HOAM at least five times (Fig. 6.2).

Characteristically, visitors from the 30–59 age group arrived with their partners, friends or family. Their family status clearly defined their needs. They look for activities for children, interesting and educational (or edutainment) programmes. Almost three-quarters of all visitors spent more than 3 h in the museum. This result was supported by the VED showing an average stay in the museum of 3.5 h. Almost every visitor spent 3 h or more in the museum, regardless of how many previous visits they had made before (Fig. 6.3). This information certainly can be a guideline for planning content and for communication development.

The duration of the visit spent in the facility compared with the total number of visits may function as a basic indicator of performance. It is assumed that longer and frequent visits indicate higher visitor appreciation and satisfaction. To find out more about this relationship the relevant

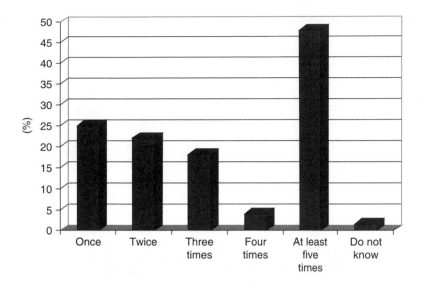

Fig. 6.2. The number of previous visits to HOAM.

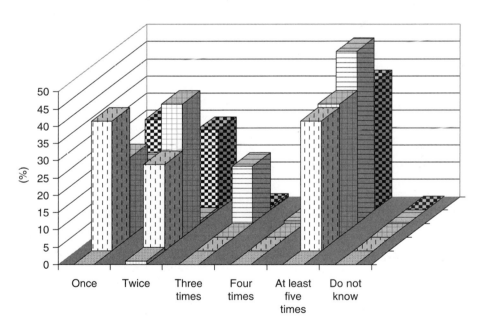

Fig. 6.3. Length of stay compared with the number of previous visits. ▨, max 30 min; ▨, approx. 1 h; ▨, approx. 2 h; ▤, approx. 3 h; ▨, more than 3 h.

data from returning and from first-time visitors were compared. Differences between the two groups were found in the demographic features such as the place of residence, the highest qualification and recent occupation. In the case of first-time visitors there was a relatively even distribution in the different qualification categories. Analysing the same data for regular visitors, we could see that repeat visitors tend to have

higher qualification levels. Certainly demographic features alone do not define the
visitor segments of the museum; therefore
one has to pay attention to other features as
well. This will take place in the next round
of data collection.

Visitor origin

Over half of the first-time visitors arrive
from the countryside. There is a drastic
drop in this ratio among regular visitors:
only 9% of the countryside inhabitants are
regular guests. More than half (56%) of the
visitors living in the countryside (i.e. not in
the Greater Budapest area) visited the
museum for a few hours, while 38% of them
devoted the whole day to discovering
HOAM. The research highlighted a remarkable finding: visitors with lower qualifications and with residence in the countryside
do not become regular visitors (Table 6.2).

Around 45% of the visitors from the
Budapest area visited all the units of the
museum, while 42% of them just walked
around. Visitors arriving from Budapest and
surroundings spend a relatively short time
travelling to and from the museum. However, those living in the countryside may
travel many hours to visit HOAM. These
visitors, therefore, are most likely to spend a
longer time in the museum.

Visit patterns within museum units

Nearly half of the visitors (44%) consciously
visit each museum unit. A fifth of the visitors returned with the purpose of seeing
those museum units that they could not
visit before. A third group of visitors (31%)
who walked round the museum saw plenty
of units, but they were not sure if they
would manage to see all the units. This
uncertainty refers to the lack of sufficient
information provided to the visitors along
the paths or at the units. This response is
alarming, since it has many related impacts,
for example:

- Lack of information increases the uncertainty of the visitor and decreases
  the feeling of comfort.
- The visitor does not feel 'looked after'.
- The visitor misses sights/attractions/
  events that would otherwise have
  increased visit satisfaction, therefore
  the visitor does not leave the museum
  with good memories that would persuade them to visit again.
- The visitors spend less time in the
  museum.
- The visitors spend less money.

These problems may not have direct impacts
on the visitor experiences, although they
are undoubtedly important. Such negative
consequences can easily be avoided by

Table 6.2. Comparison of first-time and regular visitors (for the most typical segments).

Visitor feature	First visit	(%)	At least five visits	(%)
Age group	30–39	40	30–39	35
			60–69	20
Occupation	Professionals	25	Professional	48
	Every other group	10–14	Senior management	14
			Pensioners	12
Highest qualification	Secondary school	44	Higher education	73
	Higher education	28	Secondary school	21
	Other	28	Other	6
Length of stay	3 or more hours	86	3 or more hours	88
Place of residence	Countryside	51	Greater Budapest	44
	Greater Budapest	29	Szentendre area	33
	Szentendre area	2	Countryside	9

thorough planning and organization of visitor flows and providing sufficient information about the sights.

Experiencing museum units

The VEP and VED methodology applied in this visitor research helped to determine the attractiveness of the units of the museum. Figure 6.4 represents the popularity of the museum units among visitors by comparing the findings of VEP and VED, i.e. time spent in a unit versus the number of photos taken in the units.

The research data show that 43.7% of visitors made identical pictures (at least once). The market square of the highland market town appeared to be one of the most popular themes with photographers. In these pictures, the main theme is the see-saw with kids playing. From the path and from the top of the stairs, photos were taken from different angles featuring the landscape of the highland market town area. This theme occurred the most, being represented in 300 photos. Other units, such as the Great Hungarian Plain, which offers typical picturesque amenities, such as authentic folk art, old village houses in an outstanding state, a windmill and a farmhouse with livestock, were popular themes too.

Although it is not an attraction, the entrance area of the museum was also a focus point in the analysis. Any entrance of a museum or exhibition has a special role in setting the scene. Visitors tend to base their expectations of the attraction on what they see and experience at the entrance. The importance of the first impression is immense and it is important in any museum to pay special attention to the careful planning and arrangement of the entrance area. From the results of this research it can be observed that the visitors enjoyed themselves at the entrance area. This was supported by the many photos they made of friends and relatives at this spot.

During the first half of the research period the Szüreti Sokadalom (Grape Harvest Festival) took place. The majority of the visitors arrived especially to participate in the festivities. This can be seen from the themes of the pictures, since the photos taken present this event from many angles. There were no comparable events during the second half of the research period, so the photos taken show significant changes. They captured a more varied mixture of themes, such as interpretation or folk plays. The number of pictures showing activities dropped dramatically in this phase, while photos showing buildings increased (Fig. 6.5).

The most significant differences can be found in the case of pictures of the

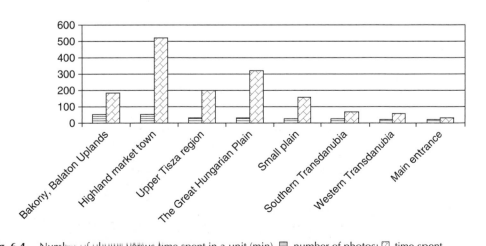

Fig 6.4. Number of photos versus time spent in a unit (min). ☰, number of photos; ▨, time spent.

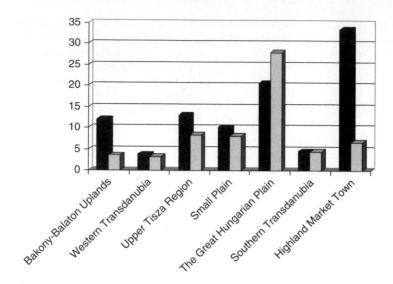

Fig. 6.5. Number of photos on days with and without events. ■, data collection on day with event; ▢, data collection on day with no event.

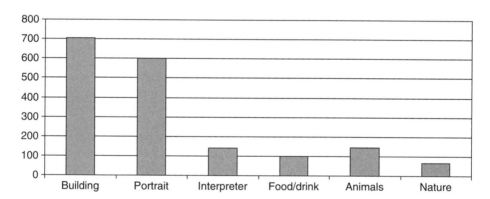

Fig. 6.6. Number of photographs by themes.

highland market town unit. During an event day the market square is full of people, interpreters and traders, and this bustle lures visitors. The square, however, remained popular even on days without events. It also can be noted that on those days the number of 'we have been there'-type photos dropped significantly. On these photos fewer people were captured and visitors focused on the details of the buildings and houses (Fig. 6.6). This may raise the question: is it acceptable for HOAM that the

core attraction, the presentation of country-side living, becomes a secondary or tertiary attraction when any event takes place?

The best experiences for visitors were gained by exploring the main sights of HOAM, such as the old village buildings, which was followed by 'gaining new experiences' in second place. According to the results, 30% of the respondents had good memories of the interpreters. This does not seem to be a high figure and leaves much room for improvement. The 135 participants

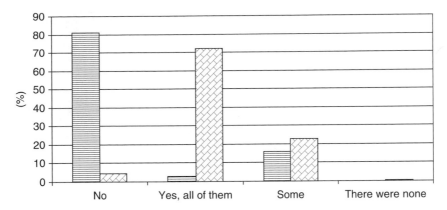

Fig. 6.7. Use of interpretive provision versus participation in group interpretive activities. ▤, group activities; ▨, interpretive provision.

in the VEP research took photos of museum staff and interpreters in more than 100 cases. This emphasizes the importance of well-trained, guest-friendly staff, who contribute a lot to the visitor experience.

Nearly 35% of visitors sought new, interactive experiences, which contrasts with the fact that large numbers of visitors did not try interactive tools and did not participate in any organized activities in the museum (Fig. 6.7).

Conclusions

From the vast amount of research data collected, some key findings are worth highlighting, especially those that were supported by the triangulation methodology.

- The events and festivals are highly appreciated and they add to the knowledge and the pleasure provided by the visit.
- Visitors have clear preferences regarding the different areas of HOAM. Two out of every three visitors have personal interaction with interpreters; therefore the role of staff in experience creation is of paramount importance.
- The buildings of HOAM are considered memorable experiences.
- Visitors tend to look at and to take photographs of anything that is new, but

show relatively low interest in taking part in group animation.

All three methods contributed to the validity of the pilot research by producing information that would not have been available otherwise, for example:

- It is now understood that the official names of the areas do not mean too much to an average visitor, especially not for first-timers. All visitors look for 'new' areas and events, and this is especially the case for loyal visitors.
- Visitors may find it difficult to see and identify the uniqueness of rural architecture: there is a tendency to make clichéd pictures of the highlights, such as the main squares, the watermill and the bridge. This aspect of visitor behaviour asks for more specific interpretation and guidance.
- Interpreters, traders and stalls prolong the duration of the visit to any area and are likely to create more memorable experiences than empty areas.

Everybody was satisfied with the methods and the outcomes of the pilot. However, all methods can be improved for the next round of data collection. The vocabulary of the questionnaire was too 'professional' and the survey team would have needed a more thorough training and guidance. Also, they were not familiar enough with the site. Without this knowledge it is sometimes difficult for them to help visitors.

The VED proved to be a very informative method, but visitors complained about the 'stress' they had to cope with during the whole visit. Some of them admitted that they forgot to fill in everything and in a few cases they lost track of their actual location. HOAM uses both numbers and names to label every area. There are, however, no site maps either at the entrances to or at the exits from the areas; therefore visitors can find it difficult to locate themselves. To overcome this problem a more thorough site description is necessary in the next version of the VED.

The VEP was a revelation to everybody in the research team, since nobody had used this method to date in Hungary. HOAM was very lucky in that visitors were curious and happy to participate in the research. The research team also had the good fortune to find a company that joined the project and provided HOAM with the cameras and CD-ROMs, which made the research project more cost-efficient. Most of the visitors who refused to participate in VEP were from the 60+ age group. The rejection was mainly due to unfamiliarity with technical things or 'gadgets', which reveals a very significant shortcoming of this method.

References

Cseri, M., Horváth, A. and Szabó, Zs. (eds) (2007) *Guide. Hungarian Open Air Museum*. HOAM, Szentendre., Hungary.

Hallo, J.C., Manning, R.E., Valliere, W. and Budruk, M. (2004) A case study comparison of visitor self-reported and GPS recorded travel routes. *Proceedings of the 2004 Northeastern Recreation Research Symposium*, GTR-NE-326.

Jacobsen, J.K.S. (2007) Use of landscape perception methods in tourism studies: a review of photo-based research approaches. *Tourism Geographies* 9, 234–253.

James, A. (2005) An introduction to visitor studies. Available at: www.alison-james.co.uk (accessed 9 June 2008).

Paálné Patkó, Gy. (2003) Communication strategy of the Hungarian Open Air Museum and its achieved results. *Ház és Ember* 16, 211–220.

Puczkó, L. and Rátz, T. (2000) *Az attrakciótól az élményig. A látogatómenedzsment módszerei*. Geomedia, Budapest.

Richard, S., Beckley, T. and Wallace, S. (2004) A picture and 1000 words: using resident-employed photography to understand attachments to high amenity places. *Journal of Leisure Research* 36, 580–606.

7 Employing the Grand Tour Approach to Aid Understanding of Garden Visiting

Dorothy Fox, Jonathan Edwards and Keith Wilkes

Introduction

Mixed methods research is arguably in the ascendancy (Brannen, 2005), blurring the boundaries between 'quantitative' and 'qualitative' research methods (see Chapter 4). Much has been written defining mixed methods research itself, and arguing the case for or against it. However, perhaps because academic journals tend to be discipline based and often incline towards particular research paradigms, there are few examples demonstrating how the elements of a mixed method design were selected. In this chapter it is shown how a mixed methods study was adapted to meet the changing circumstances of a cultural tourism research project. In doing so, a novel approach to interviewing was required and the method selected, drawn from ethnography, is described in detail.

The study cited sought to understand participation in garden visiting from a number of perspectives but principally that of the visitor. It concentrated on what lay behind the decision to visit gardens rather than the experiential aspects of a visit. It therefore moved beyond the established approach of individual agency, with its assumption of free choice, to incorporate social and material agency. Initially the project was conceived as a quantitative survey followed by qualitative interviews. This design was developed, as in many other cases, because the research project had more than one objective and hence more than one type of question needed to be answered.

An initial literature search undertaken for the study showed that the data available appeared to be limited and were largely based on visitor surveys (for example, Gallagher, 1983). This type of data provides no information on the propensity to visit a garden or about people who may wish to visit but are constrained in some way from doing so. Therefore it was decided that, on balance, a survey of residents rather than garden visitors would provide better numeric, descriptive data. Following the completion of a pilot study, a cluster survey of residents, based on postcodes in the Bournemouth (BH) area in southern England, was carried out in November/December 2002. The sample size was 932 households, from which the adult who would next celebrate their birthday was asked to complete the questionnaire to generate random sampling. A total of 345 questionnaires were completed, giving a response rate of 37%. The survey instrument included open and closed questions and the data were analysed using SPSS. At the end of the survey instrument the residents were asked if they would be willing to take part in an interview, which would provide qualitative data in a subsequent phase.

However, two amendments were subsequently made to the initial plan – adding a further quantitative and qualitative phase. First, during completion of the resident survey data analysis, a major work on visitors to gardens and their motivation was published (Connell, 2004), and it was therefore decided to add an additional quantitative phase, in the form of a garden visitor survey, so that some of the findings of Connell and the resident survey could be assessed further.

Second, as can happen in any research project, the best-laid plans may not come to fruition. Responses to the resident survey had indicated that 77 people were willing at that time (2002) to take part in further research. However, by the spring of 2005, when the interviews were able to be undertaken, only nine respondents were then willing to take part in a semi-structured interview, and the group was homogenous in terms of their gender (mainly female), age (predominantly middle-aged) and a shared interest in gardening and/or garden visiting. The research was not intended to focus on any particular group of people and therefore it was clear that these interviews, although valuable, would not sufficiently enrich the understanding of garden visiting. Therefore, the decision was taken to add a final data collection phase to the study, by carrying out a series of short interviews with visitors to a range of horticultural attractions as potential garden visitors might be found at them. All that remained was to select an appropriate form of interview.

Interviews are often perceived as the research method of choice within tourism (Jennings, 2005). However, as Jennings makes clear, not all interviews are the same. Not only do they use different methods to obtain information but also, because they have different philosophical backgrounds, they may be part of different methodologies. Three main types of interview are widely discussed in the tourism and social science literature: structured, semi-structured and unstructured interviews (for example, Finn *et al.*, 2000; Bryman, 2008) or, similarly, standardized, semi-standardized and non-standardized interviews (for example, Berg, 2007). The structured or standardized interview is normally viewed as a quantitative method and the others as qualitative methods. In considering the type of interviews to be undertaken in the current study, there was concern that researcher familiarity with the context from the earlier phases of the research could unduly influence, and hence limit, the questions asked if a semi-structured format was used. Therefore an unstructured interview format was adopted.

Generally, unstructured interviews rely on verbal accounts of social realities in which control by the interviewer is minimal: the interviewee leads the interview with their thoughts. The interviewer has an idea about themes or issues but these are used as a guide. There is no set order of questions, although the interviewer may return the interviewee to the topic if they diverge from it. Although unstructured interviews seem to fit no particular pattern, there are, in fact, many types of unstructured interviews, with Jennings (2005) describing 13 different forms.

The advantages of an unstructured interview approach, according to Jennings (2001), are the 'richness' of the description gained about a social world and the 'depth' of the data afforded by the relationship between the interviewer and interviewee. The disadvantages include the inability to extrapolate from the data to the wider population and that they are more time consuming than other interview types (Jennings, 2001). For positivist critics, there can be concerns over reliability and viability, but non-positivists argue that criteria such as trustworthiness are more appropriate in assessing whether qualitative research is valid (see Chapter 5).

Such interviews are a fundamental method in ethnography, together with participant observation and the sourcing of statistical and other records, photographs and artefacts. Ethnography is widely seen as a means of understanding a way of life from the native point of view (see Chapter 14). The study reported here, as already stated, sought the garden visitor's perspective and so drawing on the strengths of ethnography would be appropriate. Jennings (2001: 160) summarizes the principles of ethnography as:

- a focus on understanding and interpretation;
- a focus on process or negotiation of meanings;
- research undertaken in natural settings;
- social phenomena studied within the social context in which they occur, in order that a holistic perspective is gained;
- emic and etic perspectives jointly utilized;
- the identification of multiple realities/ perspectives;
- the use of multiple methods that include participant observation and interviewing; and
- non-judgemental positioning.

Spradley describes ethnography as 'the work of describing a culture' (Spradley, 1979: 3) and he refers to culture as 'the acquired knowledge that people use to interpret experience and generate social behaviour' (Spradley, 1979: 5). He argues that a concentration on shared knowledge does not eliminate an interest in customs, behaviour and artefacts but that it highlights the importance of the meaning (his emphasis) of these phenomena. In complex societies, even within the same cultural groups, there are cultural scenes, such as different professions, hobbies and neighbourhoods, and any individual is likely to have the shared knowledge of several cultural scenes and can therefore act as an informant for any of them. Gardens open to visitors are clearly a cultural scene in this respect and therefore anyone who has visited or, indeed, thought about visiting could be an informant about some aspect of participation.

Spradley's Developmental Research Sequence

Spradley (1979) argues that the best way of learning to do ethnography is by actually doing it and he proposes a 12-step process to achieve such understanding by undertaking 'ethnographic interviews'. His developmental research sequence is not described fully here, as the purpose of this chapter is not to describe ethnographic research but to show how the first four steps of his interviewing technique can be adopted for other types of research study. Despite several references to this technique, its use does not appear to have been described in detail or critiqued in any study.

The first four steps listed by Spradley are:

1. Locating an informant.
2. Interviewing an informant.
3. Making an ethnographic record.
4. Asking descriptive questions.

Step 1: Locating an informant

Spradley identifies five minimal requirements for selecting a good informant:

- The informant is thoroughly familiar with his or her culture. For example, interviewing a novice traveller will work well if one wants to understand the experience of learning to be a tourist but not if the subject of the study is tourism in general. A good informant is so familiar with their culture that they do things without thinking; it has become automatic from years of practice.
- Informants must have direct and *current* experience of the cultural scene.
- For inexperienced ethnographers in particular, informants from an unfamiliar cultural scene can make things that are run-of-the-mill to the informant stand out to the ethnographer.
- The informant has sufficient time to be interviewed.
- The informant has not already 'analysed' his or her culture in a particular way. Spradley gives an example from his study of tramps, in which a college-educated tramp used his social science background in responding to questions, defining the men on 'skid row' in standard socio-demographic characteristics, such

as race and marital status, rather than in the language of 'skid row'.

Step 2: Interviewing an informant

There are numerous speech events in different cultures, for example a job interview, sales pitch, friendly conversation or, as discussed here, an ethnographic interview. Speech events have different cultural rules relating to how they start, finish and the interaction in between. These differences enable one speech event to be distinguished from another, but there are also similarities. Spradley (1979: 58) suggests that ethnographic interviews are a 'series of friendly conversations into which the researcher slowly introduces new elements to assist informants to respond as informants'. He describes three important ethnographic elements: explicit purpose, ethnographic explanations and ethnographic questions. Ethnographic interviews, he states, tend to be more formal than friendly conversations because the interviews have a definite purpose and direction. Therefore the ethnographer gradually takes more control of the speech event, directing it in ways that will lead to an understanding of the informant's cultural knowledge. Ethnographic explanations must be given to the informant. These will include general statements about what the project is about, whether it is being recorded, etc. Finally there are the ethnographic questions.

Step 3: Making an ethnographic record

An ethnographic record consists of field notes, tape recordings and artefacts, amongst others. Spradley (1979) stresses the importance of learning the language of a culture, not only as a means of communication but also because language creates and expresses cultural reality. He emphasizes the importance of a verbatim record of what is said; otherwise the interviewer, without realizing it, will summarize and restate what the informant says. He gives the following example from his research (Spradley, 1979: 73):

(a) Informant's actual statement: 'I made the bucket in Seattle one time for pooling: I asked a guy how much he was holding on a jug and he turned out to be a ragpicker and he pinched me'. (b) Field notes entry: 'I talked to Joe about his experience of being arrested on skid row when he wasn't drunk'.

Spradley acknowledges that while at the time his condensed notes seemed adequate, he came to realize that they lost some of the most important clues to the informant's culture and language. He therefore suggests that the most effective means of making a verbatim record of an interview is to use a tape recorder, although he recognizes their disadvantages of inhibiting informants and preventing a rapport from developing.

Step 4: Asking descriptive questions

Developing rapport with informants is one of two complementary processes – the other is eliciting information. Spradley argues that an effective means of framing a question is to ask descriptive questions. As an ethnographer almost always knows who an informant is, they will also know the cultural scene with which they are familiar. Therefore, one could always ask a tourist: 'What do you do on holiday? Could you describe a typical day?'. Spradley then describes five major types of descriptive questions and several subtypes, which could be used to encourage an informant to talk about a particular cultural scene. The aim is to persuade the informant to talk extensively in their native language.

Grand tour questions

Spradley (1979: 86) begins by describing his own experience, one familiar to many ethnographers, on starting a study of a cultural scene:

> I arrived at the alcoholism treatment centre and the director asked, 'Would you like a grand tour of the place?' As we walked from building to building, he named the places and objects we saw, introduced me to people, and explained the activities in progress. I could not ask tramps to give me

a grand tour of the Seattle City Jail, so I simply asked a grand tour question: 'Could you describe the inside of the jail for me?' In both situations I easily collected a large sample of native terms about these cultural scenes.

Grand tour questions about a location are relatively easy for informants and can be extended beyond spatial aspects to temporal and sequential aspects. They can also be about events, people, activities or objects and, as Spradley (1979: 87) notes, can 'encourage informants to ramble on and on', producing a verbal description of significant features of their cultural scene. He describes four types of grand tour question:

1. *Typical grand tour questions*: the ethnographer asks the informant to generalize about a cultural scene. This encourages a description of how things usually are. For example: 'Could you describe a *typical* visit to a museum?'
2. *Specific grand tour questions*: these questions seek information about the most recent or best-known event, location, activity, etc. Spradley notes that some informants can find it difficult to generalize about a typical aspect but can easily describe something that happened recently. An example question would be: 'Could you tell me about the last time you visited a museum?'
3. *Guided grand tour questions*: this form asks the informant to give an actual 'grand tour' – for example: 'Could you show me around the museum?'
4. *Task-related grand tour questions*: as the name suggests, this is a request to the informant to undertake a simple task that could aid the ethnographic description. Using the same example, a visitor to a museum could be asked to sketch a map of the exhibits they have studied.

Mini-tour questions

Spradley (1979: 88) suggests that the responses to these grand tour questions 'offer almost unlimited opportunities for investigating smaller aspects of experience'. These smaller units of experience can be described by asking mini-tour questions, which use the same approaches as the four above but which focus on a smaller aspect. An example of a task-related mini-tour question would be to ask a visitor to a museum to demonstrate something using an interactive exhibit.

Example questions

Example questions are still more specific. The informant above, for example, could be asked to show what happens if they take a particular action with the exhibit. In Spradley's experience, this can lead to the most interesting stories that an ethnographer can learn from.

Experience questions

This final type of question is best asked after numerous grand tour and mini-tour questions have been posed, as informants can find them difficult to answer. They seek to identify unusual or atypical events rather than the more routine ones. For example, 'Could you tell me about some experiences you have had visiting a museum?'.

Native-language questions

Native-language questions are designed to encourage the informant to use the terms and phrases common to a cultural scene and remind the informant that the ethnographer wants to learn their language. The first type, a direct-language question, would be, for example, 'How would you refer to it?' or 'Is that the way most people would say it?'. These questions are particularly important if there is familiarity between the informant and the ethnographer with each other's culture. The second type, a hypothetical-interaction question, places the informant in an imaginary setting and asks them to describe what kinds of things might be said. The third type of native-language question is one in which the ethnographer asks the informant for typical sentences that contain a particular word or phrase.

With a case study using a mixed method approach, the next section will demonstrate how Spradley's interviewing techniques can be adopted in a non-ethnographic study.

Case Study: the Grand Tour Approach Applied to the Phenomenon of Garden Visiting

Introduction

In considering the type of interviews to be undertaken in the final phase of the research, the breadth and multiplicity of the experience of visitors prior to a trip to a garden was required, so the responses of many participants would be needed. This eliminated the option of long interviews with a small number of participants. Additionally, it was recognized that a visit to a garden is a social experience: Connell (2004) found only 14% of respondents visited alone, and Gallagher (1983) recorded 9%. Therefore a better understanding of the dynamics of decision making within a pair or group of visitors could be obtained by interviewing the social unit together, whether they were family or friends.

Gardens afford opportunities to talk, as only 4% of respondents in the resident survey said they did not like to talk to anybody when in a garden. Therefore the casual conversation form of interviewing described by Daengbuppha *et al.* (2006) could be effective. However, their interest was the visitor experience and interaction with heritage sites, whilst this research was more concerned with what had happened prior to the visit as much as the experiential aspects of the garden visit. Accordingly, some means of initiating the interview in such a way as to direct the participants' thoughts initially backwards in time but which would then allow for an openness of direction was required. Therefore Spradley's method of asking descriptive questions, and in particular the specific grand tour question, seemed an appropriate vehicle.

The resident survey had also shown that a quarter of respondents had indicated that they liked to talk to other visitors, and so it seemed likely that they would be willing to talk to an interviewer. Other recommendations made by Spradley would also be met: for example, a visit to a garden is usually a leisurely pursuit without the fixed start and finishing times of some other cultural attractions, so visitors would probably have time to talk. In addition, by the very act of visiting a garden or other horticultural attraction, the participants would be informants having direct and current experience of the cultural scene. The resident survey also showed that as many respondents re-visited a garden or visited different gardens repeatedly, it was likely that many participants would also be very familiar with the cultural scene.

A final requirement was that the data obtained from the interviews would need not only to complement the other phases of the research but also to be capable of integration with the existing data sets. However, the data consisted of many different types of response. For example, respondents to the surveys drew ticks, crosses or forward slashes in boxes, or circles around numbers, to indicate agreement with a researcher-provided response. They wrote in words, numbers or symbols in response to open questions and some wrote unprompted additional information about a response at the side of the questionnaire. Participants in the interviews replied not only to questions from the researcher but also spoke in response to questions or comments from their companions, and some made an unprompted comment, having answered a question but then redirected the conversation.

The challenge of the research was therefore how to consider these very different forms of data. Furthermore, the research sought to generate understanding from the data but there was also awareness that if, as argued within the study, behaviour such as garden visiting reflects social influences, then so would the responses in the data. Therefore it was decided to consider all the forms of responses from both surveys and interviews as part of a participant's explanatory repertoire. Linguistic repertoires are 'a set of descriptive and referential terms which portray beliefs, actions and events in a specific way' (Wooffitt, 1993: 292). Similarly they are defined as 'clusters of terms, descriptions and figures of speech' by Sarantakos (2005: 310).

Potter and Wetherell (1987: 149) were concerned with the way language is used to

give an account of behaviour and introduced the notion of 'interpretative repertoires'. They defined a repertoire as
'constituted through a limited range of terms
used in particular stylistic and grammatical
constructions' and interpretative repertoires
as 'recurrently used systems of terms used
for characterizing and evaluating actions,
events and other phenomena'. Repertoires
are not conceptualized by them as intrinsically linked to social groups, nor does an
individual draw on the same repertoire in
different situations. Hermes (1995: 8) uses
'interpretative repertoires' to understand
how women's magazines become meaningful in everyday life. She suggests that: 'Repertoires are the cultural resources that
speakers fall back on and refer to. Which
repertoires are used depends on the cultural
capital of an individual reader.'

Furthermore, the participants' explanations were accepted at face value; they were
their explanations. Therefore, although they
did not explain garden visiting per se, they
did contribute to an understanding of the
phenomenon.

Data collection

When it became apparent that there might
be difficulties in obtaining a suitable sample
of volunteers from the resident survey, a
pilot scheme of 19 short individual or group
interviews, based on Spradley's developmental research sequence approach, was
carried out at Compton Acres, a privately
owned garden overlooking Poole Harbour
in southern England. The specific grand
tour question 'What made you come to
Compton Acres today?' was used to start the
interviews, further questions, as suggested
by Spradley, followed, to encourage participants to expand on their initial response.

Thereafter, further sets of interviews
using the same technique were carried out
at five other attractions, selected purposefully to be representative of the horticultural
attractions sector. The first was in West Sus-
sex at Wakehurst Place, described as 'Kew's
garden in the country' and owned by the
National Trust but administered by the
Royal Botanic Gardens, Kew. The remain-
ing sites were all in Dorset. They were a
mature cottage garden, opened under the
auspices of the National Gardens Scheme (a
charitable organization); the Bournemouth
Pleasure Gardens, publicly owned gardens
located in the town centre; Stewarts Gardenlands, the first 'garden centre' in the UK,
and a craft and garden show, a relatively
small, professionally run show.

Additionally, interviews were carried
out with members of a Dorset allotment
association, either on the day before or during a coach trip to Wakehurst Place, as part
of that set of interviews. In each location the
sample was chosen purposively, but with
an element of randomness to be as inclusive
as possible. At Compton Acres, the craft and
garden show, Stewarts Gardenlands and
Wakehurst Place, the interviewer remained
at one location and approached the next
group passing upon the completion of each
interview. At the cottage garden, at the allotment association plots and on the coach
trip, the interviewer selected a particular
area and then interviewed every individual
or group in that area. In the Bournemouth
Pleasure Gardens both techniques were
used, the first in the lower gardens (because
too many people pass by at one time to ran-
domly select a group) and the second in the
central gardens (because far fewer people
walk by).

All the interviews were recorded with
the participants' consent and recordings
were then transcribed. The process was iterative, with one set of interviews being transcribed and coded before the next set was
carried out, so that the findings that emerged
could be incorporated in subsequent mini-
tour questions if an opportunity arose. The
visitor interviews were analysed collectively with the data from the nine resident
interviews.

Examples of questions and responses

Following the specific grand tour question,
'What made you come to Compton Acres (or

Wakehurst Place, etc.) today?', a typical response and subsequent question was:

> Interviewee: I've been before but we're holidaying with friends and they've never been before so I brought them to have a look.
>
> Interviewer: Was there anything special about the garden that you wanted them to see? (Specific mini-tour question.)
>
> Interviewee: Uh, just everything really.

Another interview beginning in the same way, but lasting longer, progressed as follows:

> Interviewee: Um, visiting friends in Verwood, and uh, they had heard about the gardens and wanted to come and investigate.
>
> Later:
>
> Interviewer: And when you visit gardens, why do you like to go? (Experience question.)
>
> Interviewee: Oh, it's very much a very peaceful pastime looking at gardens and great for ideas for your own garden, although it might be small, you can still scale down what you see to fit your own garden.
>
> Interviewer: Have you ever copied an idea, have you actually done it? (Example question.)
>
> Interviewee: Yes.
>
> Interviewer: Can you tell me …
>
> Interviewee: Um, we've gone for, um, living in Cornwall, we get quite a lot of good mild weather and we've gone for more um, more oriental sort of looking things, we've got a fern tree, ah that's obviously going to the Eden Project, on our doorstep … generally sort of just picking up on those sort of things and making things more interesting, Acers and things and very much getting into scaling down what you see in the garden.

Analysis of the interview data

The initial consideration regarding the data analysis was the type of analysis to be adopted. Sarantakos (2005: 344) states that qualitative analysis '… aims to transform and interpret qualitative data in a rigorous

and scholarly manner … Beyond this there is simply no consensus as to how qualitative analysis should proceed, or what makes an acceptable analysis.'

Seale (2004) suggests that there are five main forms of qualitative analysis: conversation, discourse, semiotic, grounded theory and qualitative thematic analysis. Conversation and discourse analysis (Rapley, 2004; Potter and Wetherell, 1987, respectively) are more concerned with the way in which the data are expressed rather than their content. A semiotic analysis is concerned with uncovering the processes of meaning production and how signs are designed to have an effect upon the perceivers of those signs (Bryman, 2008). Qualitative thematic analysis (Miles and Huberman, 1994; Seale, 2004) and a form of grounded theory analysis (Glaser, 1978) therefore informed the analysis in this research (see also Chapter 10).

Secondly, there was the practical issue of whether or not to conduct the analysis with the aid of computer software and, if so, which program to use. The principal arguments for using software packages are that they can add rigour by making analysis more systematic and transparent (Kelle, 1995). In contrast, concerns are concentrated on the possibility that a researcher can become alienated or distanced from the data by the technology (Weitzman, 2000). As the interviews were carried out, transcribed and coded by one researcher, the possibility of alienation was reduced compared with analysis carried out by different people. Therefore, computer-assisted qualitative data analysis software (CAQDAS) was used, and having considered the merits and availability of the packages available, NVivo was chosen.

Miles and Huberman (1994) describe three components of analysis, which they argue are simultaneous: data reduction, data display, and conclusion drawing and verification. These stages were undertaken using the NVivo software as an analytic tool. The first of several stages carried out was section coding, by which NVivo 'autocodes' sections of the text under a particular heading. The references of speakers were used as headings to enable the identification of everything that each person said, as opposed to the document, which contained the interviewer's and other companions' speech as well. Additionally, everything which an interviewee said about that particular visit was coded 'this visit' to distinguish it from other visits to horticultural attractions. Both these actions facilitated searching at a later date.

Punch (2005: 200) suggests that there is a wide range of possibilities when assigning codes to data:

> At one end of the continuum, we can have prespecified codes or more general coding frameworks. At the other end, we can start coding with no prespecified codes, and let the data suggest initial codes .... Nor ... does it need to be an either-or decision. Thus, even when guided by an initial coding scheme, we can be alert to other labels and categories suggested by the data.

In the current research pre-specified codes were derived from the findings of the quantitative phases. But as the qualitative phases were designed to elaborate and inform the data derived from the quantitative findings, the latter form of coding described by Punch (2005), in which additional categories are subsequently created, was employed. In NVivo, coded segments of text are copied to a node, and any text can be coded as many times as the analyst requires.

Memos were created and linked to a node (using a DocLink in NVivo). Glaser (1978: 83) defines a memo as '... the theorizing write-up of ideas about codes and their relationships as they strike the analyst while coding'. Memos were created of the analyst's reflections on the related literature, difficulties in understanding the interviewee's meaning, patterns that were emerging and also contradictions, etc. Memos were also made regarding the analyst's thoughts on the node contents. This occurred either sporadically (as referred to by Glaser) or systematically. On completion of the coding of the first set of transcripts (those from Compton Acres) and after completion of each subsequent transcript, one or two nodes were reviewed in order through the tree hierarchy. Each segment of text coded at a node was assessed as to whether all the segments

were consistent and whether the label given to the node accurately reflected its contents. If not, other notes were then added and the data was re-coded to the new node. NVivo allows for the easy merging, movement, relabelling and re-coding of nodes, so as the memos developed (all entries were dated) various changes were made to the nodes.

Data display includes the organization and concentration of the data, and the NVivo software offers several means of doing this – in this study the nodes were constructed and displayed in a tree hierarchy. Concurrently with the data reduction and display, tentative conclusions were drawn. These were then tested using the information directly from the nodes or by using the search facility in NVivo. The actions of creating an initial coding framework, the development of further codes, reflection on the contents of the nodes recorded in the memos and either constantly referring back to the literature already reviewed or, on occasion, by seeking out new sources were therefore iterative.

A summary of responses to the grand tour question

The participants' explanatory repertoires revealed individual processes as well as other phenomena or structures that afford garden visiting and highlighted the importance of the natural and the social in addition to individual agency in deciding to visit a garden. One source of data that provided this information was the responses to the grand tour question: 'What made you come to (place x) today?' This question was not only the opening question to all participants in the visitor interviews but was also included as an open question in the visitor survey that had been undertaken at Compton Acres.

The written answers in the visitor questionnaire were always brief and many included two explanations, for example 'enjoyed previous visit + lunch' and 'like gardens, easy to reach from Bournemouth' (the nearby coastal resort). The oral responses were longer and again often included more than one explanation. All the written

Table 7.1. The explanatory categories given in response to the 'grand tour' question (visitor survey).

Explanatory category	Example quote
Individual agency	To study the gardens
Revisiting	Been here before many years ago
Social agency	My friend suggested it
Personal description	We love gardening and visiting gardens
Weather	Sunny day
Locality	Local to where I'm staying
Occasion	Mother's birthday trip
Indeterminate	Obviously a mistake

and oral answers could be assigned to one of eight explanatory categories (examples taken from the visitor survey are presented in Table 7.1).

The analysis of these initial responses and the answers given to the subsequent 'Spradley' descriptive questions, together with the findings of the other data sets, enabled an in-depth understanding of participation in garden visiting to emerge. Detailed findings regarding the influence of, first, the weather and, secondly, family and friends are reported in Fox and Edwards (2008) and the findings in full are given in Fox (2007). By way of example, the findings relating to one of the explanatory categories, i.e. 'occasion', are detailed here.

The participants' explanations of their visit often referred to a temporal element. Time was either seen as 'ordinary', in which case they spoke in terms of its availability, or it was considered as 'special' in some way, i.e. an occasion. Having the time to visit was an influence that many participants mentioned:

> Interviewee (woman at the cottage garden): … we've been going to visit this garden for ages and never got round to it. So today, we said right, we're going to drop everything and go! So we did and came here.

Some participants spoke more specifically about how they had the time to visit gardens or about how the opening times of gardens limited their visiting. Those that open as event attractions are particularly

restricting: the cottage garden had opened for 1 week in April and then again in August 2005, when the interviews were carried out. Some of the visitors revealed why they were there that day:

> Interviewee: But this one we saw advertised, well in the 'yellow' book, [a guide book] saw earlier in the year and then I said oh we've missed that one, so it'll have to be later in the year.

> Interviewer: Oh, because it was open in April, wasn't it?

> Second interviewee: … We missed that, so we figured …

> Interviewee: We must do it now; we must do it this week.

The natural environment also has its own 'calendar':

> Interviewee (woman at Wakehurst Place): We normally come Easter time, so of course it's nice now. I mean we usually come when the rhododendrons are out … We went down to Mottisfont Abbey, gorgeous roses. It's just the right time of the year.

Therefore a different type of 'special event' arises when a visit to a permanently open garden is made at a particular time. However, some participants discussed attraction-visiting practices, which amount to routine visiting. For example, one retired couple revealed how if it is a Thursday they will often visit a garden. For other participants, a socially mediated occasion can prompt a visit, as demonstrated here:

> Interviewer: What made you suggest Compton Acres today?

> Interviewee: Today, Father's Day.

> Interviewer: … do you usually go out on Father's Day or special days out?

> Interviewee (woman): Yep, all the time.

Participants also mentioned that Mother's Day, birthdays and anniversaries could prompt visits. However, some interviews carried out at the garden centre on the spring bank holiday Monday gave the impression that bank holidays seem to afford time rather than the affective elements of the personal occasions:

> Interviewer: And what made you come today rather than ...

> Interviewee (woman at Stewarts Gardenlands): Bank holiday really. We're both off work.

Conclusion

Spradley (1979) developed a strategy for undertaking interviews, which included a form of questioning – descriptive questions – as part of his approach to ethnographic research. In this chapter it has been shown how using descriptive questions can be incorporated into a mixed method for aiding understanding of visitors to gardens. Replicating this form of unstructured interviewing suited not only the objectives of the research but also the context. Particularly, it allowed for limited researcher bias and was very flexible. Additionally, it not only enabled interaction between participants but also facilitated children and teenagers to contribute to the research, with the approval and in the company of their parents. However, as noted above, it is a time-consuming method, particularly as there can be periods of conversation that, whilst not directly relevant to the study, are necessary in developing rapport. As in any research method there are ethical and quality issues that need to be considered, but which have not been discussed here due to space limitations. None the less, this study offers practical and useful guidance for similar explorations of cultural attractions.

Acknowledgements

The research reported in the case study was undertaken for the first author's doctorate, supervised by the other two authors. In addition, she would like to acknowledge the contribution and support of Dr Stephen Wallace of Plymouth University.

References

Berg, B.L. (2007) *Qualitative Research Methods for the Social Sciences,* 6th edn. Pearson Education, London.

Brannen, J. (2005) *Mixed Methods Research: a Discussion Paper*. The Economic and Social Research Council, National Centre for Research Methods. Available at: /www.bournemouth.ac.uk/cap/documents/Methods ReviewPaperNCRM-005.pdf (accessed 15 May 2006).

Bryman, A. (2008) *Social Research Methods*, 3rd edn. Oxford University Press, Oxford.

Connell, J. (2004) The purest of human pleasures: the characteristics and motivations of garden visitors in Great Britain. *Tourism Management* 25, 229–247.

Daengbuppha, J., Hemmington, N. and Wilkes, K. (2006) Using grounded theory to model visitor experiences at heritage sites: methodological and practical issues. *Qualitative Market Research: an International Journal* 9, 367–388.

Finn, M., Elliott-White, M. and Walton, M. (2000) *Tourism and Leisure Research Methods*. Pearson Education, Harlow, UK.

Fox, D. (2007) Understanding garden visitors: the affordances of a leisure environment. PhD thesis. Bournemouth University, Poole, UK.

Fox, D. and Edwards, J. (2008) Managing gardens. In: Fyall, A., Garrod, B., Leask, A. and Wanhill, S. (eds) *Managing Visitor Attractions*. Butterworth-Heinemann, London, pp. 217–236.

Gallagher, J. (1983) *Visiting Historical Gardens: a Report on Contemporary Garden Visiting and its Lterature*. Leeds Polytechnic, Leeds, UK.

Glaser, B.G. (1978) *Theoretical Sensitivity: Advances in the Methodology of Grounded Theory*. The Sociology Press, Mill Valley, California.

Hermes, J. (1995) *Reading Women's Magazines*. Polity Press, Cambridge, UK.

Jennings, G. (2001) *Tourism Research*. John Wiley and Sons Australia, Milton, Queensland, Australia.

Jennings, G. (2005) Interviewing: a focus on qualitative techniques. In: Ritchie, B.W., Burns, P. and Palmer, C. (eds) *Tourism Research Methods: Integrating Theory with Practice*. CAB International, Wallingford, UK, pp. 99–117.

Kelle, U. (1995) Introduction: an overview of computer-aided methods in qualitative research. In: Kelle, U. (ed.) *Computer-aided Qualitative Data Analysis*. Sage Publications Limited, London, pp. 1–17.

Miles, M.B. and Huberman, A.M. (1994) *Qualitative Data Analysis*, 2nd edn. Sage Publications Limited, London.

Potter, J. and Wetherell, M. (1987) *Discourse and Social Psychology: Beyond Attitudes and Behaviour*. Sage Publications Limited, London.

Punch, K.F. (2005) *Introduction to Social Research*, 2nd edn. Sage Publications Limited, London.

Rapley, T. (2004) Analysing conversation. In: Seale, C. (ed.) *Researching Society and Culture*, 2nd edn. Sage Publications Limited, London, pp. 383–396.

Sarantakos, S. (2005) *Social Research*, 3rd edn. Palgrave Macmillan, Basingstoke, UK.

Seale, C. (2004) Coding and analysing data. In: Seale, C. (ed.) *Researching Society and Culture*, 2nd edn. Sage Publications Limited, London, pp. 305–321.

Spradley, J.P. (1979) *The Ethnographic Interview*. Wadsworth Group, Belmont, California.

Weitzman, E.A. (2000) Software and qualitative research. In: Denzin, N.K and Lincoln, Y.S. (eds) *Handbook of Qualitative Research*. Sage Publications Limited, London, pp. 803–820.

Wooffitt, R. (1993) Analysing accounts. In: Gilbert, N. (ed.) *Researching Social Life*. Sage Publications Limited, London, pp. 287–305.

8 Multi-method Research on Ethnic Cultural Tourism in Australia

Jock Collins, Simon Darcy and Kirrily Jordan

Introduction

Australia has more immigrants than most Western societies today (OECD, 2007), with communities drawn from most corners of the globe (Collins, 1991, 2008). As a consequence, Australia's major cities have become very cosmopolitan places (Burnley, 2001). When the opening ceremony for the Sydney 2000 Olympic Games was held, there was a community living in Sydney to match every national flag engaged in the athletes' procession. The 2006 Australian census revealed that 60% of Sydney's population were first- or second-generation immigrants. Australian cities such as Sydney, Melbourne, Brisbane and Perth have a cosmopolitan feel, most evident in the great variety of restaurants and cafés, providing food from menus derived from all continents. In all these cities, and others like them around the Western world, immigrant entrepreneurs have clustered in certain suburbs, so that ethnic precincts, such as Little Italy, Chinatown, Little Korea or Little Turkey, emerge.

The growth of the cultural and tourism industries is an important characteristic of modern developed economics like Australia. These industries intersect in the field of 'cultural tourism'. Cultural tourism is now recognized as an important agent of economic and social change in contemporary Western societies such as Australia. Cultural tourism includes tourism to traditional cultural attractions such as museums and galleries, but it also incorporates new forms of tourism associated with cultural activities. They include, but are not limited to, cultural attractions related to the urban ethnic diversity that accompanied immigration to countries such as Australia. The cultural tourism possibilities of ethnic diversity are relatively underdeveloped in the literature. The research reported in this chapter was designed to produce results that begin to redress this gap in our understanding of cultural tourism. This chapter discusses the methodological approaches appropriate for the study of what we call 'ethnic cultural tourism', i.e. tourism that is related to the cultural diversity that accompanies immigration.

The central research issue addressed in this chapter is: what methodologies and research methods and instruments are appropriate to investigate dimensions of cultural tourism related to ethnic precincts in Australia's major cosmopolitan cities? Ethnic precincts are neighbourhoods with clusters of immigrant entrepreneurs that have developed a reputation for, and an identity as, a place in the city to experience minority ethnic cultures, with ethnic food, goods and festivals being the main attractors. They are

often 'branded' by local government authorities, given ethnic makeovers in the public
spaces of the precincts and marketed to
locals, visitors and tourists.

The research projects that we report on
were designed to develop case studies of
how, in a range of urban settings, ethnic cultural heritage can be developed into an
effective part of interpretive tourist attractions for destination areas.

Section two of this chapter develops an
interdisciplinary theoretical framework
for this research. Any research project is
shaped by its theoretical points of departure. The section reviews the sometimes
overlapping literatures of immigration
studies, tourism studies, cultural geography, immigrant entrepreneurship and regulation theory to present an interdisciplinary
theoretical framework that will shape the
research design and the research instruments. Section three then develops a range
of quantitative and qualitative research
methodologies and research instruments
for the ethnic precinct case studies. Section
four briefly summarizes the results of this
research, reflects on the research methodology and identifies gaps in need of further
research.

Ethnic Cultural Tourism and Ethnic Precincts: Theoretical Points of Departure

The growth of the cultural tourism market

As the experience economy becomes the
focus of postmodern conceptualizations of
place and space (Darcy and Small, 2008), the
cultural and tourist industries intersect to
create unique destination experiences, of
which cultural tourism is but one of a number that have been identified in Australian
tourism strategy (Commonwealth Department of Industry, Tourism and Resources,
2005). Cultural tourism is recognized as an
important agent of economic and social
change in Europe and elsewhere (Richards,
1996, 2007). Cultural tourism includes tourism to traditional cultural attractions, such

as museums and art galleries, ballet and
opera, but it also incorporates new forms of
tourism associated with cultural activities.
They include, but are not limited to, cultural
attractions related to the urban ethnic diversity that accompanied immigration to countries such as Australia (Collins, 2006). One
site of ethnic cultural tourism is ethnic precincts such as Chinatowns, Little Italys,
Korea towns, Little Saigons and so on in
major cosmopolitan cities such as Melbourne
(Collins *et al.*, 2001) and Sydney (Collins
and Castillo, 1998), attracting visitation from
national and international tourists. Other
forms of cultural tourism are event-specific
(tall ships) or linked to subcultures such as
the gay community (Sydney's gay and les-
bian mardi gras).

As Richards notes, there has been a
growth of cultural tourism as a consequence
of both increased tourism demand and the
growing supply of cultural attractions: 'As
cultural markets become increasingly globalized, so competition between cultural
attractions for a share of the cultural tourism market will also intensify' (Richards,
1996: 18–19). He identifies key questions
for tourism that emerge from the rise of the
importance of 'traditional' and 'new' cultural industries:

> Who are the tourists who use these cultural
> facilities? Why do they engage in cultural
> tourism? How great is the demand for
> cultural tourism? What elements of culture
> attract cultural tourists? Whose culture is
> being consumed by the cultural tourists?
> Few previous studies have attempted to
> answer these basic questions.

Ethnic cultural tourism

This chapter reports on the methodological
processes of developing research instruments
and recruiting informants for a research
project designed to address the questions
Richards raises, but each time replacing
what he terms cultural tourism with ethnic
cultural tourism. For this research the case
studies were drawn from three cities and six
sites that each had an ethnic cultural heritage: Sydney (Chinatown, Finger Wharf, Art

Gallery), Melbourne (Chinatown, Little Italy) and Perth (Northbridge). These case studies sought to explore the intersection between traditional and new cultural landscape precincts, and take, as points of departure, the questions raised by Richards: Who are the tourists who take part in ethnic cultural tourism? Why do they so? What are their responses to landscapes of ethnic cultural tourism? A comparative methodology is adopted for this research. The underlying principle is that it is not possible to identify unique aspects of a phenomenon such as ethnic cultural tourism unless it is compared with other dimensions of cultural tourism

The broader questions are related to the opportunities that ethnic cultural landscapes in Australia offer for current and future patterns of Australian tourism and the policy implications for the Australian tourism industry in relation to the increasingly important ethnic cultural tourism phenomena. The field of ethnic cultural tourism is underdeveloped in Australia at the level of theory, research and policy development. Yet international research suggests that ethnic cultural tourism has significant potential in attracting new tourists. The present research project was designed as a scoping study with a view to setting out the parameters involved in ethnic cultural tourism research in Australia. It aimed to identify how ethnic heritage and contemporary cultural diversity impact on visitor experience and on local communities. The objective was to assist the Australian tourism industry in understanding the growing importance of cultural tourism by developing a number of case studies of cultural landscapes tourism in three Australian states.

Cultural landscapes is a term with very broad meaning. It refers in part to the way in which traditional cultural industries – 'high culture' activities such as museums, art galleries, opera and ballet, and 'popular culture' activities such as film, music, restaurants and shopping – are a central part of national and international tourist activities and attractions in Australia. The term also refers, in part, to the way that the ethnic

diversity of Australian society and its built and social environments shape the dynamics of Australian tourism. Australia is one of the most culturally diverse nations in the world today: it has more immigrants and greater ethnic diversity than any other Western nation (Collins 1991, 2000). These two dimensions of cultural landscapes, of course, intersect and interact. This can be seen, for example, in the proliferation of 'foreign' film festivals in major Australian cities, of museum events or art gallery exhibitions related to immigrant cultures, and in the way that immigrant communities have pioneered the Australian wine industry in regions such as Griffith and New South Wales, or in the tourist attraction of Chinese heritage in places such as Young in New South Wales and Ballarat in Victoria, and the festivals and eating and shopping experiences in Sydney's and Melbourne's Chinatowns.

A Review of Cultural Tourism Literature

The tourist experience

Our first point of departure is the literature related to the tourist experience (Selwyn, 1996; Urry, 2002; Selby, 2004) and the way that the cultural economy and the images and experience of place (Suvantola, 2002) shape the tourist experience. The tourism experience consists not only of a collection of tourism facilities, or real economy experiences, but also of a set of symbolic economy experiences (Urry, 2002; see also Chapter 5, this volume). The latter involves the consumption of signs, symbols, festivals and spectacles used in creating aestheticized spaces of entertainment and pleasure. This has led researchers to explore the links between ethnic heritage, cultural diversity and urban tourism as crucial components of the cultural capital of post-industrial society (Kearns and Philo, 1993; Lash and Urry, 1994). In discussing the 'symbolic economy', Zukin (1995) points to the role of ethnic diversity in shaping place and space, relating it to a tendency to commodify cosmopolitan life-styles and turn them into a vital resource for the prosperity and growth of cities. One of the contradictions of globalization is that local difference and place identity become more important in a globalized world. Ethnic heritage, cultural diversity and urban tourism become links between the cultural capital of post-industrial cities and the tourism marketing and commodification of those experiences (Kearns and Philo, 1993; Lash and Urry, 1994; Zukin, 1995). Hoffman (2003: 96), interestingly, observed that 'multiculturalism and diversity have recently become a positive demographic characteristic for business and tourism', indicating that ethnic diversity in ethnic precincts is one aspect of the symbolic economy. City planners, place marketers, tourist guides, and food and culture critics play a role in simultaneously advertising and promoting ethnic precincts and cultural diversity in the city while, at the same time, reshaping the very image of culture and ethnicity in a way that maximizes the appeal to tourists (Halter, 2000; Selby, 2004).

Old cultural landscapes of tourism

Cultural tourism, of course, entails many things: from 'cultural' activities such as viewing exhibitions at museums and attending operatic performances to those activities associated with visiting historic building edifices and viewing ethnic festivals. When examining cultural urban tourism phenomena, the terms 'ethnic tourism' (cf. Hitchcock, 1999), 'heritage tourism', 'cultural tourism', 'urban tourism' (cf. Chang, 2000) and even 'eco tourism' (cf. Gibson *et al.*, 2003) are regularly used interchangeably.

The literature on traditional or 'old' cultural landscapes of tourism, such as museums and art galleries, is fairly well established. Richards (1996: 15) presents data to show that there has been a second 'museum boom' in Europe since the early 1980s, with a rapid growth in that time in the number of museums. This has been accompanied by a growth of 'specialized

museums', with some 2500 museums identified in the UK alone (Richards, 1996: 16). Examples of new specialized museums can be found in London (Museum of the Moving Image, Theatre Museum, Design Museum), in Brussels (Cartoon Museum), in Amsterdam (Sex Museum, Pianola Museum, Cannabis Museum) and in many other cities across Europe. As MacDonald (1992: 163) has observed, the 'new' museums have partly been created as a response to the deficiencies of the old: 'The failure of mainstream museums (to reach a wider audience) is one reason why we are seeing growing numbers of specialized museums designed for specific audiences, such as children, indigenous peoples and specific ethnic communities'.

New cultural landscapes of tourism

As the literature on traditional or 'old' cultural landscapes of tourism is so established, this scoping project can make its strongest contribution to the literature on cultural landscapes of tourism by focusing on one form of the new cultural landscapes of tourism: that of ethnic diversity as a consequence of immigration to Australia and other countries. In particular, we are interested to explore ethnic precincts as important sites for the new cultural tourism. As a consequence, this literature review will concentrate on ethnicity as a critical axis of new cultural landscapes of tourism (Rath, 2007).

The most highly developed interdisciplinary theoretical framework for the study of urban ethnic tourism that draws on these elements is regulation theory, which has become central to the new tourism literature (Costa and Martinotti, 2003: 67–68; Fainstein *et al.*, 2003). Fainstein *et al.* (2003) explore the way that four types of regulatory frameworks – regulation of visitors to protect the city, regulation of the city for the benefit of the visitors and the tourism industry, regulation of tourism labour markets, and regulation of the tourism industry itself – structure relations within the urban tourist milieu and provide a framework for a historical and contemporary comparative analysis of global urban tourism. This regulation theory approach 'places tourism within a complex matrix of economic, political, cultural and spatial interactions and illustrates the interplay of sectors and scales – local, regional, national and international' (Fainstein *et al.*, 2003: 240). The authors also stress the importance of studying the linkages and processes inherent in the city tourist experience, 'without sacrificing the possibility of agency or overlooking the complex role of culture'.

The conceptual framework for this exploration of the (contradictory) nature of ethnic precincts and their relation to tourism draws on a broad-ranging interdisciplinary literature (Collins, 2007), addressing issues of the cultural economy (Zukin, 1995), international tourism (Suvantola, 2002; Urry, 2002), the urban and cultural geography of ethnic place and space in the city (Burnley, 2001), ethnic economies (Light and Gold, 2000), immigrant entrepreneurship (Waldinger *et al.*,1990; Rath, 2000; Kloosterman and Rath, 2003) and the marketing of ethnicity (Halter, 2000).

Various authors draw attention to the spatial aspect of ethnic and cultural consumption, more particularly to places of consumption (shopping malls, high streets, ethnic precincts). Urry (2002: 137) notes how tourist experiences are shaped by the intersections of class, gender and ethnicity, and that:

> Ethnic groups are important in the British tourist industry... and in some respects play a key role ... In recent years certain ethnic groups have come to be constructed as part of the 'attraction' or 'theme' of some places, giving as an example the case of Manchester around 'its collection' of Chinese restaurants in a small area.

These spatial links between tourism and ethnic diversity are not new, of course. For example, Judd (2003) describes the rise of tourist enclaves that accompanied the rise of grand tourism in the mid-19th century as the historical precursors of today's places of consumption. Hoffman (2003: 97) argues that: 'The pursuit of ethnic branding reflects the fact that minorities are the fastest growing (new) consumer population.'

The demand side of ethnic precinct tourism

Research into ethnic precincts and tourism puts greater emphasis on the demand side, or the consumer/tourist side, of the ethnic economy. Most of the research into immigrant entrepreneurship in the past two decades has concentrated on the supply side of immigrant enterprises: the establishment of the enterprise, the division of labour, employment relations, marketing and business success (Collins *et al.*, 1995; Collins, 2003). This is important because different regimes of regulation and governance (state, federal and local) play an important role in shaping patterns of immigrant entrepreneurship (Kloosterman and Rath, 2001, 2003), and therefore the supply of ethnic businesses and precincts. In Australia, the development of ethnic precincts such as Sydney and Melbourne's Chinatowns has been extensively shaped by local government authorities.

Yet, in order to fully understand ethnic tourism, it is necessary to conduct new research into the demand side of ethnic entrepreneurship, often mentioned but not investigated in the literature. Since ethnic restaurants are a significant legacy of minority ethnic communities in the Australian built environment, the cultural significance of eating ethnic food (Gabaccia, 1998) and the 'critical infrastructure' required to support ethnic economies and the development of ethnic precincts (Zukin 1995, 1998) come into focus. Important questions emerge then: Who eats Chinese or Italian food? Where and why? What role do restaurant and food critics play in this regard? The cultural symbolism of eating Chinese or Italian food, for example, also needs exploring in this context. What cultural interaction occurs in Chinese restaurants? What symbolism and décor are used by entrepreneurs to signify to the public that they are eating in an 'authentic' Chinese or Italian precinct restaurant? What constitute 'authentic' Chinese/Italian cultural experiences from the point of view of the customers, and how do they vary according to the ethnicity and tourist status of the customer? Gabaccia (1998: 229–230) views American taste for ethnic food (and music) as central to the American identity:

> Key to identity and culture in both American music and eating is the tension between people's love for the familiar and the pleasure they find in desiring, creating and experiencing something new ... Consumers' preferences for multi-ethnic food and multi-ethnic music remain an important expression of their identities as Americans.

The authenticity of ethnic precincts

According to Bryman (2004), the opposite of authenticity is Disneyfication. He refers to the centrality of theming in contemporary consumption places and of the contradictions of such theming attempts:

> Critics of theming often disapprove of the use of symbols of nostalgia for thematic cues. Drawing on faux designs and histories, theming in terms of nostalgic references is often depicted as presenting a sanitized history, one that removes any reference to hardship and conflict in the cause of consumption.
>
> (Bryman, 2004: 52)

While Bryman looks at the theming of restaurants, malls and other places, he does not look specifically at ethnic theming. The examples of ethnic precincts such as Sydney's Chinatown show the complexities of government (local and state) involvement in creating 'authentic' façades, highlighting the relationship of the state to different factions within the ethnic community. This involves what MacCannell (1973, 1999) calls 'reconstructed ethnicity' and 'staged authenticity'. Is it possible for local authorities to help develop ethnic precincts that do not collapse into a 'Disneyfication' of ethnicity? Is it possible to develop ethnic precincts in cities such as Sydney without necessarily reproducing white stereotypes of the ethnic Other?

The other key aspect of the authenticity of ethnic precincts relates to the custom of the precinct and the events that occur there. Certainly the presence of Italian immigrants as customers walking along the streets and eating in the restaurants of a Little Italy may contribute to its authentic feel, just as the large number of visibly Asian customers in the Chinatowns of cities may help to provide a similar 'authentic' feel. When Italy wins or loses World Cup soccer matches, Little Italy is where you will find happy or sad Italian supporters. This authenticity is boosted by the role of the ethnic precinct as the place where ethnic festivals are held. Sydney and Melbourne's Chinatowns both hold a series of events to mark the Chinese New Year, while other ethnic precincts host ethnic community events, national days and other public celebrations of ethnic diversity (Collins and Castillo, 1998: 169).

Tourist safety in ethnic precincts

The issue of tourist safety is central to any government tourist strategy. No one wants to go to a place where their or their family's safety is put at risk. Control and surveillance are thus embedded in the development of tourism in general, as well as in terms of potential tourist precincts such as ethnic precincts. Body-Gendrot (2003: 39) emphasizes the importance of 'techniques of social control and security' that mega-event tourism, such as Olympic Games or World Cup soccer events, require, while Judd (2003: 23) points out that building tourist places as fortress spaces is one response to managing issues of tourist safety. Borrowing from Foucault, Edensor (1998: 41) notes that there is a 'remorseless surveillance through panopticon visual monitoring' in enclosed public spaces such as shopping malls. Shopping is encouraged but, as Judd argues, 'aimless loitering is discouraged or forbidden' (Judd, 2003: 29).

There are a number of aspects of control and surveillance that relate to ethnic precincts. The first is the historical construction of minority immigrant communities as criminal (Collins *et al.*, 2000), so that the places and spaces where they concentrate attract a criminal reputation. This is reinforced by the way that racism, prejudice and xenophobia depict immigrant minorities as the criminal 'Other', who are a threat to the safety of the host society (Poynting *et al.*, 2004). Ethnic precincts of minority immigrant groups are thus constructed as places of crime, such as gambling, drugs and prostitution, and of criminal gangs, at the same moment that they become exotic ethnic places.

Ironically, this criminal feel can also be an attraction to tourists. Chinatowns the world over have always had a criminal aspect. In New York's Chinatown, Chinese tongs, or gangs, are involved in crime and control the streets. According to Kinkead (1993: 47), in the first decades of the 20th century tourists: 'went to Chinatown to ogle vice: guidebooks warned of the immorality and filth of the quarters. The sightseers hired guides to show them opium dens, slave girls, and sites of lurid tong murders. Bohemians visited to smoke opium and drift away into hazy dreams.'

Mixed Methods for Investigating Cultural Tourism in Ethnic Precincts

The theoretical framework developed above shapes the methodologies and research instruments required to investigate ethnic cultural tourism. In general this research needs to generate a greater understanding of the production, consumption and development of cultural landscapes by tourists and visitors as well as locals. Specifically, we employed mixed methods of quantitative and qualitative methodologies in the fieldwork that we conducted in sites of successful ethnic cultural tourism. The quantitative methodology focused on a random survey of 100 tourist consumers in each ethnic precinct ($n = 579$), conducted via interviewer-completed questionnaires following the 'next person' technique (Veal, 2006). The sample size was dictated by the resources provided for the scoping study from the Sustainable Tourism Cooperative Research Centre. The surveys analysed the impressions, expectations and activities of the tourists in each precinct. Some insights into

ethnic-based tourism within tourism precincts were gained through a statistical analysis of the total sample from all the precincts while other insights were provided through individual precinct sample analysis. While the statistical analysis of each precinct was limited by the relatively small sample size ($n = 100$), it did still allow analysis by frequency, cross-tabulation, chi-square, *t*-tests and ANOVA (analysis of variance). In order to situate the tourist surveys within the broader context of the political economy of ethnic tourism in these Australian cities, the quantitative research was completed with qualitative methodologies focusing on the way that producers (ethnic entrepreneurs), consumers and what Sharon Zukin (1995) calls the 'critical infrastructure' (local government authorities, ethnic community organizations, place marketers, media, tourist interpretation, etc.) shape ethnic precincts.

A number of key aspects of ethnic cultural tourism require investigation. First, it is important to identify tourist/consumer subjectivity about the ethnic tourist experience, including ethnic precincts. This makes it important to survey tourists in ethnic precincts and other ethnic cultural sites to get their opinion on matters such as authenticity, atmosphere, experience, food, cultural iconography and the like. In other words, the theoretical framework shapes the questions to be asked of tourists and hence the development of the survey as a research instrument. The questionnaire also needs to record background information on the tourist, such as country of residence, age, gender and their length of stay, and explore issues such as how the tourist heard about the site, what attracted them to the site and their impressions of the tourist experience, including issues of interpretation and authenticity. Matters of research design then come into play. Our comparative methodology required us to conduct surveys in each of the ethnic cultural tourist sites in Sydney, Melbourne and Perth. It was also important to design questions that have been covered in broader visitor surveys for other sites, in order to allow comparisons to be made and to attempt to investigate the uniqueness of the ethnic cultural tourist experience. In addition, attention was paid to the numbers to be surveyed – pilots of 100 were conducted in each site – and issues related to randomness: time of day, day of week and gender.

Regulation theory and the work of Sharon Zukin (1995, 1998) led us also to focus on the other major stakeholders that shape the ethnic cultural tourist experience. We conducted key informant interviews with the local government authorities under whose remit the cultural precinct falls, because they are key players in the formation of and development of the precinct. Interviews were also conducted with the immigrant entrepreneurs in the ethnic precinct and the ethnic community organizations and tourist site operators located there. The interviews were then undertaken with place marketers from local and state government. For example, we held close discussions with the numerous government agencies with a role in redeveloping and revitalizing Perth's Northbridge as a centre for tourism and leisure. The City of Perth, Town of Vincent, East Perth Redevelopment Authority, State Department of Premier and Cabinet, and Western Australian Police were all involved in these efforts. The multitude of stakeholders necessitated a lengthy period of immersion in the field.

In contrast, in Sydney's Chinatown, the main government players were limited to the City of Sydney and Tourism New South Wales. Along with the Chinatown Cultural Advisory Committee – established by the City of Sydney as a conduit to tap into Chinese community views – these bodies were concerned mainly with the promotion of the annual Chinese New Year festival. The literature suggests that annual events – in our case studies on either ethnic festivals such as Chinese New Year celebrations or the F1 Grand Prix in Melbourne's Little Italy – are important both in the cultural identification of the precinct and in the marketing of the precinct. Observations, interviews and photos of these events were collected; user surveys of the events conducted by other parties were consulted to get further insights into the events themselves and their tourist dimension.

Additional site observations for each case study were structured at various times of the day and week to provide an overview of (changing) customer and use patterns in the ethnic precinct. Photos were used to collect images of the ethnic iconography and ethnic façades of the precincts. The public representations of the precincts were collected from the stakeholder management information systems, including annual reports, corporate plans, brochures, advertising and newspaper articles. The fieldwork also involved content analysis of tourist representations in local media, contemporary and archival arts and cultural heritage representations, participant observation and in-depth interviews of tourists and visitors (consumers) and key informants in a selection of urban cultural landscape precincts. Of particular importance to this investigation are issues of theming, access, authenticity, commodification and spatial consumption. Importantly, our approach also recognized that other 'actors', such as residential communities, arts practitioners, historians and the like, are important contributors to the cultural heritage of these precincts.

The analysis needed to explore the contradictions that often accompany increased tourism, including issues of authenticity. To this end we sought out the history of the development of the cultural landscape tourism site and the impressions and experience of the tourism developers regarding a range of matters related to cultural landscape tourism, including interpretation and marketing. In doing so we sought to identify the different viewpoints of the various actors about the cultural landscape tourism in their area. As well as relying on surveys and in-depth interviews, we interrogated the local newspaper, community, family and other archives to investigate the different discourses and representations of the cultural tourism landscape and the immigration stories that underlie them. We found that views of authenticity and the appropriateness of ethnic theming varied considerably among our respondents.

For example, in Sydney's Chinatown, most survey participants – whether Chinese or non-Chinese – responded positively to the Chinese arches and other 'traditional Chinese' symbols in the streetscape. However, other symbols created clearly divided opinion. In particular, the Golden Water Mouth sculpture, billed by some as a positive symbol of Australian multiculturalism, since it incorporates both Chinese and Australian elements, is strongly opposed by many within the Chinese community, who argue that it is bad feng shui. This confirms Meethan's (2001: 27) analysis that symbols of ethnicity are 'multivocal, that is, they have the capacity to carry a range of different, if not ambiguous and contradictory meanings'. It also confirms the importance of consumer surveys and on-the-ground qualitative research in understanding the tourist experience from multiple perspectives.

The result of this quantitative and qualitative research method, derived from a clear theoretical foundation, is an innovative and original exploration of the tourist dynamics in each case study precinct as cultural landscapes of tourism, including issues related to interpretation of the precincts. The ensuing discussion examines the implications of the study for the precinct stakeholders. Central to this discussion is the importance of developing a broader interdisciplinary understanding of the ethnic precincts so as to fully develop the potential of interpretive experiences.

Research Outcomes

An important outcome of our research into cultural tourist precincts is a better understanding of the dynamics of cultural landscapes of ethnic tourism and our understanding of the way in which the built environment is shaped by cultural practices of ethnic minorities. Contributing to this outcome is a road-tested and revised visitor survey instrument (see Appendix 8.1), which could be utilized in research into other cultural landscapes of tourism in urban and rural areas. The strengths of the instrument are the inclusion of a number of open-ended responses that provide a

comparison of the ethnic interpretation between the tourism precincts. However, at the same time this adds significantly to data entry work. The research team suggests that the analysis of the open-ended response sets is undertaken in two ways:

- a verbatim record of each open-ended response is kept for the dual purpose of qualitative analysis and for precinct managers, who may interpret the results in a more instrumental way for improved management practice; and
- developing a coding scheme for use within the quantitative analysis package.

The refined instrument, together with the basic survey of the ATLAS Cultural Tourism Research Project (see Chapter 2), offers a basis for comparative analysis of like or contrasting sites. As already identified, for future precinct research the sample size needs to be increased to provide for a more detailed and precise statistical analysis of individual tourism precincts and comparative analysis between tourism precincts.

Our major finding is that Australia's multicultural past and the cosmopolitan nature of contemporary urban Australia provide a great potential for tourism in urban and rural areas in Australia, a potential that is untapped when compared with more traditional cultural tourist precincts, such as the Art Gallery of New South Wales and Woolloomooloo's Finger Wharf. In particular, our research suggests that ethnic precincts provide a great potential for future tourist attraction. Table 8.1 presents the mean of response for five attitudes statements as to respondent experience of the precincts on a scale of 1 strongly agree to 7 strongly disagree. All mean scores suggest the ethnic precinct experience was a positive one for the visitor. The two strongest responses were that 95% of survey respondents reported that they agreed or strongly agreed that they would like to visit the precinct again and 93% would recommend it to friends. However, as Fig. 8.1 shows, there were variations of the means for the statements across precincts, with a greater standard deviation occurring across the ethnic cultural precincts than the traditional cultural precincts of the Art Gallery of New South Wales and Woolloomooloo Finger Wharf. This tourist potential of ethnic precincts and ethnic heritage, which we call ethnic cultural tourism, is, as yet, untapped in Australia. While ethnic precincts hold great tourist potential, they require more effective partnerships between ethnic entrepreneurs, local government authorities, regional, city and state tourism and development boards, and local ethnic communities in order to maximize this potential.

Table 8.1. Mean response to attitude statements (scale: 1, strongly agree to 7, strongly disagree).

	No. of responses	Mean score
Like to visit again	477	1.83
Would recommend to others	478	1.97
Met my expectations	476	2.46
Memorable experience	479	2.84
Had little effect on me	479	4.93

Ethnic festivals and major events provide key opportunities for the advertising, promoting and branding of cultural landscape tourist sites to national and international tourists and sustaining greater tourist visitation to these sites throughout the year. Yet, these same events pose challenges to the local ownership and authenticity of the sites as government players step in. While not suggesting a generalized outcome of encouraging the marketing of localized events for sustaining tourism, it must be recognized that doing so has challenges for those involved in the production of the event at the local level.

Finally, we point to the importance of further research into cultural landscapes of tourism if their tourist potential is to be realized. While ethnic precincts hold great tourist potential, maximizing this potential will require more effective partnerships between ethnic entrepreneurs, local government authorities, regional, city and state tourist and development boards, and local ethnic communities. We believe that more research into what we call 'cosmopolitan

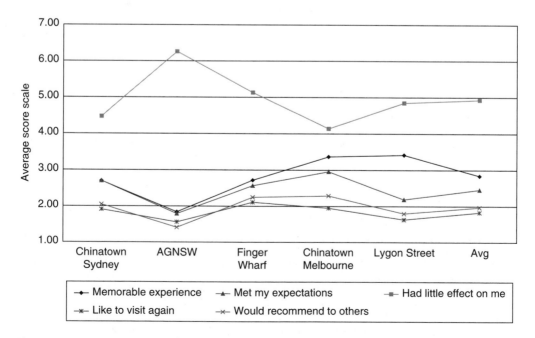

Fig. 8.1. Mean response to attitude statements by location. Scale: 1, strongly agree to 7, strongly disagree.

tourism' in both urban and rural sites in Australia would reap great rewards for the Australian tourism industry. Our scoping study revealed the potential; further research would consolidate the gains made in this regard.

Acknowledgements

The research reported here was funded by an ARC linkage grant and a grant from the Sustainable Tourism Cooperative Research Centre.

References

Body-Gendrot, S. (2003) Cities, security, and visitors: managing mega-events in France. In: Hoffman, L.M., Fainstein, S.S. and Judd, D.R. (eds) *Cities and Visitors: Regulating People, Markets, and City Space*. Blackwell Publishing, Oxford, UK, pp. 39–52.

Bryman, A. (2004) *The Disneyization of Society*. Sage, London.

Burnley, I. (2001) *The Impact of Immigration on Australia: a Demographic Approach*. Oxford University Press, South Melbourne, Australia.

Chang, T.C. (2000) Singapore's Little India: a tourist attraction as a contested landscape. *Urban Studies* 37, 343–368.

Collins, J. (1991) *Migrant Hands in a Distant Land: Australia's Post-war Immigration*. Pluto Press, Sydney.

Collins, J. (2000) Immigration and immigrants: ethnic inequality and social cohesion. In: Boreham, P., Stokes, G. and Hall, R. (eds) *The Politics of Australian Society: Political Issues for the New Century*. Longman, Sydney, pp. 302–316.

Collins, J. (2003) Australia: cosmopolitan capitalists down under. In: Kloosterman, R. and Rath, J. (eds) *Immigrant Entrepreneurs: Venturing Abroad in the Age of Globalisation*. New York University Press, New York, and Berg Publishing, Oxford, UK, pp. 61–78.

Collins, J. (2006) Ethnic diversity and the ethnic economy in cosmopolitan Sydney. In: Kaplan, D. and Li, W. (eds) *Landscapes of the Ethnic Economy*. Rowman and Littlefield, Lanham, Maryland, pp. 135–148.

Collins, J. (2007) Ethnic precincts as contradictory tourist spaces. In: Rath, J. (ed.) *Tourism, Ethnic Diversity and the City*. Routledge, London, pp. 52–67.

Collins, J. (2008) Globalisation, immigration and the second long post-war boom in Australia. *Journal of Australian Political Economy* 61, 244–266.

Collins, J. and Castillo, A. (1998) *Cosmopolitan Sydney: Explore the World in One City*. Pluto Press, Sydney.

Collins, J., Gibson, K., Alcorso, C., Tait, D. and Castles, S. (1995) *A Shop Full of Dreams: Ethnic Small Business in Australia*. Pluto Press, Sydney.

Collins, J., Noble, G., Poynting, S. and Tabar, P. (2000) *Kebabs, Kids, Cops and Crime: Youth Ethnicity and Crime*. Pluto Press, Sydney.

Collins, J., Childs, T., Mondello, L. and Breheny, J. (2001) *Cosmopolitan Melbourne: Exploring the World in One City*. Big Box Publishing, Sydney.

Commonwealth Department of Industry Tourism and Resources (2005) *Tourism White Paper – a Medium to Long Term Strategy for Tourism*. CDITR, Canberra, Australia.

Costa, N. and Martinotti, G. (2003) Sociological theories of tourism and regulation theory. In: Hoffman, L.M., Fainstein, S.S. and Judd, D.R. (eds) *Cities and Visitors: Regulating People, Markets, and City Space*. Blackwell Publishing, Oxford, UK, pp. 53–71.

Darcy, S. and Small, J. (2008) Theorising precincts: disciplinary perspectives. In: Hayllar, B., Griffin, T. and Edwards, D. (eds) *City Spaces – Tourist Places: Urban Tourism Precincts*. Elsevier, Oxford, UK, pp. 63–91.

Edensor, T. (1998) *Tourists at the Taj: Performance and Meaning as Symbolic Site*. Routledge, London.

Fainstein, S.S., Hoffman, L.M. and Judd, D.R. (2003) Making theoretical sense of tourism. In: Hoffman, L.M., Fainstein, S.S. and Judd, D.R. (eds) *Cities and Visitors: Regulating People, Markets, and City Space*. Blackwell Publishing, Oxford, UK, pp. 239–253.

Gabaccia, D.R. (1998) *We are What We Eat: Ethnic Food and the Making of Americans*. Harvard University Press, Cambridge, Massachusetts.

Gibson, A., Dodds, R., Joppe, M. and Jamieson, B. (2003) Ecotourism in the city? Toronto's Green Tourism Association. *International Journal of Contemporary Hospitality Management* 15, 324–327.

Halter, M. (2000) *Shopping for Identity: the Marketing of Ethnicity*. Schocken Books, New York.

Hitchcock, M. (1999) Tourism and ethnicity: situational perspectives. *The International Journal of Tourism Research* 1, 17–32.

Hoffman, L.M. (2003) Revalorizing the inner-city: tourism and regulation in Harlem. In: Hoffman, L.M., Fainstein, S.S. and Judd, D.R. (eds) *Cities and Visitors: Regulating People, Markets, and City Space.* Blackwell Publishing, Oxford, UK, pp. 91–112.

Judd, D.R. (2003) Visitors and the spatial ecology of the city. In: Hoffman, L.M., Fainstein, S.S. and Judd, D.R. (eds) *Cities and Visitors: Regulating People, Markets, and City Space.* Blackwell Publishing, Oxford, UK, pp. 23–38.

Kearns, G. and Philo, C. (1993) *Selling Places: the City as Cultural Capital Past and Present.* Pergamon Press, Oxford, UK.

Kinkead, G. (1993) *Chinatown: a Portrait of a Closed Society.* Harper Perennial, New York.

Kloosterman, R. and Rath, J. (2001) Immigrant entrepreneurs in advanced economies: mixed embeddedness further explored. In: Kloosterman, R. and Rath, J. (eds) *Journal of Ethnic and Migration Studies* 27. Special issue on 'Immigrant entrepreneurship', 189–202.

Kloosterman, R. and Rath, J. (2003) *Immigrant Entrepreneurs: Venturing Abroad in the Age of Globalisation.* New York University Press, New York, and Berg Publishing, Oxford, UK.

Lash, S. and Urry, J. (1994) *Economies of Signs and Space.* Sage, London.

Light, I. and Gold, S.J. (2000) *Ethnic Economies.* Academic Press, San Diego, California.

MacCannell, D. (1973) Staged authenticity: arrangements of social space in tourist settings. *American Sociological Review* 79, 589–603.

MacCannell, D. (1999) *The Tourist: a New Theory of the Leisure Class,* 3rd edn. Schocken, New York.

MacDonald, G.F. (1992) Change and challenge: museums in the informational society. In: Karp, I., Kreamer, C.M. and Lavine, S.D. (eds) *Museums and Communities: the Politics of Public Culture.* Smithsonian Institution Press, Washington, DC, pp. 158–181.

Meethan, K. (2001) *Tourism in Global Society: Place, Culture, Consumption.* Palgrave, New York.

OECD (2007) *International Migration Outlook SOPEMI – 2007 Edition.* OECD, Paris.

Poynting, S., Noble, G., Tabar, P. and Collins, J. (2004) *Bin Laden in the Suburbs: Criminalising the Arab Other.* Federation Press, Sydney.

Rath, J. (2000) *Immigrant Business: the Economic, Political and Social Environment.* Macmillan, Basingstoke, UK, and St Martins Press, New York.

Rath, J. (2007) *Tourism, Ethnic Diversity and the City.* Routledge, London.

Richards, G. (1996) Introduction: cultural tourism in Europe. In: Richards G. (ed.) *Cultural Tourism in Europe.* CAB International, Wallingford, UK, pp. 8–20. Available at: www.tram-research.com/cultural_tourism_in_europe.PDF (accessed 5 August 2009).

Richards, G. (2007) *Cultural Tourism: Global and Local Perspectives.* Haworth Press, Binghampton, New York

Selby, M. (2004) *Understanding Urban Tourism: Image, Culture and Experience.* IB Tauris, New York.

Selwyn, T. (1996) *The Tourist Image: Myths and Myth Making in Tourism.* John Wiley and Sons, Chichester, UK.

Suvantola, J. (2002) *Tourist's Experience of Place.* Ashgate, Aldershot, UK.

Urry, J. (2002) *The Tourist Gaze,* 2nd edn. Sage Publications, London.

Veal, A.J. (2006) *Research Methods for Leisure and Tourism: a Practical Guide,* 3rd edn. Pearson Education Limited, Harlow, UK.

Waldinger, R., Aldrich, H., Ward, R. and Associates (1990) *Ethnic Entrepreneurs: Immigrant Business in Industrial Societies.* Sage, London.

Zukin, S. (1995) *The Cultures of Cities.* Blackwell, Cambridge, UK.

Zukin, S. (1998) Urban lifestyles: diversity and standardization in spaces of consumption. *Urban Studies* 35, 825–839.

Appendix 8.1. Survey instrument for ethnic precincts.

Cultural Landscapes Survey

This survey is part of a project being conducted by researchers at UTS, Monash University and UNSW. It seeks to understand people's experiences of the (name of site). The survey is anonymous and you will not be identified in any way. Are you over 18? Can I take a few minutes of your time to complete this survey?

Part A: Your Visit to this Area

1. How often have you visited (name of site)?

☐ Daily
☐ Several times a week
☐ Weekly
☐ Fortnightly
☐ Monthly

☐ Every few months
☐ Yearly
☐ Once every 2 to 3 years
☐ First visit
☐ Other: _____

2. When do you mainly visit (name of site)?

☐ Weekdays
☐ Weekends
☐ Holidays

☐ Special events
☐ Other: _____

3. How did you first hear about (name of site)?

☐ Live near here
☐ Friends/family
☐ Newspaper/magazine
☐ TV
☐ Radio
☐ Banner/poster

☐ Brochure/pamphlet
☐ Hotel staff
☐ Tour company
☐ Always known about it
☐ Just wandered in
☐ Website: _____
☐ Other: _____

4. How many people are accompanying you today?

☐ Alone
☐ One other
☐ Two others

☐ Three others
☐ Four others
☐ Five + others

5. What is their relationship to you?

☐ Family
☐ Friends
☐ Colleagues

☐ Tour group
☐ Other: _____

(continued)

Appendix 8.1.   *Continued.*

6. What are your reasons for visiting here today?
(tick all responses)

☐ Business engagement   ☐ Educational reasons
☐ Work here   ☐ Hotel located here
☐ Shopping   ☐ Relaxation/time out
☐ Eating   ☐ Thoroughfare
☐ Social engagement   ☐ Special event: _____
☐ Sightseeing/interest   ☐ Other: _____
☐ Cultural experience

Part B: Your Experiences in this Area

I would now like to ask you about the physical form of (name of site).

7. What do you like most about the architecture and physical features of (name of site)?
(record key words)

_____   _____
_____   _____
_____   _____

8. Are there things you don't like about the architecture and physical features of (name of site)?
(record key words)

_____   _____
_____   _____
_____   _____

I would now like to ask you about the way you feel when moving around (name of site).

9. What do you like most about the general atmosphere of (name of site)?
(record key words)

_____   _____
_____   _____
_____   _____

10. Are there things you don't like about the general atmosphere of (name of site)?
(record key words)

_____   _____
_____   _____
_____   _____

11. Generally do you feel safe or unsafe when in this area?

☐ Safe
☐ Unsafe

(continued)

Appendix 8.1.   *Continued.*

12. What are your reasons for feeling (safe or unsafe) in this site?

_____

_____

_____

_____

13. Have you been to similar places in other cities?

☐ Yes
☐ No

The next questions ask you to use a scale to indicate how strongly you agree or disagree with a number of statements (give respondent card with scale)

14. Using the scale I have given you, can you tell me how strongly you agree or disagree with the following statements? (Circle a number from 1 to 5)

This visit has been a memorable experience for me
Strongly Agree 1   2   3   4   5   6   7 Strongly Disagree
(Name of site) has had little effect on me
Strongly Agree 1   2   3   4   5   6   7 Strongly Disagree
My visit to (this site) has met my expectations
Strongly Agree 1   2   3   4   5   6   7 Strongly Disagree
I would recommend (this site) to others
Strongly Agree 1   2   3   4   5   6   7 Strongly Disagree
I would like to visit (this site) again
Strongly Agree 1   2   3   4   5   6   7 Strongly Disagree

15. Can you suggest ways of improving your experience of (name of site)?

_____

_____

_____

_____

_____

Part C: Yourself

This is the last section. It asks for some basic demographic details (give respondent card with list of options).

16. Looking at the items on the card, which of the groups best describes your situation?

☐ Young, single, living at home
☐ Young, single, living alone or in shared accommodation
☐ Midlife, single
☐ Young/midlife, couple no kids
☐ Parent with youngest child aged 5 or less
☐ Parent with youngest child aged 6–14

(continued)

Appendix 8.1. *Continued.*

☐ Parent with youngest child aged 15 or older
☐ Older, working, single
☐ Older, non-working, single
☐ Older, working, married person
☐ Older, non-working, married person

17. Do you mind telling me your age?

☐ 18–19	☐ 30–34	☐ 45–49	☐ 60–64
☐ 20–24	☐ 35–39	☐ 50–54	☐ 65–59
☐ 25–29	☐ 40–44	☐ 55–59	☐ 70 +

18. How would you describe your ethnicity or cultural background?

_____
_____

19. Where is your place of residence?

_____
_____

20. (If Australian resident) **What is the postcode for the area you live in?**

Write postcode: _____

21. (If not local) **How long have you been away from your usual place of residence?**

☐ 1 night or less
☐ More than 1 night

22. (If reside overseas) **Where did you first hear about (name of site) – in Australia or overseas?**

☐ Australia
☐ Overseas

23. And finally, do you have any other comments about (name of site) that you'd like to add?

_____
_____
_____
_____
_____
_____

(continued)

Appendix 8.1.   *Continued.*

_____

_____

24. (Note the gender of the respondent)

☐ Female
☐ Male

That completes the questionnaire. Thank you very much for your time and cooperation.

END OF QUESTIONNAIRE

Interviewer notes

Note any other comments, characteristics etc of the interview which you feel may be pertinent data for the analysis.

_____
_____
_____
_____
_____
_____
_____
_____

9 Tracking the Urban Visitor: Methods for Examining Tourists' Spatial Behaviour and Visual Representations

Deborah Edwards, Tracey Dickson, Tony Griffin and Bruce Hayllar

Introduction

Understanding the places tourists visit, the time they spend and the services they utilize can provide valuable information for many engaged in the management or study of tourism. This information can be used for such purposes as informing location choices for restaurants, accommodation or attractions in order to maximize exposure to visitor traffic. Government agencies and destination managers can use the information to inform planning decisions, redirect visitor flows to avoid overcrowding, minimize adverse impacts on sensitive sites, concentrate marketing activities, inform transport policies and more broadly distribute expected benefits. In addition, there is the opportunity to reflect on how design, signage and even marketing may influence how tourists engage with an urban destination.

Collection and evaluation of data on tourists' spatial behaviour can be difficult because of the labour-intensive nature of methods such as large surveys, traffic and people counts, travel or trip diaries, and observation. Global positioning system (GPS) technology now makes it possible to track the paths tourists are taking accurately and to provide greater understanding of the socio-spatial behaviour of tourists.

One of the problems for researchers in this area is that the rate of technology development can, at times, exceed the pace at which studies can be developed, conducted and reported on. The extant literature is minimal; thus researchers may be better informed by web-based materials than relying upon published academic papers to inform their practice in this area. In writing about this study, we wanted to make the process accessible to readers, to demonstrate that research can be creative and flowing. By reflecting on our experiences, we felt that we could provide a basis for other researchers to explore and possibly experiment with their own process. Therefore, this chapter details the journey for improving our understanding of the spatial behaviour of urban tourists. Our intention is to present the whole process, things that went well and things that did not. However, it is worth noting that by the time this chapter is published, new technologies or innovations of existing technologies may have moved the potential research applications to a whole new realm.

The Global Positioning System and Web 2.0 Applications

One of the authors of this paper viewed a television programme in 2005 on the use of pervasive technologies in urban environments. Pervasive technologies may be categorized as: mobile, such as phones and personal digital assistants (PDAs); fixed, such as displays in bus stops or asynchronous transfer modes (ATMs); and embedded, such as traffic monitors. Some of these technologies make use of GPS. GPS is a precise positioning tool that started as a navigation concept and has grown to an operational system of 24 NAVSTAR earth-orbiting satellites (McDonald, 2002). The growing importance of global satellite navigation systems is reflected in the European Commission's investment into the European regional augmentation of GPS (EGNOS) as well as the development of the European global navigation system called GALILEO (Directorate-General Energy and Transport, 2007). Navigation satellites allow any person who owns a device that incorporates a GPS receiver to determine their longitude, latitude and altitude anywhere on Earth. For location positioning at least three satellites are required. Over the past 10 years, and particularly in the last 3, the development of products that incorporate GPS capabilities has expanded at a rapid rate. Uses of GPS have extended to include both commercial and scientific applications. Commercially, GPS is used as a navigation and positioning tool in aeroplanes, boats and cars, and for almost all outdoor recreational activities, such as cycling, hiking, fishing and kayaking.

Web 2.0, a term that has focused attention on how businesses may use the Web more creatively and strategically, is also providing access to other evolving programs, including Google Earth and Flickr. Google Earth is a virtual globe program that maps the planet by the superimposition of images obtained from satellites, aerial photography and GIS (geographic information systems). Google Earth displays satellite images of varying resolution of the Earth's surface, allowing users to see things like houses and cars from a bird's eye view. The degree of resolution available is variable and is based somewhat on the points of interest and population bases, but most land (except for some islands) is covered in at least 15 m of resolution.

Google Earth allows users to search for addresses, enter coordinates or use the mouse to browse to a location. Flickr is an image- and video-hosting website, Web services suite and online community platform. The site enables users to share images and videos and to geotag images to locations by linking the data and time information from the photo to location information from a GPS or map (Geotag, 2007).

GPS and Web 2.0 are exciting technologies that we believe offer products and platforms that could enhance tourism research. We felt that these tools could assist us to better understand how tourists navigate the urban environment, what trails they take during their visit, why they have taken a particular trail, what barriers they encounter, what modes of transport they use and what memories they take away with them. It was research that was intended to augment an ongoing study into visitor experiences, expectations and needs in relation to urban environments. We hoped that data captured from the mobile devices would provide us with information on places travelled, distance travelled and stopping times, building a picture of visitors' spatial behaviour. The ability to overlay the information on to a satellite map for a visual representation of tourist trails was a feature we were looking forward to exploring.

The Research Project

Project partners

Given the potential of the above technologies, we decided to experiment with GPS and a range of more traditional methods, including photography, questionnaires and debriefing interviews, to conduct two small-scale projects investigating the spatial behaviour of urban tourists in two Australian cities, Canberra and Sydney.

We had already received funding for a study on expectations and needs (Edwards *et al.*, 2007), but additional funds were sought to cover the purchase of devices and the cost of participant incentives. A proposal was developed and expressions of interest sought from a number of commercial organizations and two state tourism offices (STOs). Whilst interested in the tracking concept, the industry was reluctant to make a monetary commitment. The two STOs, however, were excited by the project, as they saw the potential for applied benefits in urban tourism planning. Subsequently they both provided funding, which enabled us to push ahead with the visitor-tracking pilot.

The Technology is Out There: Let's Use It!

GPS offers several advantages over the traditional methods, as it allows the precise and continuous tracking of individuals and provides spatially rich data, including velocity and timing information (O'Connor et al., 2005). Studies have, for example, been carried out in Copenhagen (Shoval and Isaacson, 2007), in Tel Aviv–Jaffa and in the German city of Heidelberg (Freytag, 2003). The latter study found that visitors to Heidelberg focus mainly on the historically and culturally rich old city centre, neglecting other areas and attractions further afield. Visitor behaviour and movement have also been tracked in specific tourist settings, such as theme parks, where Kempermann et al. (2004) recorded significant differences between first-time visitors and repeat visitors. It was found that new visitors try to get to as many attractions as possible, whereas repeat visitors are more selective and focused (see Chapter 6). Arrowsmith and Chhetri (2003) undertook a pilot study using handheld GPS receivers to monitor the movement patterns of tourists through a national park in south-west Victoria, Australia, and Ten Hagen et al. (2006) captured the spatial behaviour of 65 tourists to the inner city of Görlitz, Germany. Unfortunately, none of the articles indicated the type of devices that were used.

The use of GPS technology was an area in which none of the authors had any previous experience. Consequently, we were confronted with a steep learning curve. What we required was an easy-to-use device

that was able to track tourists in densely built urban environments. We faced significant challenges – Australia had yet to catch up with technological advances in the European Union and some parts of Asia, and there were significant limitations with available devices in Australia. They were overly expensive, not easy to use, had limited tracking ability in urban environments or were not suitable for tracking people. Nor did we have the skills to build our own add-ons. We trawled journals for articles on visitor tracking, the Internet for prospective devices and talked with colleagues in our own school and other universities.

One of the authors attended a technology convention where there were many devices for vehicle tracking, but none were tailored for people tracking or would meet the particular needs of this study. The answer, however, came some months later from our own colleagues in sport, who were using a GPS device, the GPSports SPI Elite, to monitor athlete performance on a football field. One of the authors, an avid cyclist, then heard about a newly released device in Australia that was being used by cyclists to track their performance, the Garmin Forerunner 305. Both devices work by locking on to any three of 24 satellites that orbit the earth, requiring them to be carried or worn in such a way that they are in view of the sky and continually receiving a signal from at least three satellites at any one time.

The GPSports SPI Elite is tracking technology primarily designed for sporting clubs, athletes and recreational sport enthusiasts. The device records time, speed, distance, position, altitude, direction and heart rate, as well as acceleration in three planes. An analysis program comes with the device. The health faculty at the University of Canberra had already purchased an additional ten devices for use in an alpine study of ski patrollers, investigating the role of hydration in balance and injury prevention. We borrowed a device and trialled it in Sydney. In order to monitor heart rate and to be accessible to the sky, the device normally sits in a pouch on a pair of straps that is worn on the back, similar to a harness. We didn't need to monitor tourists' heart rates and we didn't want to ask tourists to wear a harness, therefore we trialled the device by carrying it in our pockets and handbags. Although we found the device worked quite well and generally gave us the information we needed, care would need to be taken by participants to carry the device in such a way that it was in view of the sky and receiving a signal. The device had some advantages. First, it was not 'attractive' as it had a single on/off button with no other outwardly discernable features and required a special recharger and software to run: there would thus be no reason for someone to steal it. Additionally, it was a robust unit, originally designed to handle heavy impacts in a professional football environment. It was an Australian-designed product with the company based in the Australian Capital Territory. Unfortunately the cost was prohibitive at AU$2000 (€1200) a unit.

The Garmin Forerunner 305 is also designed for athletes and recreational sport enthusiasts. The device records time, speed, distance, position, direction and heart rate. It is worn on the wrist like a watch, providing a consistent view of the sky. It is a commercial product, which comes with its own software or is compatible with other software. This compatibility feature was a bonus as we found a free program downloadable from the Web, 'Zone Five Software', which was very user friendly and incorporated a number of features that would prove helpful for data collection. We undertook a small

trial and found that the information was similar to that of the SPI Elite. Its cost was considerably less at AU$500 (€300) per unit, and we felt that being able to wear the device on the wrist would be less troublesome for participants than having to carry a device. However, its compact nature and ease of use also raised concerns about whether we would get them back if our respondents saw the value in what they were wearing.

Finally, we decided to use both devices, the Garmin 305 GPS receivers in Sydney and the SPI Elite in Canberra. It was a pragmatic decision as the University of Canberra offered us the use of their GPSports SPI Elite at no cost. An overview of the advantages and disadvantages of each device is set out in Table 9.1.

Cameras

Our initial plan was to purchase disposable cameras for each person to use, and then to pay for processing, at an estimated cost of AU$25 (€15) each. But when we calculated the cost to purchase the cameras and then process them for 80 participants, it became apparent that, in the long run, it would be cheaper to purchase ten relatively inexpensive digital cameras. This was a decision that provided us with further flexibility as we were able to upload images on the tourists' return and to talk to them about their

Table 9.1. GPSports SPI Elite versus Garmin 305.

GPSport SPI Elite	Garmin 305
High cost per unit (*c.* AU $2000)	Lower cost per unit (*c.* AU $500)
Low risk of being stolen as it requires a specialized program to run and a unique recharger	High risk of being stolen as it can easily be used, but needs a battery charger to maintain
Shorter battery life, *c.* 8 h	Longer battery life, *c.* 10 h
Robust, able to take any knock	Not as robust
Supplied harness not simple to wear	Easy to wear on wrist
Can be used in various sport and tourism contexts	Can be used in various sport and tourism contexts
Ten units can be recharged in one suitcase-sized unit	Each unit needs to be separately recharged
Software supplied is not user friendly, but local support is available	Software, supplied and downloaded, is user friendly
Australian-owned company	Overseas-owned company

experiences. As with the Garmin watches, there was always a risk that people would wish to take the camera, not just the photos!

The Study Locations and Venues

Participants were recruited from three venues located in Canberra, in the Australian Capital Territory, and in four venues located in Sydney, New South Wales.

Canberra is a purpose-built city, designed as Australia's capital in 1908. Major roads follow a wheel-and-spoke pattern rather than a grid. The city centre is laid out on two perpendicular axes: a water axis stretching along Lake Burley Griffin and a ceremonial land axis stretching from Parliament House on Capital Hill north-eastward along ANZAC Parade to the Australian War Memorial. Canberra is organized into a hierarchy of seven districts divided into smaller suburbs. Most suburbs have a 'town centre' that is the focus of commercial and social activities.

Sydney is the site of earliest European settlement in Australia. Sydney's central business district (CBD) is a densely urbanized location that extends southwards for about 3 km from the Harbour Bridge to Central Station. On the east side it is bounded by a chain of parkland that extends from Hyde Park through the Domain and Royal Botanic Gardens to Farm Cove on the harbour. The western side is bounded by Darling Harbour, a popular leisure and nightlife precinct. George Street serves as the CBD's spine and main north–south thoroughfare.

The choice of venue for recruiting participants in both cities was moderated by the venue's geographic location within the city, its management's willingness to participate, access to wireless Internet connection and the level of accommodation offered. Seven venues were selected:

- Canberra City YHA Backpackers Hostel;
- Hotel Kurrajong Canberra;
- Pavilion on Northbourne Canberra;
- Sydney Central YHA;
- Bondi Beachouse YHA Sydney;
- Y Hotel Hyde Park Sydney; and
- Y Hotel City South Sydney.

Canberra City YHA is right in the centre of the Canberra CBD, within 5 min of the interstate bus terminal and within walking distance of major shopping centres. The Hotel Kurrajong is a five-star establishment in a heritage-listed building, approximately 5 km south-east of the centre of Canberra. It is positioned adjacent to what is known as The Parliamentary Triangle and is within easy driving distance of Canberra's main attractions. The Pavilion on Northbourne Hotel is a four-star hotel located 2 km north of the city centre. It is within easy driving distance of Canberra's major attractions.

Sydney Central YHA is located in a heritage-listed building opposite Central Railway Station at the southern end of the CBD. It is accessible to most of the city's major attractions, such as the Opera House, Harbour Bridge, The Rocks, Darling Harbour and Centrepoint Tower. Bondi Beach YHA is located at the southern end of Sydney's famous Bondi Beach. Visiting the CBD from this hostel requires the use of public or private transport. Y Hotel Hyde Park is a three-star bed and breakfast hotel located on the eastern side of the CBD, opposite Hyde Park and Oxford Street. It is within walking distance of Darling Harbour, China Town, city shops, the Opera House, Paddington and The Rocks. Y Hotel City South is a three-star bed and breakfast hotel on the southern edge of the city, close to Prince Alfred Park, Sydney University, Central Railway Station and Broadway.

Geographic locations of the venues are indicated on Figs 9.1 and 9.2. We were satisfied with the range of geographic locations in Canberra – north of the city, in the centre of the city and south of the city. These locations offered three distinct starting points for tourists' engagement with the city. However, in Sydney we were not as pleased, as three of the venues were located in the same southerly direction from the city centre. Several weeks were spent trying to obtain permission to conduct the study from venues in other geographic locations within the city. Each time the response was the same: hotels were excited by the project but ultimately they were concerned about the impact of the research on the overall enjoyment of their guests.

Fig. 9.1. Canberra data collection venues: 1, Pavilion on Northbourne; 2, Canberra City YHA Backpackers Hostel; 3, Hotel Kurrajong.

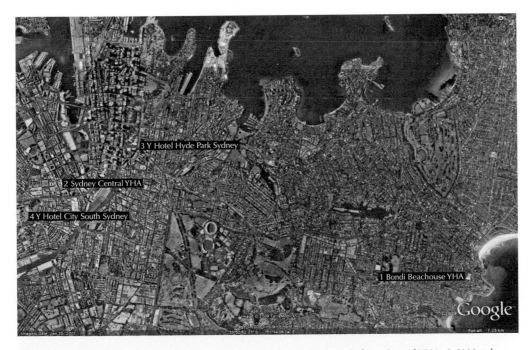

Fig. 9.2. Sydney data collection venues: 1, Bondi Beachouse YHA; 2, Sydney Central YHA; 3, Y Hotel Hyde Park; 4, Y Hotel City South.

Administration

As this was new territory, there were some concerns as to how the recruitment of participants would go. On the evening before data collection, information letters were distributed in each venue, advising guests of the project, their requirements and an incentive for taking part. Visitors were recruited the following morning. Depending on the location (Canberra or Sydney), they were asked to wear or carry a GPS tracking device that would record their location, time, speed, distance and direction for that day. Visitors were provided with a digital camera and asked to take images as though they were using their own camera. There was no limit to the number of images they could take, the type of image taken or objects of interest.

To support the tracking pilot a questionnaire was designed to capture demographic information about participants, along with their purpose for visiting, the activities they engaged in, mode(s) of transport used during the day and any barriers they encountered.

Upon returning to their accommodation at the end of the day, a debriefing was conducted with each participant. The debriefing comprised three parts: participants were asked to complete the questionnaire; their images were uploaded on to a laptop and reviewed with a researcher; and the data collected from the GPS devices were downloaded and their tracks were overlayed on to a Google Earth Map of either Canberra or Sydney for a visual representation of the participant's trail. This was facilitated by having wireless Internet access at each venue. The researcher reviewed the track with the participant, taking notes of any way-finding difficulties, the participant's reasons for choosing sites and their activities of interest. Participants enjoyed actively participating in the study. Various groups would stay on after their interview to view other people's trails and to share their experiences. Participants wanted the data to be personalized and trails were labelled using their first names. Figures 9.3 and 9.4 represent an individual's trail in Canberra and Sydney, respectively.

Fig. 9.3. Individual tourist trail in Canberra.

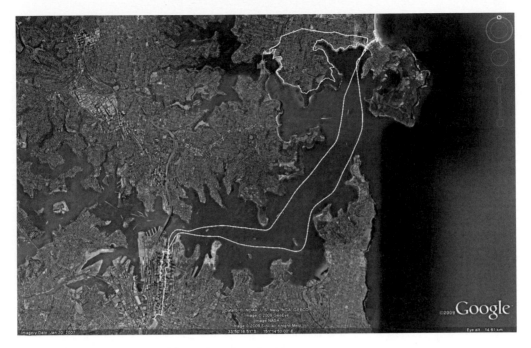

Fig. 9.4. Individual tourist trail from Sydney Central YHA.

A limiting factor in the number of people approached was the availability of the technology, which was budget-constrained. We only had ten cameras and ten GPS devices for each site. The collation of the data afterwards was also constrained by the number of research assistants and laptops available. A total of 80 participant groups were recruited, resulting in 74 useable trails. A number of issues were encountered during data collection in both Canberra and Sydney. The Garmin watches have a timer, which needs to be turned on to enable tracking. In two instances, the researcher neglected to turn the timer on and the trails were not collected. In another two instances participants fiddled with their watches and this prevented their trails being captured. In Canberra the devices were more problematic. Because people carry them in pockets or handbags, some devices had difficulty locking on to the satellites. In addition, if the person spent a prolonged period indoors, such as inside the War Memorial or the Art Gallery, the SPI Elite would automatically switch off. With only a small LED indicator,

it was difficult for people to know that the device needed restarting.

The software supporting the GPS devices enabled the overlaying of trails on to Google Earth. This technology provided clear evidence of the path taken, speed travelled (which assists in determining if the mode of transport was motorized or non-motorized) and time of day. Trails can be overlayed individually or collectively on to one map, showing individual trails or the intensity of activity along particular paths. An advantage of the Garmin software was that each route could be separately colour coded, enabling easier visual analysis of the data. Ultimately, the Garmin watches and software proved more user-friendly and reliable for participants and researchers alike.

In terms of digital photography, participants were instructed to use the cameras as they would normally. This resulted in the collection of 3093 images – 1114 in Canberra and 1840 in Sydney. Later the images were loaded on to Flickr, a photo-sharing website, and participants were invited to write brief comments on their images, explaining why they took a particular photograph. We now had a significant amount of data.

Analysing the Data

The analysis of data is currently under way. Travel patterns are being examined both individually and collectively. Individual trails will be analysed for linear itinerary patterns to model tourists' spatial movements from their accommodation point. Previously, models have been developed deductively based on how factors identified from the urban transportation modelling and tourism literature might influence movement in a local destination (Lew and McKercher, 2006). The trails we captured provide sufficient detail to permit meaningful analysis that has, to date, been difficult to obtain. Comparison will also be made with previous research in Canberra using travel diaries.

Photographs were examined using content and semiotic analysis for patterns across collections and the importance of, and meanings given to, the images contained within them. In this context questions we ask will include: 'How do visitors' images compare with the dominant tourism images seen in brochures and on websites around the world?'; 'To what extent do tourists reproduce visual stereotypes in personal photographs?'; 'What are the memories that tourists to Canberra and Sydney want to take home with them?'; 'How can this knowledge and information be used to improve the marketing of Canberra and Sydney?'; 'How much do the images reflect desired or sought-after experiences in and of the city?'; and 'If holiday brochures try to sell "images of ourselves" (Jenkins, 2003), what images of themselves are tourists capturing?' (see also Chapter 6).

The nature of the study has facilitated quick 'eyeballing' of the data, enabling us to discuss early findings with our industry partners. Issues and considerations raised in these discussions have been helpful in guiding and refining further data analysis.

A further development in the research design that occurred after the data were collected was an opportunity to geotag the participants' images to their trails. This application takes the GPX[1] data and the user's photographs and matches the time the photos were taken with the times in the GPX file to find the person's location at the time the photo was taken. Viewed collectively, the geotagged images enable the mapping of images and identification of popular sites. At the time of writing, a research assistant was in the process of undertaking this task.

Reflecting on the Process

As an emerging application of available technologies in a tourism context, the knowledge generated from this study provides a basis for the future development of alternative, reliable and cost-effective methods for gathering data on the spatial behaviour of urban visitors as well as a comparison with other data collection methodologies such as travel diaries (see Chapter 6). The accuracy and detail of information about trails and the time spent in different attractions far exceeds anything that can be gathered through travel diaries or post-travel surveys. Though using such modern equipment provides a clear view, it does not negate the need to collect supporting information and feedback via other methods to help interpret the trails. We would argue, in fact, that in the context of this study it was critical. It is easy to map the results and overlay on Google Earth and show intensities of use, particularly with the Garmin software, but this neglects individual issues, motivations and serendipitous actions.

The debriefing interview gave us useful information on how people orientated themselves and their barriers to movement, which provided insights into issues such as the adequacy of directional signage and tourist information. As an example, while Canberra has many cycle paths around the city and between major attractions, few visitors used these paths. Whether that was related to pre-trip planning, access to pertinent information, availability of bike hire and bike storage opportunities or lack of signage is yet to be explored. In Sydney, participants found that elements such as signage and the challenges of public transport created difficulties for their movements throughout the city.

GPS technology presents several drawbacks. First, its unavailability or inaccuracy inside or close to buildings resulted in trails not being captured or an excessive amount of 'visual noise'. Second, the attractiveness and cost of the technology heightened insecurities over the devices being stolen. One evening a group of participants had to be locked out of their hostel, as they still had not returned the device well after the requested time. When they contacted security to gain access they were asked to return the camera and the watch. Third, on a couple of occasions the equipment failed but this was not known until participants returned to the accommodation. Fourth, the intensive nature of the study limited the number of individuals who could be simultaneously monitored. Finally, equipment, incentive and resource costs limited the duration of the study. The advantages and disadvantages of the study are presented in Table 9. 2.

Discussing participants' trails and images resulted in a personal study, one which allowed us to experience a day in their tourist lives visually and to 'walk in their shoes'. As a rule, providing personal details of participants engaged in a research study is seen as an invasion of privacy and breach of trust on the part of the researcher. However, we found it necessary to modify the project along the way to take account of participants' requests that they be known by their first names.

Future Directions

In this study, we were interested in increasing our depth of understanding of tourists' spatial behaviour in urban environments. Alternatively it is possible to explore tourist spatial movements broadly, by focusing only on the trails taken. Including both the local community and tourists in such a study would add greater breadth to analysing the way in which urban spaces are negotiated and used. Similar to the Spatial Metro Project (2008), large-scale mapping of pedestrian movement can be undertaken from parking stations and/or major transport interchanges with no debriefing or image capture.

Table 9.2. Pros and cons of GPS-based visitor tracking.

Pros	Cons
Accuracy of trails and time frames	High set-up costs for equipment
Being able to link trails to photos through geotagging	Recharging of batteries required overnight
The GPSs and digital cameras are reusable over many projects	Small sample sizes
Uploading trails and photos immediately enables researchers to capture the emotions, memories and energy of the tourists in-the-moment	Researcher-intensive activity
Overlaying the trails on to Google Earth or other mapping options aids the recall of the tourist	Difficulty in establishing a suitable base from which to recruit participants
Easy to compare trails and investigate intense areas of activity/travel	Risk of having expensive equipment stolen
	No control over when participants return to 'base'
	Equipment failures may not be identified until the tourists return to base
	GPS function is limited indoors (unless the person is near a window), underground (although entry and exit data are logged), therefore satellite signals may be distorted in built-up areas, on cloudy days and in deep valleys

In the near future, emerging technologies, such as GALILEO, and the creation of more sensitive handheld devices will help support indoor tracking, which may be of great interest to retailers, museums, galleries and indoor attractions who monitor their audience attendance, behaviour and responses to various displays or other spatial elements. New devices are being developed that will indicate the direction the person is facing, providing not only where a person went but also what they looked at and for how long.

Note

[1]GPX (the GPS Exchange Format) is a lightweight XML data format for the interchange of GPS data (waypoints, routes and tracks) between applications and Web services on the Internet.

References

Arrowsmith, C. and Chhetri, P. (2003) *Port Campbell National Park: Patterns of Use*. Department of Geospatial Science, RMIT University, Melbourne, Australia.

Directorate-General Energy and Transport (2007) GALILEO: European Satellite Navigation System. Available at: http://ec.europa.eu/dgs/energy_transport/galileo/intro/challenge_en.htm (accessed 10 June 2008).

Edwards, D., Griffin, T. and Hayllar, B. (2007) *Development of an Australian Urban Tourism Research Agenda*. Technical Report. CRC for Sustainable Tourism Pty Ltd, Gold Coast, Australia.

Freytag, T. (2003) *Städtetourismus in Heidelberg – Ergebnisbericht zur Gästebefragung 2003*. Geographical Institute of Heidelberg University, Heidelberg, Germany.

Geotag (2007) Welcome to Geotag. Available at: http://geotag.sourceforge.net/ (accessed 10 June 2008).

Jenkins, O. (2003) Photography and travel brochures: the circle of representation. *Tourism Geographies* 5, 305–328.

Kempermann, A.D.A.M., Joh, C.H. and Timmermans, H.J.P. (2004) Comparing first-time and repeat visitors' activity patterns in a tourism environment. In: Crouch, G.I., Perdue, R.R. and Timmermans, H.J.P. (eds) *Consumer Psychology of Tourism, Hospitality and Leisure*, vol. 3. CAB International, Wallingford, UK, pp. 103–119.

Lew, A. and McKercher, B. (2006) Modelling tourist movements – a local destination analysis. *Annals of Tourism Research* 33, 403–423.

McDonald, K.D. (2002) The modernization of GPS: plans, new capabilities and the future relationship to Galileo. *Journal of Global Positioning Systems* 1, 1–17.

O'Connor, A., Zerger, A. and Itami, B. (2005) Geo-temporal tracking and analysis of tourist movement. *Mathematics and Computers in Simulation* 69, 135–150.

Shoval, N. and Isaacson, M. (2007) Tracking tourists in the digital age. *Annals of Tourism Research* 34, 141–159.

Spatial Metro Project (2008) Spatial Metro Project: a network for discovering the city on foot. Available at: www.spatialmetro.org (accessed 6 March 2008).

Ten Hagen, K., Kramer, R., Modsching, M. and Gretzelb, U. (2006) Capturing the beaten paths: a novel method for analysing tourists' spatial behaviour at an urban destination. In: Hitz, M., Sigala, M. and Murphy, J. (eds) *Information and Communication Technologies in Tourism 2006*. Springer, Vienna, pp. 75–86.

10 An Application of Grounded Theory to Cultural Tourism Research: Resident Attitudes to Tourism Activity in Santiponce

Mario Castellanos-Verdugo, Francisco J. Caro-González
and M. de los Ángeles Oviedo-García

Introduction

Grounded theory (GT) is an inductive methodological approach that allows researchers to generate theories from data extracted from reality. It was developed in the 1960s by the American sociologists Glaser and Strauss (1967). Glaser defines grounded theory as a general methodology of analysis linked to data collection that uses a systematically applied set of methods to generate an inductive theory about a substantive area (Glaser, 1992: 16).

GT is a systematic procedure of data gathering and analysis that allows the generation of theories whose evidence is to be found in the behaviour, words and acts of the people researched. In this methodology the theory and the data are generated at the same time and the researcher aims, whenever possible, to not be influenced by previous work. Goulding (2002: 40) sets out the principles on which this methodology is based, according to the work of Glaser and Strauss (Glaser, 1992: 16):

- the need to get out in the field if the researcher wants to understand what is going on;
- the importance of theory grounded in reality;

- the continually evolving nature of the field experience for the subjects and the researcher;
- the active role of people in shaping the worlds they live in through the process of symbolic interaction;
- an emphasis on change and process and the variability and complexity of life; and
- the interrelationship between meaning in the perception of subjects and their actions.

The theory evolves during the research process itself and is a product of continuous interplay between analysis and data collection (Glaser and Strauss, 1967; Glaser, 1978; Charmaz, 1983; Strauss, 1987; Strauss and Corbin, 1990, 1994).

One of the essential characteristics of GT is theoretical sampling, i.e. the process of sampling events, situations, populations and responses, thus generating comparisons between samples of responses, descriptions and behaviours in the inductive generation of theory (Douglas, 2003: 49). Constant comparison is the second essential characteristic. This is made up of the exploration of similarities and differences across incidents in the data. By comparing where the facts are similar or different, the researcher can generate concepts and concept properties based on recurring patterns of behaviour (Goulding, 2002: 170). Finally it must be noted that any source of data can be useful for the research.

The basic principles of GT are described in this chapter. They are illustrated by research carried out by the authors in the tourism sector. We will thus indicate in which cases using this research method was recommended, how it is used (process) and the result that can be achieved.

The case study of Santiponce, a town of 7500 inhabitants in Andalucia, southern Spain, presents a paradoxical situation: the town has an important tourist attraction, the Roman archaeological site of Itálica, but this is largely ignored by the residents. The archaeological site of Itálica is the third most-visited monument of the Andalusian Autonomous Community, preceded only by the Alhambra of Granada and the Mosque of Cordoba. The Santiponce case has been selected because of the negative attitude of its residents, who do not consider Itálica as an opportunity for economic development through tourism (Caro and Castellanos, 2005; Oviedo *et al.*, 2007). This is in spite of the undoubted advantages of small tourism businesses for local communities (Ashley, 2000; Hampton, 2003; Richards and Wilson, 2004). The aim of this study is to understand a complex phenomenon in which a multitude of different factors intervene and to develop an explanatory model of the sustainable exploitation of tourism in a small place. Thanks to the process of abstraction, which ranges from data extracted from reality to emerging theoretical concepts and categories, GT helps us to achieve this aim.

When is the Use of GT Recommended?

Authors such as Glaser and Strauss (1967), Yin (1988), Eisenhardt (1989), Miles and Huberman (1994) and Goulding (2002) indicate that the GT methodology is appropriate when studying a contemporary phenomenon in the context of real life and when the boundaries between the phenomenon and the context are not clear. Researchers who

use this methodology wish to go beyond the mere description of a given situation, seeking the causes that bring about the phenomenon and analysing their effects. This is research that fits in with the post-positivist and interpretative focus of science and derives from symbolic interactionism (see also Chapters 3 and 14, this volume).

Following the line put forward by Glaser (1992), and given the unique character of the case selected, the phenomenon was studied without prior hypotheses. Theoretical contamination was avoided whenever possible. A set of proposals giving rise to an explanatory model were generated from observations. Generalizations, concepts or hypotheses arise from the precise examination of the data and the posterior coding and abstraction avoids the over-restriction of information in prior models. Pre-understanding may become a barrier to finding the true meaning of the data, especially when expertise gained through previous research or managerial experience tempts the researcher into premature or preconceived selective coding (Connell and Lowe, 1997). Stake (1995) is of the opinion that, with this kind of research, one may achieve a greater understanding of a particular case and gain greater clarity about a subject, a specific theoretical aspect, a phenomenon, a population or a general context.

The use of GT was considered opportune in the Santiponce case for the following reasons:

- The aim of GT is to build a theory inductively. Given that no similar cases were found in the literature, it is appropriate to facilitate understanding of the phenomenon by generating an emergent theory.
- Multiple data sources are used in GT: in-depth interviews, observation, researchers' notes, official documents, events, etc. This makes the triangulation of data easier and broadens the perspectives from which the phenomenon can be observed.
- Applying GT is especially recommended in studies of human behaviour (Goulding, 2002: 107), as in this case.

- As Goulding also suggests (2002: 107), it is a chance to apply a methodology to a discipline in which it has been little used (Connell and Lowe, 1997).

The GT Investigation Process

From analysis to theory

The most relevant characteristic of the GT investigation process is the iterative way in which the data collection and analysis are conducted simultaneously. In this way the theoretical concepts emerge from the analysis and shape it at the same time (Fig. 10.1).

Data triangulation

GT uses any type of data that the researcher may collect and which help towards the understanding of the phenomenon under study. Among the possible primary data sources are interviews, observation and field notes. Among the secondary sources is any document produced by the institutions or people researched (text books, communiqués, promotional brochures, newspapers, letters, Web pages, blogs, photographs, videos, etc.). One of the characteristics of this methodology is that it allows the combination and integration of data from different sources (Glaser, 1978: 6).

Data triangulation permits a broader vision of the studied phenomenon (see also

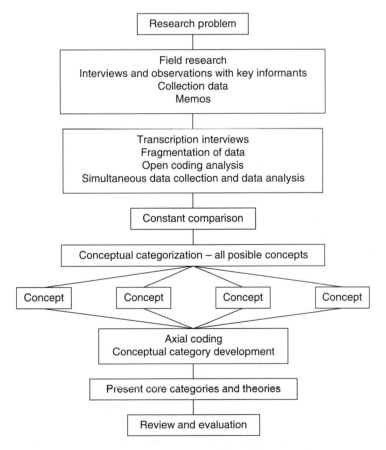

Fig. 10.1. Theory building through the research process. Adapted from Goulding (2002: 115).

Chapter 5). Egri and Herman (2000) and Herman and Egri (2002) have demonstrated the richness of explanatory power that can come from researcher triangulation when using the GT method.

Data triangulation has often been used, while not always in explicit terms, in recent qualitative tourism research (Decrop, 1999: 159). Decrop cites studies such as Markwell's (1997), which uses data from photographs and travel diaries, in addition to observation and interview transcripts, and Bramwell and Rawding's (1996) study, which triangulates data from committee papers, promotional brochures and structured interviews and mentions the possibility of describing people's non-verbal behaviour or descriptions of the environment (weather, atmosphere, setting, furniture, etc.).

In the case of Santiponce, the main types of data collection methods were in-depth interviews of key informers, observation and field notes. This information was completed by reports on the place, documents such as the strategic and tourism plan, the municipal website, institutional workshops and promotional brochures of the town and the archaeological site of Itálica.

Theoretical sampling

As in any other research, in GT the selection (quantitative and qualitative) of the people to be interviewed must be considered. In the case of GT, the sample is suggested by the phenomenon to be studied. Theoretical sampling is the process of data collection for generating theory, whereby the analyst jointly collects, codes and analyses the data and decides what data to collect next and where to find them, in order to develop the theory as it emerges (Goulding, 1998: 53). In other words, it is a process controlled by the emerging theory (Glaser and Strauss, 1967: 45; Glaser, 1978: 36).

The sample is not, therefore, determined in the research design phase, but can vary as the data collection proceeds and in accordance with the theoretical results achieved by means of the constant comparison

method. This phase of the research process is completed at the moment at which the theoretical saturation level is reached, i.e. once new informants do not add anything new to the concepts emerging (see also Chapter 13).

The theoretical sampling contributes to the flexibility of the research process. It allows the researcher to place the emphasis on one concept or another, so that compiled data reflect what happens in the field rather than being a speculation about what should have been observed (Glaser, 1978; Strauss and Corbin, 1990; Coyle, 1997).

In Santiponce, the persons interviewed were all experts with experience in managing heritage sites and/or tourism activities linked to them. Different criteria were taken into account in selecting the respondents:

- Their relevance as key informers. People who held important positions or were close to the decision-making process, in municipal tourism policy, the local tourism industry or heritage or cultural management. Interviewing executives guaranteed a greater access to strategic information.

- The interviewees should be able to offer different and contrasting visions of the phenomenon studied. If one wishes to analyse the different aspects of a problem, one has to approach it from the perspectives of different actors. Opposing positions between the interviewed persons arose with regard to specific subjects. This approach revealed latent conflicts requiring more thorough study.

- The 'snowball' technique was also used. Some of the persons to be interviewed were thus suggested by others.

- The incorporation of new interviews was stopped when the researchers found that the last two informants had not added relevant new data. Theoretical saturation was then reached as new concepts did not emerge from the interviews.

The interviews were carried out in the locations proposed by the experts, normally their workplace. Contextually relevant information could thus be gathered efficiently. In order to make the data collection easier and reduce subjectivity, two interviewers were used. All the interviews were digitally recorded and the average interview length was about 50 min. In all cases the interviewers' aim was to allow the respondents to speak openly and freely. The conversation was re-started or a new subject was introduced only when necessary. The interview was composed of the following questions:

1. Please tell me your name, position and connection with the muncipality of Santiponce?
2. How important is the tourist sector for Santiponce?
3. Could a greater impulse be given to tourism? How?
4. Is Santiponce something more than Itálica?
5. What can Santiponce offer tourists?
6. How could tourism activity in Santiponce be driven?
7. What is the role of the public institutions (town hall, provincial government, regional government)?
8. What is the role of local business people? And those from outside?
9. How would residents note the increase in tourism activity?
10. Do you have any additional comment to make?

Along with the information produced by the respondents, documents brought forward in the interviews were analysed, together with the notes taken during the research of the field, i.e. the physical and social context in which the phenomena that are the object of study take place (Rodríguez *et al.*, 1996: 103). In this phase, various appraisals (contextual) and communications (verbal and non-verbal) were gathered by the interviewers.

Each interview was accompanied by a memo, in which the interviewer clarified ideas and added codes and their possible meanings. All this information was transcribed and included in the data analysis process.

Data analysis

The data analysis process took place at the same time as the collection of data. The first step was to transcribe and prepare the documentation for information treatment with the qualitative analysis program Atlas.ti, which was selected for its appropriateness in research strategy. Atlas.ti enables a large quantity of textual information to be analysed while allowing its contextuality to be retained. Another advantage is its ease in generating graphic models that connect the categories studied (Mehmetoglu and Dann, 2003; Mehmetoglu and Altinay, 2006). Moreover, the use of this software increases both the internal and external validity of the research (Caro and Díez, 2005).

First, a line-by-line analysis of the documents was carried out in order to interpret the data. Codes were assigned to those statements that were meaningful to the research, aiming to generate the broadest range of codes possible. This phase led to hundreds of codes that were grouped to form conceptual value clusters and to identify their similarities and differences through constant comparison.

This open coding process, suggested by Strauss (1987), allows the search for concepts that help to cover the field data, overcoming the possible over-rigidity of analysis categories previously set up. By means of open coding, a set of categories emerges that is constantly broadened, modified, redefined or readapted in accordance with the new citations that are being categorized. Open coding allows similar incidents and phenomena to be compared and contrasted with each other, and, where similar, correspondingly coded (Douglas, 2003: 47). This process is termed the constant comparison method. The incidents found in the data need to be contrasted with others to validate their interpretation (Corbin, 1998). The comparison between similar or different facts enables us to generate category properties that increase the possibilities of generalization and explanation (Glaser and Strauss, 1967: 24). In this respect, Glaser's methodological approach relies primarily upon the constant comparison of different incidents, perceptions, relationships and issues, with the aim of identifying inconsistencies, contradictions, gaps in data and emerging consensus on key concepts and relationships. In grounded theory, consensus remains below the surface, until it emerges (Glaser, 1992: 95).

Next, the process of axial coding is carried out. This is a more sophisticated method of coding data, which seeks to identify incidents that have an interrelationship. It is incumbent on the researcher to specify those relationships, which are normally the product of constant comparison data (Goulding, 2002: 169).

The core codes that make up the explanatory model are developed from the axial coding. To do this, the open codes that are most closely interrelated and which support the evidence are joined together (Strauss, 1987; Strauss and Corbin, 1990). These codes can be classified as representing context, conditions, actions, interactions and outcomes (Douglas, 2003). The code grouping allows the data to be reduced to a group of explanatory categories around a key category that defines the research problem, in the present case the sustainable exploitation of tourism in a small locality.

The categories and subcategories derived from the code grouping are reflected in a tree diagram (Fig. 10.2).

The information is also codified according to the actors referred to and who are interconnected by categories emerging from the analysis of the interviews. This codification allows the study of links that are set up between them and gives rise to a framework of connections that adds to the explanation of the locality's situation. In Fig. 10.3 the different actors involved in the exploitation of Santiponce for tourism are identified.

Results

The material analysed brought forth a series of results, which are ordered in accordance with the following main categories:

- the importance of tourism;
- the attitude of the residents;
- the change in these attitudes; and
- the relationships with the institutions.

The following sections present fragments of the interviews as evidence and as an explanation of the relationships in the data.

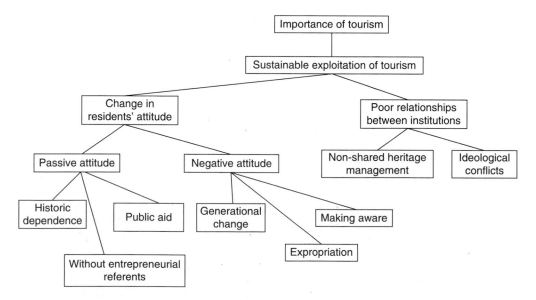

Fig. 10.2. Categories emerging from the code grouping.

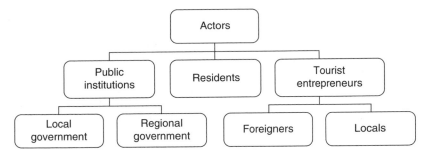

Fig. 10.3. Categories corresponding to the actors deduced from the data.

Importance of tourism as context

All the interviewees and strategic documents of the locality coincide in terms of tourism being the main axis of local development. The economic and social growth of the zone is closely linked to tourism:

> The truth is tourism can mean the way of life for the inhabitants of Santiponce, that's to say, the best way in the medium term to create richness with respect to the municipality and the inhabitants of the municipality.

> If we take away tourism from Santiponce, it won't get anywhere.

The decline of agriculture, traditionally the main source of income of the local population, along with the need for more land area for agricultural development, has led to this economic activity being abandoned. In addition, industrial activity is scarce in the area:

> Here the idea's really clear, I mean, Santiponce was kept out of the agricultural programmes because of the issue of space, minimal measures of agricultural space were needed and that didn't exist here.

> It doesn't have a municipal area, its resources are very limited, then it hasn't industry, or very little and what little it's got … four factory bays over there in that area.

The respondents also seem to agree that the involvement of the local population in tourism is closely linked to the archaeological site of Itálica and its appreciation, and that the local economy has been gradually expanding as the tourism sector at a national and world level has grown:

> Tourism here is from, I don't know, 70 years ago; it's always been a place with a lot of influence on tourism since Itálica started being visited. Tourism here is considered as a sector that has always had an effect on … sometimes 10%, at other times 30%, and I'd say now 50%.

> I believe Itálica is the biggest business this town can have as a source of work and resources, not in itself for the stable staff of workers or the companies that work in it – some are from here and others aren't – but regarding the services sector and all that's brought about by a municipality receiving 300,000 visitors a year.

Attitude of the residents

The experts agree on the need to strengthen tourism activity, but at the same time they highlight the passivity and even the aversion that local residents feel towards the archeological site in their municipality and therefore its exploitation for tourism:

> I've always been very impressed that, having this potentiality, I've never seen anyone from here, for instance, in Itálica for years. It seems like for them it's a crime or a punishment, houses were expropriated … I mean, it was always something negative for the town itself, the survival of the town was questioned; I think this fear of losing our identity as a population due to administrative pressure.

> I can't understand such a passive attitude or so reticent with regards to identifying Itálica, because it's theirs and they should claim it as a place to be proud of.

There are various explanations that the interviewees give for this attitude. One of them is the low level of education of the inhabitants, which means they are not able to appreciate the cultural richness they possess. For them the land the site occupies is not taken advantage of. So much so, that at some points in time they have even used it as a tipping ground:

> It was a totally uneducated population; they didn't see beyond the farmers; they didn't see anything but hindrances; they didn't see the positive side.

> Of course the people see that and say: 'I sowed that every year'. But they even put a concrete wall there so they couldn't see what was behind, or so the people couldn't throw rubbish there, but this is normal in a town; they throw the rubbish over the top of the wall.

The municipal authorities distrust the behaviour of their fellow citizens with respect to the appreciation of the ruins. This creates resistance to the introduction of improvements that stimulate tourism. This perception makes it difficult to delegate responsibility to the residents themselves or to get them involved in the tourism management of the locality:

> No, no, people feel like it and have good intentions; I think there's fear of the very neighbours' rejection of a statue being put up and it being stoned or broken. I've even heard about some things … but it's … and if they paint on it? Well, if they paint on it, it'll be cleaned and they can paint a façade and they can paint …

But the main issue that all the respondents agree on is the impact that the ruins have had on the urban development of Santiponce. A key moment that contributed to aggravating the negative perception about Itálica was the discovery of the Roman theatre. This discovery was the motive for expropriating a large area of the town. This was even seen as a threat to the town's very survival:

> In the '60s, the administration acted very traumatically. This town was threatened, almost to the point of disappearing. Expropriations took place. The senior

citizens of the town … you take them out of their neighbourhood, you move them, you put them out of place and they don't have a town any more; what was their street before now doesn't exist and that then brings about uprooting.

They've lived with their backs to history; they've almost been against it; they've had misgivings about it. The neighbours of Santiponce have always been afraid of their houses being bought, of them ending up being expropriated.

If an inadequate and imposed expropriation is added to this factor, without counting on the neighbours at all, and if the compensation is low and late in coming, the misgivings and fear towards everything related to the historic site grow among the population:

> There's been a very negative vision about Itálica here, especially when the theatre was found and many houses were expropriated, so there's been a very negative vision because they had finished off the town.

> When you've expropriated people, have paid them poorly and late, well … I remember a wedding I was at not long ago, and speaking with one from the town, he says: 'How are we going to like Itálica, if what Itálica has done is give us problems, we can't like Itálica'. So the town has always lived with its back to Itálica.'

What has also generated problems has been the fact that any modification or enlargement of a home has led to the discovery of archaeological remains, implying the paralysing of the work while the find was inspected or the expropriation of the land being expedited:

> We got on badly, very badly, because the administration doesn't offer solutions when they discover new finds; there's a lot of pressure on the houses, on the neighbours, curtailing many logical things but not offering solutions. There's a lot of tension.

> Then, when I've asked the town people here about it, the old people, the people have always seen Itálica as a threat, because there are people who expropriate the land and the land is there, dying laughing, and they've not been able to sow anything have

they? And when people have to build their house, they go to the town hall and in the past the mayor said: 'Cover it up as quick as you can, the culture people are coming.'

Another determining social–cultural factor is the absence of entrepreneurial spirit among the residents. They lack initiative and risk-taking capacity and do not take advantage of the privileged circumstances of the territory. Some of the experts justify this lack of initiative in terms of the historic dependence of the inhabitants:

> The town can't complain about the heritage, though the Santiponce people don't value it; until the 19th century the Santiponce people suffered a lot from being dominated in some way, first by the prior's authority then by the duke's.

Nor are there any models of entrepreneurship in the local population that incite young people to go into business. This, along with the low degree of identification with the heritage, gives rise to a very reduced entrepreneurial class:

> The same as the kids copy the basketball or football players who are the current-day aristocrats. But Santiponce has never had that; there's only one person, who they call the Marquis, who has an export company where they export everything; he gets the money, gets drunk and goes around with his mistress.

> It's not a sign of identity. The kids there have never wanted to be Itálica guides, for instance, though it would have been easy to earn a living.

But the majority refer to the clichés about the lack of entrepreneurial spirit of the Spanish and the Andalusians, always used to the support of public institutions filling this space with aid and subventions:

> There we have not only the Santiponce people problem, but the problem of the Andalusians and the Spaniards, who have a very paternalistic attitude, always waiting for the public funds to get things moving; private initiative is what brings about business, but you've got to have the idea; you've got to put forward the project and fight for it.

The experts also consider that, in addition to the lack of resources they are sometimes confronted with, the few business people in the locality have an aversion to the high risks they have to take when investing in tourism:

> I'm going to give you my opinion, the population is quite passive; they don't have business initiative; they think that as Itálica is here, Itálica has to give the money; if you just do a study and you go round, you realize there's no fast food place, a place that sells sandwiches; just imagine if they put one right here in the gateway.

The interviewees from outside Santiponce are very critical of the residents. Resentment towards the passive attitude of the Santiponce people is noted:

> In Santiponce they've always been asking for things, a thing from the monastery, or asking the friars and after asking the administration, because Itálica was there. The Santiponce people nowadays are beggars; they have never taken the initiative about anything, and it has nothing to do with being in Andalusia. They are even more always asking for things. Listen, you've got to give me this, you've got to give me something else, you've got to give me that ... But what do *you* do, what do *you* give? One-way relationship: to ask for things. They have a right to everything. They are the ones who suffer. You've got to give me something ... But what do you do to be given something? Why have I got to give *you* something and not someone else? This is very special in Santiponce ... in the end they have to have everything done, let the Ministry of Culture do it, let the provincial government do it, let the town hall do it.

What is true is that this lack of initiative affects the infrastructure of the town's services, especially around Itálica. The town hall's initiatives to involve business people have not been welcomed due to the disinterest of the business sector:

> Well, this plan tried to create a series of instruments of collaboration between the public and the private sector, and the tourism panel was set up, and in theory there were meetings every other month, every three months, something to have a

contact to make proposals, us from our point of view and them from theirs, and you know it's a bit distressing that they don't go to many meetings; we have to be behind them just for them to attend, sent them a letter; if the letter doesn't work, go to them to remind them about it and despite all that they often don't go: 'I can't, I've a lot of work, I've …'.

In general, the opinion of the experts is that business people from outside would not be badly looked upon by the residents if their activities created a source of wealth for the population. However, this could bring about the marginalization of the local population in small businesses in the submerged economy (Hampton, 2005: 751).

Change of attitude

Despite this negative attitude of the residents towards Itálica, the interviewees note how in recent years a slow but positive and irreversible change is taking place in the attitude of the inhabitants towards tourism:

The residents have changed a lot since we started the process in '97; I mean, before it was a rejection of tourism, now they simply see it, they contemplate it, they still don't take it into their arms, which would be the next point.

I would define this, if it could be defined, as a process of decanting; I mean, tourism in Santiponce has to go seeping into the surface of the most internal spaces via a pure process of decanting in time.

The proactive strategy of the municipality to increase the participation and involvement of the citizens, imbued by the spirit of the Local Agenda 21, has contributed to this new situation. This policy, resulting in the organization of training and awareness workshops, the creating of strategic planning commissions and the popularizing of the local patrimonial richness in schools has been relatively successful:

[Regarding the strategic plan] There's a participatory commission; the participation is high compared to how people here participate, which is little; it's not bad, about

20 people including business people and general public, good citizens; it's not bad.

I think things are changing a bit … they're taking part and I think this is important, that they see themselves as actors, participating in the matter, and its implication is also essential, I think, little by little …

Another influencing factor is generational change. This is bringing about the rise of a class of young people with a higher cultural level. At the same time, they are becoming aware from their schooldays:

As the young people grow up and see new realities, they are getting involved in the subject. So, we'll have to go on sowing and creating this structure.

Though there remains much to be done, a greater effort is pleaded for to sensitize the population to the importance of their heritage and for them to feel proud of the richness of their territory:

We think the first step is the knowledge of the heritage, so the first thing is for people to approach it, get to know it; this is the best way for them to appreciate it, to value it. For them to be proud of what there is in their town and to assume it as their own, to get involved. But to get involved they need to feel it. Then, I think this is the path; we must insist on knowledge; in this sense, a load of events must be promoted, matters that justify the visits, and especially for them to feel it as something that's theirs, that they don't see it as foreign to them.

The change of attitude with regard to Itálica is taking place as the residents see the improvements that are appearing in the town and, in some way, they claim the benefits of this development. The residents are starting to see some advantages in tourism:

Though these days there are people who live from tourism, who work directly, the six or eight positions that have been made are for young people, people from here, and all this has made itself felt differently.

Another key aspect is the appropriation of the archaeological site by the neighbours. Two good examples are the Via Crucis celebrations Itálica organizes annually and the fact that residents increasingly use the Roman ruins for their strolls:

> The older people enjoy Itálica a lot for strolls; many of them are retired and instead of walking along the road like they do in other towns, they have the privilege of coming to walk here every morning, so these people look at it differently; they look at the improvements and they say look what you've done, so they now see it differently.

> The Itálica Vía Crucis is a revindication of the town, which is asking to take part in Itálica and spontaneously they've invented the Via Crucis. They're starting to identify Itálica as something that's theirs.

Connections between the municipal government and the regional government

An important problem that emerges from the interviews is that of the political connections between the town hall and the regional government. In the opinion of the interviewees, the different political orientations influence public investment in the locality and the support given to local tourism by both the provincial and regional management:

> Yes, but they're reluctant; right now the town hall is run by the United Left and they curtail everything; it's lamentable.

> If the town hall, perhaps they have asked, but as we know, a United Left town hall has to ask more than a town hall of another political colour.

> When they qualified Santiponce as a touristic municipality, I reckon there were two; Fuengirola it seems to me was the one before, and Santiponce in all Andalusia; it's just that … What's happened? What's happened here is that – don't record this (joking) … if the town hall was governed by another team, the matter would be different …

Furthermore, the regional government owns and manages the site of Itálica. They decide on heritage issues, and the management has not been implemented in a participatory manner so that the opinions of

local leaders are heard. This evidently influences the way in which the town feels the presence of Itálica as something imposed. Something they have to live with but which does not belong to them:

> I think it's especially difficult because the two monuments belong to the Ministry of Culture and not to the town hall; if only there were more political harmony and more municipal participation in the life of the site and I think there should be.

There is no doubt that confrontation exists between the political institutions in charge of the management of tourism and the heritage. This makes it difficult to coordinate and exploit the synergies between the entities involved.

Conclusions from the Case Study

The economic development of Santiponce depends on the strengthening of tourism. To do this the locality relies on an exceptional heritage: the archaeological site of Itálica. However, historical, cultural, economic and political conditions have put a brake on the positive relationship between the residents and the municipality's heritage. Figure 10.4 sketches the categories and relationships that have emerged during the research and which explain this phenomenon. The dependent variables analysed are the residents' attitude and the sustainable exploitation of the heritage. The rest of the dimensions seem to be tied by positive or negative unions, through which they contribute or do not contribute to the categories they affect.

These connections are based on their nature: historical, cultural, economical or political.

Historical (1, 3, 4), since the neighbours have always depended on different types of power: the ecclesiastical and now the political. Moreover, one must add the traumatic situations the population has lived through due to the expropriation (7) of many of the houses built on important archaeological findings.

Cultural, because this relationship of dependence has generated the residents'

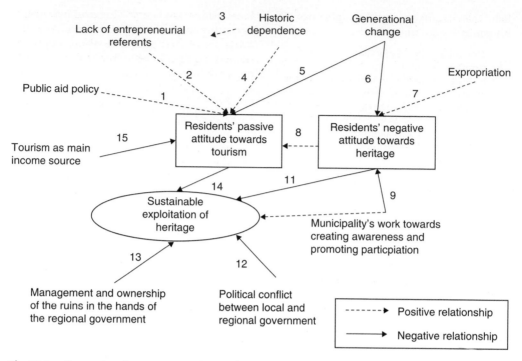

Fig. 10.4. Connections between categories. Explanatory model of the difficulties of sustainable tourism exploitation in Santiponce.

passive mentality, which has had a profound impact on their behaviour. This has also brought about the lack of entrepreneurial models among the young people of the locality (2). The generational change has, however, led to an important change of attitude regarding tourism activities (5 and 6).

Economic, in its being an outstandingly agricultural town. In the past, agriculture has always been the basic activity of the local economy, but this situation is currently unsustainable due to the more extensive land demanded by the new forms of exploitation (15).

Political, due to the complex situation of the municipal government, which is led by a party that is different from that of the provincial and regional governments (12). To this context must be added the circumstance of the ownership and management of the heritage being in the hands of the regional institutions (13).

All this framework gives rise to complex power relationships that make the sustainable exploitation of the historical–artistic heritage difficult. That is why the residents live with their backs turned to the site and even consider it to be harmful owing to the traumatic experiences they have had with the archaeological excavations (11, 14).

If one wishes to guarantee the conservation of the cultural inheritance, it is fundamental to stimulate the participation of the local population (Tosun, 2000: 626). The citizens must have the idea that the resources they have to belong to them and should feel proud of what living with such wealth means (Black and Wall, 2001). The authorities must play the role of inspirators and educators. They must consider the changing of the attitude of the residents as a long-term aim (9 and 10). At the same time, they cannot neglect the creation of conditions and infrastructure so that the neighbours appreciate the beneficial change caused by the tourist visits to Itálica and the sustainable exploitation of the site as a source of income for the local community. For these achievements to be possible, the different institutions involved must closely collaborate and coordinate their actions in order to obtain synergies in the management and exploitation of the archaeological site for tourism.

Evaluation of the Use of Grounded Theory in Tourism Research

We have been able to observe how GT helps to explain complex phenomena connected with social processes. The description of reality from evidence, and the subsequent abstraction process, contributes to the generating of concepts, categories and connections that help in the search for theoretical explanations.

However, one must remain cautious about applying this methodology, owing to the risks inherent in the researcher's interpretation of reality. That is why there is a need for methodological procedures that help to increase the validity of the research. For example, the triangulation of data or the use of tests to ensure the accuracy of the coding. It is also important to check the results obtained in the light of previous theories, so as to guarantee the study's external validity. In this study use has been made of triangulation in different ways. In the coding process the trials (test and re-test) proposed by Krippendorff (1990) have been followed. The 'devil's advocate' figure has also been used. Here a researcher from outside the team analysed the whole research process and put forward any doubts that arose.

To sum up, GT can offer a different and refreshing vision of tourism phenomena, and if based on a strict procedure of data collection and on a systematic analysis, it can give rise to generalizable explanations from a theoretical point of view, albeit not from a statistical one. Data analysis leads to the creation of theories that help to explain experiments and can be generalized in order to be used for formulating new research hypotheses.

References

Ashley, C. (2000) The impacts of tourism on rural livelihoods: experience in Namibia. *ODI Working Paper* 128, ODI, London.

Black, H. and Wall, G. (2001) Global–local inter-relationships in UNESCO World Heritage Sites. In: Teo, P., Chang, T.C. and Ho, K.C. (eds) *Interconnected Worlds. Tourism in Southeast Asia*. Elsevier Science, Pergamon, Oxford, UK, pp. 121–136.

Bramwell, B. and Rawding, L. (1996) Tourism marketing images of industrial cities. *Annals of Tourism Research* 23, 201–221.

Caro, F.J. and Castellanos, M. (2005) Agentes sociales, turismo y espacios urbanos: una aplicación de la teoría fundamentada en investigaciones de turismo. In: AECIT (ed.) *Turismo y Territorio: Conflictos, Corresponsabilidad y Estrategias de Gestión*. AECIT, Málaga, Spain, pp. 1–16.

Caro, F.J. and Díez, E.P. (2005) Investigación cualitativa asistida por ordenador en Economía de la Empresa. *Investigaciones Europeas de Dirección y Economía de la Empresa* 11(2), 45–58.

Charmaz, K. (1983) The grounded theory method: an explication and interpretation. In: Emerson, R. (ed.) *Contemporary Field Research: a Collection of Readings*. Little Brown Company, Boston, Massachusetts, pp. 109–126.

Connell, J. and Lowe, A. (1997) Generating grounded theory from qualitative data: the application of inductive methods in tourism and hospitality. *Management Research* 3, 165–173.

Corbin, J.M. (1998). Alternative interpretations: valid or not? *Theory & Psychology* 8, 121–128.

Coyle, I.T. (1997), Sampling in qualitative research. Purposeful and theoretical sampling; merging or clear boundaries? *Journal of Advanced Nursing* 26, 623–630.

Decrop, A. (1999) Triangulation in qualitative tourism research. *Tourism Management* 20, 157–161.

Douglas, D. (2003) Grounded theories of management: a methodological review. *Management Research News* 26, 47.

Egri, C.P. and Herman, S. (2000) Leadership in the environmental sector: values, leadership styles and contexts of environmental leaders and their organizations. *Academy of Management Journal* 43, 571–604.

Eisenhardt, K. (1989) Building theories from case study research. *Academy of Management Review* 14, 488–511.

Glaser, B. (1978) *Theoretical Sensitivity*. Sociology Press, Mill Valley, California.

Glaser, B. (1992) *Basics of Grounded Theory Analysis: Emergence versus Forcing*. Sociology Press, Mill Valley, California.

Glaser, B. and Strauss, A. (1967) *The Discovery of Grounded Theory: Strategies for Qualitative Research*. Aldine, Chicago, Illinois.

Goulding, C. (1998) Grounded theory: the missing methodology on the interpretivist agenda. *Qualitative Market Research: an International Journal* 1, 50–57

Goulding, C. (2002) *Grounded Theory. A Practical Guide for Management, Business and Market Researchers*. Sage Publications, Newbury Hill, California.

Hampton, M.P. (2003) Entry points for local tourism in developing countries: evidence from Yogyakarta, Indonesia. *Geografiska Annaler* 85, 85–101.

Hampton, M.P. (2005) Heritage, local communities and economic development. *Annals of Tourism Research* 32, 735–759.

Herman, S. and Egri, C.P. (2002) Triangulation in action: integration of qualitative and quantitative methods to research environmental leadership. In: Parry, K.W. and Meindl, J.R. (eds) *Grounding Leadership Theory and Research: Issues, Perspectives and Methods*. Information Age Publishing, Greenwich, UK, pp. 129–148.

Krippendorff, K. (1990) *Metodología de Análisis de Contenido: Teoría y Práctica*. Paidós, Barcelona, Spain.

Markwell, K.W. (1997) Dimensions of photography in a nature-based tour. *Annals of Tourism Research* 24, 131–155.

Mehmetoglu, M. and Altinay, L. (2006) Examination of grounded theory analysis with an application to hospitality research. *International Journal of Hospitality Management.* 25, 12–33.

Mehmetoglu, M. and Dann, G. (2003) Atlas/ti and content analysis in tourism research. *Tourism Analysis* 8, 1–13.

Miles, M.B. and Huberman, A.M. (1994) *Qualitative Data Analysis. An Expanded Sourcebook*. Sage Publications, London.

Oviedo, M.A., Castellanos, M. and Martín, D. (2007) Gaining residents' support for tourism and planning. *International Journal of Tourism Research* 10, 95–109.

Richards, G. and Wilson, J. (2004) The impact of cultural events on city image: Rotterdam Cultural Capital of Europe 2001. *Urban Studies* 41(10), 1931–1951.

Rodríguez, G., Gil, G and Garcia, E. (1996) *Metodologia de la Investigación Cualitativa*. Aljibe, Malaga, Spain.

Stake, R.E. (1995) *The Art of Case Study Research*. Sage Publications, Thousand Oaks, California.

Strauss, A. (1987) *Qualitative Analysis for Social Scientists*. Cambridge University Press, Cambridge, UK.

Strauss, A. and Corbin, J. (1990) *Basics of Qualitative Research: Grounded Theory Procedures and Techniques*. Sage Publications, London.

Strauss, A. and Corbin, J. (1994) Grounded theory methodology: an overview. In: Denzin, N. and Lincoln, Y. (eds) *Handbook of Qualitative Research*. Sage Publications, London, pp. 273–285.

Tosun, C. (2000) Limits to community participation in the tourism development process in developing countries. *Tourism Management* 21, 613–633.

Yin, R. (1988) *Case Study Research: Design and Methods*. Sage Publications, Beverly Hills, California.

11 Tales from the Field: Video and its Potential for Creating Cultural Tourism Knowledge

Tijana Rakić

Introduction

This chapter aims to promote innovative qualitative approaches in general and the use of visual methods in particular within cultural tourism research. It does this because a great number of cultural tourism researchers seem to have long had a preference for quantitative rather than qualitative research methods and a tendency to use a 'standardized scheme or pattern' (Schutz, 1964 in Feighey, 2003: 78) in their respective research projects. Throughout the chapter, I argue that researcher-created video, an innovative visual research technique in the social sciences and humanities (Banks, 2001; Pink, 2001a, 2007; Crang and Cook, 2007; Rakić and Chambers, 2007a,b, 2009), can be used alongside traditional qualitative research methods in creative ways in order to create new, visual knowledges in the field of cultural tourism research.

The mode by which researcher-created video is used in research is influenced, among other things, by different theoretical approaches and therefore the first part of the chapter explores the current state of (cultural) tourism research. It also explores the more traditional approaches to research, such as positivism and post-positivism, and the more innovative approaches, such as critical theory and constructivism. What follows then is a rather brief exploration of the key differences between these approaches and their influence on research methodologies, as well as on visual methods. Entrenched throughout this discussion is an attempt to encourage researchers to engage in qualitative (visual) research projects that are thoroughly underpinned on both a theoretical and a practical level.

In attempting to depict the potential of researcher-created video and its use within the study of (cultural) tourism, I then go on to elucidate the context of my most recent (visual) research project: an interdisciplinary study underpinned by constructivism, which focuses on the relationships between world heritage, tourism and national identity at the Athenian Acropolis. The exploration of the project, as well as the role played by researcher-created video as a complementary fieldwork technique, demonstrates the potential that video created by researchers can have in studying not only motivations, perceptions and experiences but also practices of visitors to cultural sites.

While including a discussion on the ethical issues the use of video in academic research might imply, as well as a discussion on the fit of video with different methodological approaches, I use a number of examples from the field to demonstrate the importance that an innovative research technique might have in contributing to the existing body of knowledge. Namely, in a research project that relied on the use of a wide variety of methods, ranging from the collection and semiotic analysis of (visual, textual and audiovisual) tourist materials and a year-long (visual) ethnographic fieldwork that included audiovisually recorded participant observation, interviewing, diary keeping and mapping of visitor movements, the use of video proved to be of crucial significance – video footage created in the field enabled me not only to tackle the research question in a new way but also to create new, visual knowledges.

Finally, considering the emerging importance of visual methods across the social sciences and humanities and the role new technologies have in academic research, I also attempt to encourage cultural tourism researchers to follow developments in other fields and explore the potential innovative approaches and techniques might have in their studies. Visual techniques such as researcher-created video facilitate deeper and richer understanding of the phenomena under study. Given that cultural tourism research projects are, by definition, concerned with cultural aspects of tourism, interpretative approaches and visual techniques are particularly relevant for this type of research.

The Role of Innovative Approaches in Cultural Tourism Research

Research projects in cultural tourism seem to have been, similarly to other projects in the wider field of tourism studies, largely marked and 'heavily dominated by positivist approaches' (Pritchard and Morgan, 2007: 12), deductive rather than inductive research, and quantitative rather than qualitative or mixed methods (see also Walle, 1997 and Riley and Love, 2000). Although such approaches have their place (Pernecky, 2007; Rakić and Chambers, 2007a), these will not necessarily be appropriate in all situations, especially within studies that seek to 'explore questions of meaning and

understanding', or involve interpretation or an inquiry into 'multiple realities associated with lived experience' (Goodson and Phillimore, 2004: 30). In addition, the exclusive or even simply overwhelming reliance on positivist and post-positivist approaches and quantitative methods in the study of tourism might also imply that the areas of inquiry are limited and that social 'reality' is oversimplified (Walle, 1997).

According to Pritchard and Morgan (2007), even if tourism as a field of inquiry has grown and matured along with the expansion of the tourism industry, it has unfortunately 'not always brought increased innovation and diversity', but rather it brought 'a greater volume of research which is mainly confirmatory and reproductive' (Pritchard and Morgan, 2007: 12). Indeed, it seems that these practices have resulted in the current situation in tourism studies where '... many key contributors to the tourism field have become stale, tired, repetitive and lifeless' (Franklin and Crang, 2001: 5).

Nevertheless, studies in tourism that have utilized innovative research methodologies and methods have been appearing in what seems to be the time when 'pioneering research methodologies and innovative methods are most needed' (Pernecky, 2007: 211). Tourism researchers seem to be becoming all the more involved with alternative approaches such as critical theory and constructivism, engaged in conducting inductive rather than deductive studies, and relying on the use of qualitative rather than quantitative methods. In addition, the very dominance of positivist and post-positivist approaches, which has for so long marked much of the scholarly tourism research, is increasingly being challenged, and researchers are being encouraged to use new approaches (see, for example, Phillimore and Goodson, 2004a; Ateljevic *et al.*, 2007).

Whereas more researchers in tourism seem to engage in qualitative research, according to Phillimore and Goodson (2004b: 5) they have 'in the main, used qualitative research as a set of methods rather than a set of thinking tools'. However, qualitative research need not be taken as a strictly prescribed set of methods that will bring the same results in all situations. Quite the contrary, in order for qualitative research to generate the desired results, it needs to be seen as a 'set of thinking tools' that will be influenced by the theoretical approach or the paradigm taken, namely the ontology, epistemology and methodology of the researcher.

Goodson and Phillimore (2004: 34) define a paradigm as a researcher's 'basic set of beliefs that define their worldview' consisting of their ontology or the definition of reality, their epistemology or the theory of knowledge and their methodology or 'the theory of the method' (Jamal and Hollinshead, 2001: 67). In a nutshell, in order to have their studies thoroughly underpinned, researchers need to ask themselves:

1. In terms of ontology: 'What is the nature of reality and therefore what is there that can be known about it?'.
2. In terms of epistemology: 'What is the nature of the relationship between the knower or would-be knower and what can be known?'.
3. In terms of methodology: 'How can the inquirer (would-be knower) go about finding out whatever he or she believes can be known?' (Guba and Lincoln, 2004: 21–22).

A particular set of ontological (i.e. realism versus relativism) and epistemological (i.e. objectivism versus subjectivism) standpoints that researchers adopt will then only inform their methodology and methods rather than strictly prescribe them. Taking into consideration the word strictures and the main focus of this chapter, both of which prevent a deeper exploration of the main paradigms, what follows is a rather brief and very simplified description of the main differences between the different approaches.

Positivism and post-positivism, even though they are two distinct paradigms, are often perceived as having much in common – both share a realist ontology or the 'belief that there exists a reality out there, driven by immutable natural laws' (Guba, 1990: 19), and both subscribe to an objectivist epistemology. One of the key differences is that under positivism, which adopts naïve realism, the findings are seen as absolutely

'true', while under post-positivism, which adopts critical realism, the findings are seen as 'probably true' reflections of the 'real' world (Guba and Lincoln, 2005). In both cases, however, researchers are not perceived as central within the research process. Critical theory, on the other hand, acknowledges the centrality of the researcher within the research process and subscribes, from a subjectivist epistemological position, to critical realism in terms of its ontology. While they do not seek to create 'a distance between the knower and what is known' and thus believe that findings are influenced and mediated by the values of the researcher, critical theorists assume 'that there is indeed a reality but one which cannot be fully apprehended' (Chambers, 2007: 108). Finally, a constructivist paradigm is marked by a relativist ontology and a subjectivist epistemology, i.e. there is a belief that realities are multiple, created in the minds of individuals and that knowledge is constructed (see also Guba, 1990). Within this paradigm, researchers are seen as central to the research process and their voices, along with the voices of their informants, are often included.

In terms of the different methodologies or 'theories of the method' (Jamal and Hollinshead, 2001: 67), it is important to bear in mind that methods are simply 'tools' within a particular methodology, which is in turn informed by the theoretical approach or the paradigm. As such, it is possible that a particular set of methods that has been successfully used in one study will not necessarily be entirely suitable for another similar study, especially considering that methods as 'tools of inquiry' will also need to fit the research topic and context, disciplinary background as well as the skill set of the researcher.

Visual methods, as innovative research techniques in the social sciences and humanities, are mostly perceived as belonging to the qualitative spectrum of methods (i.e. see Banks, 2001; Pink, 2001a; Crang and Cook, 2007; Rakić and Chambers, 2007a,b, 2009; Rose, 2007; Stanczak, 2007). However, as with other methods, the different approaches taken will inform the way in which visual research is conducted as well as the way in which data are interpreted. In the context of researcher-created video for example, researchers whose work is underpinned by an objectivist/positivist or post-positivist approach on the one hand might prefer to use minimal camera movements, very long shots, not appear in their footage and later use little or no editing. On the other hand, researchers whose work is underpinned by a subjectivist/constructivist or critical theory approach might prefer to rely somewhat more on the use of camera movements and shorter shots, occasionally appear in and edit their footage as well as use author-reflexive narrative. In terms of interpretation, researchers whose work is underpinned by an objectivist/positivist or post-positivist approach will mostly believe 'that what is "seen" by the visual researcher is a "true" representation of reality' and negate their role in interpreting the footage. Researchers whose work is underpinned by a subjectivist/constructivist or critical theory approach though will mostly believe 'that the researcher is inextricably implicated' (Rakić and Chambers, 2007a: 245) in the production and interpretation of visual representations of reality (which, in the case of a constructivist approach, will be seen as local, co-constructed and plural). Although theoretically visual methods can be used from different perspectives and some influences of the different approaches can overlap, subjectivist relativism was argued to be the most viable position (see Rakić and Chambers, 2009).

That said, in this attempt to inspire other researchers to rely on innovative approaches and use visual methods in order to create new visual knowledges in the field of cultural tourism research, what follows are not the findings but rather a reflexive account of my most recent research project, an interdisciplinary research project underpinned by constructivism and within which, alongside the more traditional qualitative methods, I also used visual methods. Indeed, the use of visual methods, specifically video, as a complementary fieldwork technique enabled me not only to tackle the research question in a new way but also to create new visual knowledges in the field of (cultural) tourism research.

The Study Context: Exploring the Relationships between World Heritage, Tourism and National Identity at the Athenian Acropolis

In brief, this interdisciplinary research, based on (visual) anthropology and (cultural) geography, and philosophically underpinned by constructivism, focuses on the relationship between world heritage, tourism and national identity at the Athenian Acropolis. The reasons for studying the relationship between world heritage, tourism and national identity in the particular case of the Athenian Acropolis were manifold. First and foremost, having lived in Greece for several years as a non-Greek national, I had developed a great interest in Greek national identity, history and tourism, and my knowledge of the local language and culture became exceptional. What this implied in terms of this research was that as a UK- based researcher with an extensive knowledge of the Greek language and culture I would encounter minimal barriers during my field research in Greece. Second, and probably most important, no similar previous study had been made of the Athenian Acropolis, which seemed to be an ideal case study. This is because the Acropolis is believed to symbolize the world heritage idea (UNESCO, 2006) and to embody the Greek nation (Yalouri, 2001), while at the same time it is also the most visited cultural heritage site in Greece (Kontrarou-Rassia, 2007).

The significance of this project lies both in its contribution to the understanding of the relationship between world heritage, tourism and national identity and in its contribution to exploring the potential of using innovative visual methods in the social sciences (i.e. see Banks, 2001; Pink, 2001a; Pink *et al.*, 2004; Crang and Cook, 2007; Rose, 2007; Stanczak, 2007) and specifically in (cultural) tourism research (i.e. see also Rakić and Chambers, 2007a,b).

The practical aspect of this research was an investigation of the role that the Athenian Acropolis, as an important world heritage site and as an internationally well-known tourist attraction, plays in the construction of Greek national identity. This 'construction' of Greekness would be ascertained through an investigation of the way the Acropolis is represented in tourism materials. Importantly, the research also involved an investigation into the 'consumption' of this constructed sense of Greekness by the visitors to the site. The complexity of this research topic and its preoccupation with meanings, representations, interpretation and perceptions, as well as with multiple realities of the lived visitor experiences, implied that I would need to rely on innovative rather than more traditional approaches, engage in qualitative rather than quantitative methods and inductive rather than deductive research. Adopting, as I had, a constructivist paradigm meant that this research was also marked by a relativist ontology, subjectivist epistemology, hermeneutical methodology and qualitative research methods (see Fig. 11.1).

Put very simply, in this project, 'reality' was treated as relative, personally and collectively constructed (i.e. plural), and 'knowledge' as subjective, co-created and situated (i.e. context dependent). In addition, the constructivist paradigm also implied that this research was interpretative (i.e. concerned with the interpretation of deep and often multi-layered meanings) and that it relied largely on qualitative methods. In addition and in contrast to many other studies of tourism, the researcher was not perceived according to a positivistic or a post-positivistic fashion, as a person in search of 'objective universal truths', where she had very little or no impact on the creation of knowledge, but rather as a person central to this process of context-specific knowledge creation and her voice as only one of many that influenced the research process (see also discussion on interpretative approaches in Jamal and Hollinshead, 2001).

Underpinned by these theoretical understandings, this research involved roughly four, often overlapping, phases. The first phase was a critical review of the literature on the historical emergence of the Acropolis as a symbol of Greekness, as a world heritage site, and as a tourist attraction. The second phase involved the collection and semiotic analysis of (visual, textual and audiovisual) tourist materials, an analysis that sought to interpret symbolic resonances of the Acropolis contained in tourism materials such as postcards, guidebooks and governmental promotional campaigns. The third phase involved a year-long (visual) ethnographic fieldwork at the Acropolis, when I engaged in audiovisually recorded participant observation, interviewing, diary keeping and mapping of visitor movements. The fourth and final phase of the research involves the analysis of the materials, editing the footage and writing up the thesis. Visual methods and researcher-created video, with which this chapter is primarily concerned, were thus a crucial element of this project, in terms of both analysing visual materials from secondary data (i.e. still and moving images contained in tourism materials) and creating visual data in the field (i.e. video and photography), data later used for analysis, presentations at conferences, as part of lectures and as footage used for the editing of a documentary on the same topic.

PARADIGM
-constructivist-

↓

ONTOLOGY
-relativist-

↓

EPISTEMOLOGY
-subjectivist-

↓

METHODOLOGY
-hermeneutic-

↓

METHODS
-qualitative-

Fig. 11.1. Methodological process (adapted from Pernecky, 2007: 222).

Embarking on a (Moving Image) Visual Ethnographic Fieldwork: Ethical Issues, Filming Permissions and Equipment

Embarking on a year-long ethnographic field-work, within which video would be used as a complementary ethnographic research technique, means that several important issues have to be considered, including ethical issues, acquiring filming permissions and choosing adequate equipment.

Ethical issues are becoming increasingly important for academic researchers, who are often being requested to submit various types of research project approval forms, many of which include an assessment of ethical issues. Ethical considerations will also often be a personal responsibility that researchers using filmic approaches might feel towards their informants. In particular, considering that video footage allows little or no anonymity (see also Rakić and Chambers, 2007a,b, 2009), researchers embarking on a (moving image) visual ethnographic fieldwork might need to ask themselves:

1.   Is filming at a particular location common practice or might it be seen as an intrusion into privacy and social life?
2.   Do I need an official licence to film there?
3.   How could I, as a researcher conducting participant observation, inform people present that filming is taking place?
4.   How will I go about acquiring informed consent from my informants?
5.   Do I need to keep the contacts of my informants and will I, in the future, wish to show any of the visual outputs of this research to them?
6.   What will I do with the footage after the fieldwork and how could that make an impact on the lives of the people appearing in it?

For this moving image, visual ethnographic fieldwork at the Athenian Acropolis, filming within this public space was a standard practice and my presence with a camera would not be seen as a major intrusion into the privacy of individuals present or into their social life. A filming permission from the Greek Ministry of Culture was nevertheless needed, and although I was unable to personally inform the often thousands of people present at the site, I was none the less obliged to notify the guards that filming would be taking place upon each of my arrivals. Owing to the nature of the visit to this open-space world heritage site, a visit which often lasted as little as 30–40 min and which took place under various weather conditions, my informants or the visitors to the site could not have been possibly expected to read and sign a traditional informed consent form. Instead they were told, often on camera, what the project was about and asked whether they would like to contribute by participating in an interview. As the footage would subsequently be used both for analysis and to create an ethnographic documentary (later used for teaching, sent to film festivals and possibly also mailed to informants), we also exchanged contacts. Lastly, during the editing process, using close-ups of clearly recognizable people who seem to be engaging in what might be considered as private activities was also avoided.

Finally, depending on the desired outcomes of such a moving image, visual ethnographic project, researchers might also need to consider whether footage produced in the field will be used purely for the purposes of analysis and possibly also for inclusion within conference, seminar or lecture presentations, or whether they also hope to create an ethnographic documentary from it (see also Rakić and Chambers, 2007b). These issues are very important as they might help determine not only the type of equipment (i.e. amateur versus semi-professional or professional video cameras) and the budget (an amateur video camera might cost less than £500 (€600), while three times as much might be needed for a semi-professional one), but also the level of film-making skills researchers will need to operate the equipment with ease. Considering that I had some experience in ethnographic film-making (see Rakić and Karagiannakis, 2006) and that the footage produced at the Acropolis was to be used both for analysis and for the creation of an ethnographic documentary, I acquired and worked mostly with a semi-professional camera, while I often also used an external microphone to ensure a higher quality of sound. Semi-professional and professional cameras, however, tend to be bulkier, and as such these will not be ideal in all situations within ethnographic fieldwork. This being the case, along with the semi-professional camera, I also used a good-quality amateur camera, footage from which, if needed, could also be used for the documentary.

None the less, not all researchers will necessarily wish to create a documentary and, importantly, researchers might wish to use video footage created in the field in a myriad of different ways. To be precise, the exact mode by which researchers will decide to create and use video footage will depend on and be informed by their approach, academic discipline, skill set, research context, desired outcome and budget. That said, a good-quality, compact, user-friendly amateur video camera, possibly also accompanied by an external microphone, might be more than any researcher embarking on such fieldwork might need (see also Rakić and Chambers, 2007b).

Tales from the Field: Researcher-created Video as a Complementary Ethnographic Fieldwork Technique

Based on my interdisciplinary readings in ethnography and visual methods (i.e. Banks and Morphy, 1997; Cook, 1997; Valentine, 1997; Edensor, 1998; Galani-Moutafi, 2000; Kearns, 2000; Pauwels, 2000, 2004; Banks, 2001; Crang, 2001; Pink, 2001a, 2006; Pink *et al.*, 2004; Harper, 2005 ; Crang and Cook, 2007; Rose, 2007) and some previous experience in conducting visual ethnographic fieldwork (Rakić and Karagiannakis, 2006), I embarked on my journey to Athens. Once there, I would spend innumerable hours at the Acropolis throughout the year, conducting overt and covert participant observation, interviewing, mapping visitor movements and their activities, writing my fieldwork diary and, importantly, filming.

As mentioned earlier, throughout the fieldwork I made extensive use of both

a compact amateur camera and a semi-professional one. The amateur camera, on the one hand, was ideal for covert audio-visually recorded participant observation, as I was often perceived as yet another tourist taking a video of her visit to the Acropolis. (Although filming without the written permission of the archaeological service of the Greek Ministry of Culture within the archaeological site of the Athenian Acropolis is prohibited, filming with an amateur video camera is not heavily policed. As a result, many visitors use their video cameras at the site). The semi-professional camera on the other hand was ideal for overt audiovisually recorded participant observation, interviewing and panoramic shots of Athens as well as for high-quality shots of the actual site and its surroundings (many of which were needed for the documentary). Thus, filming was a central part of both my participant observation and interviewing but played no major role in my diary keeping, or in fact in mapping visitor movements and activities.

In particular, filming proved to be an invaluable tool as a part of both covert and overt participant observation. Other than the fact that it successfully 'camouflaged' me as a tourist/visitor, thus enabling me to successfully blend with visitors present at the Acropolis, video-taking was also instrumental in allowing me to film visitor activities, favourite spots, experiences and comments, all footage later used for analysis as well as for editing of the film. During these filming sessions I also kept notes in my fieldwork diary, descriptions of these filming sessions, but also 'thick' descriptions of other (non-filmed) observations such as visitor activities, comments, patterns of movements, volume of visitation, etc. In addition, I also kept notes on my position as a relatively young, white, female researcher in the field as well as of any relevant more 'theoretical' thoughts, such as the corporeal, embodied, multi-sensory nature of the visit to the site. Coupled with these notes (later transcribed and used as data within the analysis), video footage of my participant observation was not only a vivid (audiovisual) representation of the filming sessions at the Acropolis (allowing me to observe and interpret social life in greater detail) but it was also, in its own distinct way, an (audiovisual) extension of my fieldwork diary.

Filming was also crucial as a part of interviewing sessions. What became apparent shortly after the first few interviews was that the presence of a video camera and the fact that informants knew that this would also result in an ethnographic documentary was seen by many as a vehicle of empowerment, allowing for their voices to be heard. In that sense, at least as a part of this particular research project, the fact that all interviewing took place with the assistance of a video camera (and sometimes also with the assistance of another camera operator) served as a motivator for visitors to engage in an interview. The footage of these interviews, similarly to the footage of participant observation, would later be used for analysis as well as for editing of the film. These audiovisually recorded interviews, later also transcribed for the purposes of analysis, were much more than just 'thick (audiovisual) descriptions' of the interview context. The audiovisual recordings allowed me re-view these interviews as many times as was necessary during the analysis stage. Other than re-hearing the actual dialogue, these recordings also enabled me to revisit and take into account other interview-specific contexts, such as facial expressions, gestures and the weather, all of which allowed a deeper understanding and interpretation.

A few filming-related questions, however, still remain unanswered. These include:

1.   Did filming on its own allow me, the researcher, to gain knowledge and understanding otherwise inaccessible?
2.   What exactly, other than richer recordings from the field, did filming offer as a part of an academic research project?

Although, within this particular project, filming per se did not allow access to knowledge and understanding otherwise inaccessible (i.e. such as through the utilization of traditional ethnographic techniques), it did,

however, allow access to deeper and richer understanding of the phenomenon under study. Interestingly, Pink (2001a: 17) also maintains that visual methods 'cannot be used independently of other methods' but, rather, that these could be added to the existing methods in ethnography (Pink, 2007).

In addition to offering a deeper and richer understanding of the phenomenon under study, in this project, filming in the field also offered the possibility of producing innovative audiovisual research outputs that could be 'used for a range of academic and pedagogic purposes', such as inclusion of video in conferences, seminars and lecture presentations (Rakić and Chambers, 2007b: 1). Confirming this point further is the fact that, although the editing of the Acropolis film was still a work in progress at the time of writing this chapter, a 2-min video clip made from the footage as a preliminary edit has already been shown at academic conferences, research methods seminars and used for (cultural and heritage) tourism-related teaching at a number of universities.

Video and its Potential in Creating Cultural Tourism Knowledge

The potential of visual methods in general and video in particular has been widely recognized across the social sciences and humanities. Harper (1989, 2003, 2005), Pauwels (2000, 2002, 2004), Banks (2001), Pink (2001a,b, 2004a,b, 2006, 2007), Rose (2003, 2007), El Guindi (2004), Crang and Cook (2007, see Chapter 7 on filmic approaches) and Stanczak (2007) are some of many authors of the more recent texts on visual methods. In fact, visual methods are said to be on the rise across disciplines (Rakić and Chambers, 2007a), with 'a series of new publications across the social sciences and humanities' revealing 'a thriving interdisciplinary interest in visual research methods' (Pink, 2006: 15).

However, it seems that tourism researchers, which include researchers in cultural tourism, 'have yet to follow the lead offered by their counterparts outside the field but are beginning to engage tentatively with some of the issues' (Phillimore and Goodson, 2004b: 21). Although interesting studies that include other visual methods have been appearing recently, to date, very few tourism researchers have included researcher- or informant-created video in their studies. Hopefully, this, and other calls for inclusion of visual methods in general and video in particular in the study of tourism (Feighey, 2003; Rakić and Chambers, 2007a,b, 2009; Walter-Pockok *et al.*, 2008), will result in a greater appreciation and wider use of video among (cultural) tourism researchers.

An inclusion of researcher-created video as a complementary technique in the study of cultural tourism, as I have tried to argue throughout this chapter, might imply that our understanding and knowledge will be deepened and widened, video being a rich recording format which includes both the visual and the acoustic dimension. This knowledge might include, but is not limited to, the nature of the embodied multi-sensory visitor experiences and visitor perceptions, as well as the meanings cultural sites and events might have for them. Having used researcher-created video as a complementary technique, cultural tourism researchers could then include excerpts of these in their conference and lecture slides, or even use these to create a documentary, disseminating in such a way the (audio-)visual knowledge to wide and diverse audiences (see also Rakić and Chambers, 2007a). The value of visual (academic) knowledge is, among numerous other authors in the social sciences, also commented on by Rose (2003) in the context of geographical knowledge. While putting an emphasis on the 'visual' nature of geographical knowledge and the role of the visual in the production of this knowledge, she suggests that 'the type of image, the practices of audiencing and the spaces of display can intersect to produce the academic geographer as a powerful producer of knowledge' (Rose, 2003: 218).

The importance of visual methods and new technologies in the academic world, along with this and other calls for inclusion of innovative visual methods in the study of

tourism, will hopefully prompt researchers in this field to engage in exploring the potential that innovative techniques might have within their studies. In fact, 'knowledge about the world is increasingly articulated visually' and 'visual technologies (photograph, film, video, television, digital images and so on) increasingly form part of many individuals' everyday experience' (Feighey, 2003: 76). This being the case, researchers in the field of (cultural) tourism might wish to 'follow the lead offered by their counterparts outside the field' (Phillimore and Goodson, 2004b: 21) and seek to include innovative methods such as researcher-created video, methods that, in some situations, might prove to be slightly more adequate in tackling, and later also representing, the knowledge about some of the phenomena under study.

Conclusions

Given the dominance of traditional approaches and methods, this chapter aimed to promote innovative approaches, visual methods and the use of researcher-created video among researchers involved in the study of cultural tourism. While claiming that traditional approaches and methods in the study of cultural tourism have and will continue to have their place, I have argued that knowledge and understanding of the phenomena under study could be broadened and deepened through a wider use of qualitative approaches and innovative methods.

Despite the fact that the innovative approaches and methods discussed in this chapter have been widely used across the social sciences and humanities, taking on board any new method, including complementary research techniques such as researcher-created video, involves a series of considerations that, ideally, should not be approached lightly. For the particular case of researcher-created video as a complementary technique, which was also the main focus of this chapter, these considerations include theoretical underpinnings and their impact on the overall methodology as well as on the particular method in question, its fit with other methods as well as with the research topic and context and, importantly, ethical issues that the use of a video camera in the field might imply.

An interdisciplinary research project underpinned by constructivism that focuses on the relationships between world heritage, tourism and national identity at the Athenian Acropolis was a basis for the exploration of researcher-created video and its potential in the study of cultural tourism. The discussion surrounding the practicalities involved in preparing for and subsequently creating video in the field, such as securing a filming licence and considering ethical issues that might be involved, as well as choosing the appropriate equipment, aimed at providing essential guidance for researchers who might wish to introduce similar methods in their projects. Within the Acropolis project, which relied on a variety of qualitative methods such as semiotic analysis of (visual, textual and audiovisual) tourist materials and a year-long (visual) ethnographic fieldwork at the Acropolis, which in turn included audio-visually recorded participant observation, interviewing, diary keeping and mapping of visitor movements, researcher-created video proved to be invaluable. Although, in the wider context of this research, filming in the field per se did not allow access to knowledge otherwise inaccessible through, for example, traditional ethnographic techniques, it did, however, allow access to deeper and richer understanding of the phenomena under study. It also offered a possibility of producing new audio-visual research outputs that could be readily used for a variety of academic and pedagogic purposes. Among all the methods, researcher-created video, an innovative, complementary research technique in the social sciences and humanities, was the one that allowed me to approach the topic in a new way and, importantly, to create new visual knowledges in the field of cultural tourism research.

I hope that in its own modest way this chapter will prove useful in providing some inspiration and guidance to other researchers in the field of cultural tourism in their endeavours to introduce innovative techniques, such as researcher-created video, in their studies.

Acknowledgements

My thanks are due to Donna Chambers for her comments on earlier versions of this chapter. Special thanks are due to Yorgos Karagiannakis for his assistance with some of the camera work at the Acropolis and editing some of the footage, as well as his comments on earlier versions of this chapter. In addition, I am very grateful to the Alexander S. Onassis Public Benefit Foundation for funding my fieldwork in Athens, as well as to Napier University Business School and the School of Marketing, Tourism and Languages for awarding their funding for various parts of this project. Lastly, I am also grateful to the Greek Ministry of Culture for approving my application for a filming licence at the Acropolis.

References

Ateljevic, I., Pritchard, A. and Morgan, N. (eds) (2007) *The Critical Turn in Tourism Studies: Innovative Research Methodologies*. Elsevier, Oxford, UK and Amsterdam.

Banks, M. (2001) *Visual Methods in Social Research*. Sage, London.

Banks, M. and Morphy, H. (eds) (1997) *Rethinking Visual Anthropology*. Yale University Press, New Haven, Connecticut.

Chambers, D. (2007) Interrogating the 'critical' in critical approaches in tourism research. In: Ateljevic, I., Pritchard, A. and Morgan, N. (eds) *The Critical Turn in Tourism Studies: Innovative Research Methodologies*. Elsevier, Oxford, UK, pp. 105–120.

Cook, I. (1997) Participant observation. In: Flowerdew, R. and Martin, D. (eds) *Methods in Human Geography: a Guide for Students doing a Research Project*. Longman, Harlow, UK, pp. 127–150.

Crang, M. (2001) Field work: making sense of group interviews. In: Limb, M. and Dwyer, M. (eds) *Qualitative Methodologies for Geographers*. Arnold, London, pp. 215–233.

Crang, M. and Cook, I. (2007) *Doing Ethnographies*. Sage, London.

Edensor, T. (1998) *Tourists at the Taj: Performance and Meaning at a Symbolic Site*. Routledge, London.

El Guindi, F. (2004) *Visual Anthropology: Essential Method and Theory*. AltaMira Press, Oxford, UK.

Feighey, W. (2003) Negative image? Developing the visual in tourism research. *Current Issues in Tourism* 6, 76–85.

Franklin, A. and Crang, M. (2001) The trouble with tourism and travel theory? *Tourist Studies* 1, 5–22.

Galani-Moutafi, V. (2000) The self and the other: traveller, ethnographer, tourist. *Annals of Tourism Research* 27, 203–224.

Goodson, L. and Phillimore, J. (2004) The inquiry paradigm in qualitative tourism research. In: Phillimore, J. and Goodson, L. (eds) *Qualitative Research in Tourism: Ontologies, Epistemologies and Methodologies*. Routledge, London and New York, pp. 30–45.

Guba, E.G. (ed.) (1990) *The Paradigm Dialog*. Sage, London.

Guba, E.G. and Lincoln, Y.S. (2004) Competing paradigms in qualitative research: theories and issues. In: Hesse-Biber, S.N. and Leavy, P. (eds) *Approaches to Qualitative Research*. Oxford University Press, Oxford, UK, pp. 17–38.

Guba, E.G. and Lincoln, Y.S. (2005) Paradigmatic controversies, contradictions, and emerging confluences. In: Denzin, K. and Lincoln, Y.S. (eds) *The SAGE Handbook of Qualitative Research*, 3rd edn. Sage, London, pp. 191–217.

Harper, D. (1989) Visual sociology: expanding the sociological vision. In: Blank, G., McCartney, J. and Brent, E. (eds) *New Technologies in Sociology: Practical Applications in Research and Work*. Transaction Publishers, New Jersey, pp. 81–112.

Harper, D. (2003) Reimagining visual methods: Galileo to Neuromancer. In: Denzin, N.K. and Lincoln, Y.S. (eds) *Collecting and Interpreting Qualitative Materials*, 2nd edn. Sage, London, pp. 13–26.

Harper, D. (2005) What's new visually? In: Denzin, N.K. and Lincoln, Y.S. (eds) *Collecting and Interpreting Qualitative Materials*, 2nd edn. Sage, London, pp. 176–198.

Jamal, T. and Hollinshead, K. (2001) Tourism and the forbidden zone: the underserved power of qualitative enquiry. *Tourism Management* 22, 63–82.

Kearns, R.A. (2000) Being there: research through observing and participating. In: Hay, I. (ed.) *Qualitative Research Methods in Human Geography*. Oxford University Press, Oxford, UK, pp. 103–121.

Kontrarou-Rassia, N. (2007) Culture: going down [in Greek]. In: *Eleytherotypia*. Newspaper published on 17 January, Athens.

Pauwels, L. (2000) Taking the visual turn in research and scholarly communication. *Visual Sociology* 15, 7–14.

Pauwels, L. (2002) The video- and multimedia-article as a mode of scholarly communication: toward scientifically informed expression and aesthetics. *Visual Studies* 17, 150–159.

Pauwels, L. (2004) Filmed science in search of a form: contested discourses in anthropological and sociological film-making. *New Cinemas* 2, 41–60.

Pernecky, T. (2007) Immersing in ontology and the research process: constructivism the foundation for exploring the (in)credible OBE? In: Ateljevic, I., Pritchard, A. and Morgan, N. (eds) *The Critical Turn in Tourism Studies: Innovative Research Methodologies*. Elsevier, Oxford, UK and Amsterdam, pp. 211–226.

Phillimore, J. and Goodson, L. (eds) (2004a) *Qualitative Research in Tourism: Ontologies, Epistemologies and Methodologies*. Routledge, London.

Phillimore, J. and Goodson, L. (2004b) Progress in qualitative research in tourism: epistemology, ontology and methodology. In: Phillimore, J. and Goodson, L. (eds) *Qualitative Research in Tourism: Ontologies, Epistemologies and Methodologies*. Routledge, London, pp. 3–29.

Pink, S. (2001a) *Doing Visual Ethnography*. Sage, London.

Pink, S. (2001b) More visualising, more methodologies: on video, reflexivity and qualitative research. *Sociological Review* 49, 585–599.

Pink, S. (2004a) In and out of the academy: video ethnography of the home. *Visual Anthropology Review* 20, 82–88.

Pink, S. (2004b) Introduction: situating visual research. In: Pink, S., Kürti, L. and Afonso, A.L. (eds) *Working Images: Visual Research and Representation in Ethnography*. Routledge, London, pp. 1–12.

Pink, S. (2006) *The Future of Visual Anthropology: Engaging the Senses*. Routledge, London.

Pink, S. (2007) Walking with video. *Visual Studies* 22, 240–252.

Pink, S., Kürti, L. and Afonso, A.L. (eds) (2004) *Working Images: Visual Research and Representation in Ethnography*. Routledge, London.

Pritchard, A. and Morgan, N. (2007) De-centering tourism's intellectual universe, or traversing the dialogue between change and tradition. In: Ateljevic, I., Pritchard, A. and Morgan, N. (eds) *The Critical Turn in Tourism Studies: Innovative Research Methodologies*. Elsevier, Oxford, UK, pp. 11–28.

Rakić, T. and Chambers, D. (2007a) Creating tourism knowledge: an exploration of the use of visual techniques. In: Harris, C. and van Hall, M. (eds) *2nd International Critical Tourism Studies Conference – the Critical Turn in Tourism Studies: Promoting an Academy of Hope? CD-ROM Conference Proceedings*. Wagenigen University, University of Wales, and Institute for Tourism, Zagreb, Split, Croatia, pp. 242–251.

Rakić, T. and Chambers, D. (2007b) Researcher with a movie camera: visual ethnography in the field. In: *6th International Symposium on Aspects of Tourism – Gazing, Glancing, Glimpsing: Tourists and Tourism in a Visual World CD-ROM Conference Proceedings*. University of Brighton, Eastbourne, UK, pp. 1–13.

Rakić, T. and Chambers, D. (2009) Researcher with a movie camera: visual ethnography in the field. *Current Issues in Tourism* 12, 255–270.

Rakić, T. and Karagiannakis, Y. (2006) *Of Holidays and Olives*. A 38-min ethnographic documentary. Pitch-DarkProductions, UK and Greece.

Riley, R. and Love, L. (2000) The state of qualitative tourism research. *Annals of Tourism Research* 27, 164–187.

Rose, G. (2003) On the need to ask how, exactly, is geography 'visual'? *Antipode* 35, 212–221.

Rose, G. (2007) *Visual Methodologies: an Introduction to the Interpretation of Visual Materials*, 2nd edn. Sage, London.

Stanczak, G.C. (ed.)(2007) *Visual Research Methods: Image, Society and Representation*. Sage, London.

UNESCO (2006) World Heritage List: Acropolis. http://whc.unesco.org/en/list/404/ (accessed 9 February 2006).

Valentine, G. (1997) Tell me about ... using interviews as a research methodology. In: Flowerdew, R. and Martin, D. (eds) *Methods in Human Geography: a Guide for Students doing a Research Project*. Longman, Harlow, UK, pp. 110–126.

Walle, A. (1997) Quantitative vs. qualitative tourism research. *Annals of Tourism Research* 24, 524–536.

Walter-Pockok, N., Zahra, A. and McIntosh, A. (2008) Proposing video diaries as an innovative methodology in tourist experiences. In: *CHME Research Conference 2008 Conference Proceedings*. University of Strathclyde, Glasgow, UK, pp. 610–622.

Yalouri, E. (2001) *The Acropolis: Global Fame, Local Claim*. Berg, Oxford, UK.

12 Using Photo-based Interviews to Reveal the Significance of Heritage Buildings to Cultural Tourism Experiences

Gregory Willson and Alison McIntosh

Introduction

Currently, modern society is argued to be afflicted by an 'experience hunger', whereby people actively seek out experiences and consume goods and services more for the 'experience' they provide than any tangible element (Pine and Gilmore, 1999). As a result, 'experience' has moved from being seen largely as a value-added aspect of goods and services to the very core of tourism (Van Manen, 1990; Prentice *et al.*, 1998; Pine and Gilmore, 1999; McIntosh and Siggs, 2005; O'Dell, 2005; Pearce, 2005). Within the published cultural tourism literature, there has been a marked growth in attention placed on exploring tourists' experiences, or the experiential consumption of tourism (for example, Silberg, 1995; Beeho and Prentice, 1997; Prentice *et al.*, 1998; Willson, 2006, unpublished thesis; Willson and McIntosh, 2007). Experience has been defined as 'the subjective mental state felt by participants during a service encounter' (Otto and Ritchie, 1996: 166), or 'events that engage individuals in a personal way' (Bigne and Andreu, 2004: 692). Thus, experience can be viewed as the subjective mental state felt by individuals (Beeho and Prentice, 1997; Palmer, 1999). As experiences are highly personal, subjective, intangible, multi-phased and multi-dimensional,

their exploration presents a number of challenges to scholars, particularly in terms of what methodological approach is able to capture the richness of the experiences gained by tourists most accurately.

Traditionally it has been argued that tourism researchers have largely been influenced by positivist and scientific paradigms in terms of deciding how knowledge may best be collected (Botterill, 2001; Jennings, 2001). Arguably, quantitative methods situated around a positivist paradigm are unable to sufficiently reveal tourists' experiences, because they cannot capture the subtleties of the subjective experience (McIntosh, 1998; Jennings, 2001; Noy, 2004; Ayikoru and Tribe, 2005; McIntosh and Siggs, 2005). While qualitative research methods were once regarded as 'methodologically vulnerable' by some (Walle, 1997), Simonson *et al.* (2001: 260) suggest that, with regard to tourism research, 'looking ahead, it is reasonable to expect that the intensity of the postmodern–positivist debate will diminish'. Indeed, many recent studies of tourists' experiences are demonstrating a noticeable trend away from the traditional positivist approach to more interpretive, qualitative and reflexive modes of enquiry, as researchers seek to yield a more 'complete' and 'lived' account of tourists' experiences (Ateljevic *et al.*, 2005; Tribe, 2005). Increasing numbers of scholars are embracing imaginative and creative research methods that serve the questions pursued rather than restricting the scope of enquiry (Beyer, 1992; Ateljevic *et al.*, 2005; Uriely, 2005; Willson and McIntosh, 2007). Importantly, innovative research techniques can help reveal the layers of personal meaning and experience, and hence deepen scholarly knowledge of cultural tourism. There is particular value in exploring qualitative differences in cultural tourism experiences, especially with regard to how culture adds value to tourists' experiences of a region/destination, not just in terms of expressed cultural motivation and activity. Within this, there is a need to explore, in a holistic sense, the rich narratives that give meaning to the wider cultural tourism experience. Eliciting narratives, for example, can provide insight into how lived experiences interact with wider societal processes, and the personal significance of experiences to tourists' lives (Trapp-Fallon, 2003; Noy, 2004).

In the context of the above discourse, this chapter outlines and critically discusses the innovative qualitative research methods used by the present authors to examine tourists' experiences of the heritage buildings in Hawke's Bay, New Zealand. Heritage buildings are buildings that are regarded as representing shared roots and the origins of our identities or belongings (Gordon, 2004). Specifically, this chapter examines the use of a hierarchical probing technique based on the laddering theory applied in marketing research, and the use of photograph-based interviews to facilitate deeper personal narratives from tourists and to elicit the layered meanings attached to their experiences. This contributes to a deeper understanding of cultural tourism, as it elicits the significance and added-value nature of cultural tourists' experiences within a destination generally, such as the value that tourists place on their experiences of heritage buildings within a wider townscape. In contrast, much previous research has examined tourists' experiences in specific attraction or environmental settings (Prentice *et al.*, 1993; Masberg and Silverman, 1996; Powe and Willis, 1996; Beeho and Prentice, 1997; Bharath *et al.*, 2004). These perspectives do not wholly

elicit the personal meaning and positioning of gained experiences within tourists' wider travel narratives.

The Study

The research area

Hawke's Bay is a largely rural region on the east coast of New Zealand's North Island, with a population of approximately 148,000 people and with two main cities, Napier and Hastings (Statistics New Zealand, 2006). The profile of Hawke's Bay's tourists is similar to other regions in New Zealand, although Hawke's Bay attracts a comparatively high proportion of younger tourists to the region: indeed, 36% of international tourists to the region are aged between 20 and 35 (Tourism Research Council New Zealand, 2005). It was deemed an appropriate case study region because it has a high concentration of heritage buildings, and visiting heritage buildings is the most popular cultural activity amongst international tourists to the region (Colmar Brunton Social Research Agency, 2003). Specifically, Hawke's Bay has a large number of art deco and Spanish mission heritage buildings, many of which were constructed after a devastating earthquake hit the area in 1931 (Art Deco Trust, 2005). Most of these buildings are preserved and protected by the New Zealand Historic Places Trust and The Art Deco Trust, who aim to identify, educate and raise awareness of the social, economic, cultural, historical and spiritual importance of the heritage buildings in the region. Art deco buildings are said to 'express all the vigour and optimism of the roaring twenties, and the idealism and escapism of the grim thirties' (Art Deco Trust, 2005), and are characterized by bright geometric shapes, sunbursts, fountain designs and repeating patterns. The Spanish mission style originated in California and reflects the unique architectural style of Spanish missionaries of the time (Art Deco Trust, 2005). Hawke's Bay was one of five New Zealand regions to receive cultural tourism funding and support from the New Zealand

Government in 2003 to facilitate cultural tourism development (Art Deco Trust, 2005). Through exploring the personal meaning of tourists' experiences of the heritage buildings in the region, the authors' research sought to strengthen support for preservation and promotion of the buildings, to explore, using in-depth interviews, the experiences gained by international tourists from Hawke's Bay's heritage buildings and, in particular, to garner a deep understanding of the personal meaning these experiences had for individual tourists.

The research population and data collection

Sixty-six in-depth interviews were conducted with international tourists visiting Hawke's Bay. International tourists only were sampled because international tourism to Hawke's Bay is projected to grow at a significantly higher rate than that of domestic tourism; for instance, by 2011 international overnight visits are predicted to grow by 35.8%, compared with 6.6% domestically (Tourism Research Council New Zealand, 2005). As a large proportion of respondents were from the UK, the USA and Australia, the researchers generally did not encounter language or cultural barriers.

Convenience sampling was used in data collection. This form of sampling has been used in a number of studies of tourists' experiences (Turley, 2001; Lau and McKercher, 2004; Morgan *et al.*, 2005). Predominantly, 'on the street' locations were selected for sampling, owing to the relatively short length of stay of international tourists in Hawke's Bay (Statistics New Zealand, 2006). Specifically, tourists were interviewed mainly along Napier's Marine Parade and in the vicinity of Napier and Hastings' information centres. These locations were selected as they are arguably the regions' primary areas of tourist flow and provided the researchers and respondents numerous comfortable and quiet places to sit and talk. Further, the chance of under- or over-representation of a certain group was minimized due to the selection of these different

locations. All interviews were tape-recorded and later transcribed by the researchers to ensure validity and to further familiarize the researchers with the recorded information. To ensure confidentiality, all respondents were given pseudonyms. These transcripts were later analysed multiple times by the researchers through content analysis, to ensure that themes were developed from the words of tourists themselves. It was felt that it was pertinent to gather information even from international tourists who had not spent much time in the region, as this would allow results to emerge as to whether respondents gained experiences through the region's heritage buildings even without having visited them and to facilitate a holistic view of tourists' experiences, i.e. a general narrative about their time in the region so far. However, respondents needed to have spent some degree of time in the region to be able to share their experiences, and therefore those that stated they had 'only just' arrived in the region were not interviewed.

The following sections review the implementation, contribution and potential limitations of interviewing supported with the use of photographs and a hierarchical probing technique associated with the laddering theory – termed here 'photo-based interviews' – as an innovative qualitative method to address the key study aims: to gain rich and personal insight into tourists' experiences of heritage buildings in Hawke's Bay.

The photo-based interviews

Sixty-six photo-based interviews were conducted with international tourists between June and December of 2005; each interview lasted for approximately 20–45 min. Forty-four photographs of attractions in Hawke's Bay were taken by the principal researcher and placed into a compact handheld photo album, which was then used to prompt open conversational-style interviews with respondents. The photographs reflected a wide range of experiences that tourists can gain while visiting Hawke's Bay (Figs 12.1–12.8). If too many photographs are presented to tourists, there is a risk of them losing attention and being presented with too much information, and thus it has been advocated that when using photo-based interviews, a 'modest' number of photographs should be included in the sample (Fairweather and Swaffield, 2001). The number of photo-

graphs selected by the current authors (44) was similar to that of previous experiential studies employing photographs, for example Fairweather and Swaffield (2001, 2002).

Perhaps surprisingly, the use of photographs to assist in revealing respondents' experiences is a relatively new research

Fig. 12.1.   Napier's beach.

Fig. 12.2.   Napier's Soundshell.

Fig. 12.3. Marineland aquatic centre.

Fig. 12.4. Vintage car outside art deco building.

technique in tourism studies, but it is gathering momentum as its true value to research is realized. Tourism scholars have applied photograph-based methodologies in different ways, but the consensus is that photograph-based methodologies are able to elicit rich insight into tourists' experiences (Albers and James, 1988; MacKay and Fesenmaier, 1997; Markwell, 1997; Fairweather and Swaffield, 2001; Garlick, 2002). For example, Fairweather and Swaffield (2001) explored tourists' experiences of Kaikoura,

Fig. 12.5.   Art deco style, Napier.

Fig. 12.6.   Art deco style, Napier.

New Zealand, through combining photographs with the Q method, which involves ranking photographs in order of preference. They were able to determine which photographs of Kaikoura respondents liked most and least, and concluded that photographs 'produced rich and subtle interpretations of a complex phenomenon in an easily understood format' (p. 227). While the ranking of photographs was not implemented in the current study, researchers should not be afraid to experiment with implementing a

Fig. 12.7. Spanish mission style, Hastings.

Fig. 12.8. Spanish mission style, Hastings.

photograph-based methodology that best befits their research direction.

In the current study, the photographs were taken on one of the researchers' personal cameras, as photographs downloaded from a tourism web page may be overly biased, as essentially these are the images the region wants tourists to see and are the focus of promotional imagery. The photographs included various photographs of different styles of heritage buildings, natural scenery, specific tourist attractions such as vineyards and Napier's aquarium, and other 'everyday' features of the region such as significant shopping areas. There are, however, a great deal of experiences available to international tourists in Hawke's Bay, and Denzin and Lincoln (2003) note that with photographic methodologies, issues such as observer identity, the subject's point of view and what to photograph become problematic. In the event that the authors had omitted important photographs, respondents were asked directly if they were to take photographs of their experiences in the region, what they would take them of. Their response was then compared with the photographs taken by the researcher and aimed to minimize any bias the researcher may have had with regard to what they felt the main experiences of Hawke's Bay were. No respondent noted that they would have taken alternative images, although it is difficult to determine the validity of this response. Some respondents did have cameras with them, and, upon reflection, the researchers could perhaps have asked respondents to share the photographs they had taken and then compare these to their sample. Photographs presented to respondents were purposefully 'ordered' within the album so that photographs of heritage buildings were not all placed together or appearing at the front of the album, in order to eliminate any visual 'bias'.

The photo-based interviews were conducted over a number of different months, days of the week and times of day, including the shoulder and main tourism seasons, to enhance sample representativeness. Prior to introducing the use of photographs in these interviews, a brief introductory discussion with respondents was held and 'ice-breaker' questions were asked including: 'What have been your favourite experiences in Hawke's Bay so far?' and 'How long have you been in Hawke's Bay?'. The purpose of these questions was to 'ease' respondents into the discussion and to establish rapport with respondents. A relaxed environment where good rapport is established between researchers and respondents is important in an interview situation. Indeed, it is argued that in-depth subjective accounts of personal experiences can be facilitated only if the respondents feel at ease with the researcher and the style of the questioning (Miller and Glassner, 2004). It was felt that good rapport was achieved with respondents, as many respondents liked to share jokes or continue discussions after the interview was completed. The researchers observed that the refusal rate to the photograph-based interviews was slightly lower than that of previously conducted semi-structured interviews: the use of photographs made some people curious and thus more willing to participate in the research. No respondents commented that they did not like the use of photographs, although it is possible that for some people, photographs hold little or no significance to their travel experiences; this could be explored in future research.

Following the introductory 'ice-breaker' questions, respondents were asked to choose as many photos from the album that they felt most represented their experiences of Hawke's Bay. Respondents were not asked to select a pre-determined number of photographs, such as to choose the top five images that best represented their experience, as it was felt that for some respondents only one or two photographs may have represented their experiences of the region, while other respondents may have wished to choose, for example, nine or ten photographs. While this is different from the technique used in Fairweather and Swaffield's (2002) study, where the purpose of asking respondents to choose a set number of photographs (six) was to allow for ranking to occur, this was not an aim of the current study, and thus asking respondents to select a set number of photographs was deemed not appropriate. Rather, a meaningful response was sought that reflected the respondent's own selection of which photographs, and how many, were relevant. Respondents generally selected between three and five representative photographs, and a high proportion ($n = 46$; 70.8%) of respondents selected at least one photograph of a heritage building. The most popular photograph depicted a vintage car in front of an art deco building (Fig. 12.4); respondents noted that the vintage car 'completed' the image and made the 1930s' heritage building experience more authentic.

After respondents had selected their photographs, they were asked to discuss why they had chosen those photographs and whether they had any stories or experiences they could share about the images they had selected. If respondents did not explain their reasons for choosing each photograph, they were prompted to clarify their reasons for selection, in order to ensure important information was not overlooked. Respondents were also asked why they had, or had not, included any heritage buildings in the selection of their photographs and their reasons for this. This question acted as a 'lead-in' to a more focused discussion on the influence of heritage buildings in shaping the experiences they had gained. In particular, the key questions asked were: 'What have these buildings added to your experience of the region?' and 'Have you got any stories/experiences you can share with me about the buildings in particular?'. The questions were designed to facilitate open-ended inductive discussion, and the laddering technique was often applied to probe responses (as will be discussed later in this chapter).

The authors advocate the use of photographs in cultural tourism research, as they provided a richness of data that brought the different dimensions of the experience and personal narratives to the fore. Notably, the photographs helped build rapport with respondents to yield information that might not otherwise have been gained, especially when used in conjunction with an interview probing technique such as the laddering technique. To illustrate, a number of respondents discussed the colours of the heritage buildings and referred to the photographs to illustrate their point. A number of respondents noted that they most enjoyed the buildings that were brightly coloured or 'pastel' coloured. Indeed, when selecting photographs of Hawke's Bay's heritage buildings in response to the question 'Which of these photographs most represent your experiences of Hawke's Bay?', most respondents chose photographs that were brightly coloured. Through prompts such as 'Why are the colours of the buildings meaningful

to you?' and 'Why is that important to you?', rich data emerged. For example, it was found that, for some, the colours of the heritage buildings evoked nostalgic experiences of their childhood or helped to transport them to a 'magical fantasy land', 'free from the stresses of modern life'.

The photographs allowed respondents to transport themselves back to the experience to recall it more accurately. This is a pertinent finding, in that a key consideration of the study of tourists' experiences is that there is often 'slippage' or 'leakage' in memory when one is asked to recall a certain experience (Denzin and Lincoln, 1994; Beeho and Prentice, 1997). Potentially, photographs can reduce the impact of this. In some instances, the photo-based interviews also elicited deep emotional responses from respondents. Emotion too is a key element of experience (Richins, 1997; Schanzel and McIntosh, 2000; Bigne and Andreu, 2004). A number of respondents found that certain aspects of the presented photographs acted as a trigger to their memories. For example, one respondent noted that the doors on one of the photographed buildings she had experienced had reminded her about a cinema that she used to visit when she was young. Another respondent became tearful at one of the photographed buildings (Fig. 12.6) because it reminded her of her childhood and, in particular, the time she had spent with her father, who had recently passed away. The emotion the photographs stirred for this respondent can be illustrated from her quote:

> I come from northern England and I used to go on holidays when I was young and I remember the art deco back then (*pauses and speaks with emotion in her voice*): I wish I could have brought my dad here; he would have loved it; it reminds me of where I grew up (*sees photograph of Napier's theatre and gets teary*). Gosh, look at the entrance to that building and the beautiful designs; that is exactly like the theatre my dad used to take me to when I was a young girl!

Through eliciting emotional responses such as this, the photographs helped the authors to delve deeply into the layered experiences of respondents and uncover the personal, and often highly significant, meaning of these experiences to tourists' lives. This finding adds support to Ziller (1990), who suggests that photographs help to yield rich descriptions and embellish stories of a phenomenon.

The photo-based interview method, as discussed in this study, does, like all other research methods, have limitations. Ideally, the researchers envisioned providing respondents with a disposable camera and asking them to capture their own experiences of the region, in the hope of facilitating further inductive analysis; at the end of their time in the region they would then return for an interview. This would essentially remove the chance for researcher bias in what photographs were taken and would ensure that tourists' experiences were grounded in the realities they themselves described (Prentice et al., 1998). While respondents were asked if they would have taken any alternative photographs to the researchers, this approach is still not ideal, as the researchers still have control over, for example, the type, size, number, angles and presentation of photographs. Conversely, allowing the researcher to have control over the selection of images enables commonalities to be measured across the sample in order to, for example, ensure that the incidence of specific attractions, such as heritage buildings, can be evaluated within tourists' experiences of a region.

As an alternative to photographs, video could be considered as a method to 'explore the narratives of experiences and lived cultural practices of tourists and of their foci' (Feighy, 2003: 82). The potential of video in exploring tourists' experiences is, like photographs, under-researched, but it is thought to offer enormously rich visual insight, which is important in 'experience-rich tourism research' (Feighy, 2003; see also Chapter 11). Owing to financial constraints, and the fact that most respondents did not spend long periods of time in the region, these approaches were not taken, but they are recommended for future exploration.

However, no one approach is likely to be wholly ideal, as tourists themselves are likely to 'edit' some of the photographs or other visual imagery they share with researchers. In particular, tourists may not choose to share certain photographs that they feel present them in ways they do not want to be seen (Prosser, 1992). Researchers must also be aware of the ethical issues associated with visual methods. Specifically, Sontag (1977) argues that through sharing photographs and discussing why they have been selected and the personal meaning of them, tourists are seeing themselves in ways they have not previously thought of. As such, researchers must show caution in their approach and respect to respondents' reported experiences; it may be that, in some cases, tourists may be unearthing thoughts and feelings that are challenging and cause them to question or relive aspects of their lives. As noted in the current research, personal memories of respondents' pasts were revealed through the photographs, and this process could potentially be cathartic or traumatic to the individual.

Application of Laddering Technique Principles to In-depth Interviewing

As mentioned above, in order to probe more personal responses to the photographs, the photo-based interviews employed the principles of the laddering technique (Reynolds and Gutman, 1988; Botterill, 2001; McIntosh and Thyne, 2005). The laddering technique has been used in a number of previous studies that have sought to elicit the experiential dimensions of tourism (for example, Botterill and Crompton, 1996; Beeho and Prentice, 1997; McIntosh and Prentice, 1999; Botterill, 2001; McIntosh and Siggs, 2005; McIntosh and Thyne, 2005). It is associated with means–end theory (Gutman, 1982), which focuses on the linkages between product attributes (means), their consequences for consumers and the personal values these consequences reinforce (ends) (Reynolds and Gutman, 1988). This technique has been widely used in marketing to help respondents think critically about a product's attributes and their personal motivations

(Reynolds and Gutman, 1988; Gengler and Reynolds, 1995); that is, it is used as an interview probing technique to link people's values with their consumption. The probes are designed to force people up the 'ladder' of abstraction, from the concrete 'means' of first-response reasons to more abstract 'ends' or personal values of their actions. To illustrate the means–end chain, Gengler and Reynolds (1995) note that a brand of dog food may be 'dry and crunchy' (attribute). The dog owner believes that these attributes will consequently give their dog 'cleaner teeth' (benefit). This consequence allows the owner to fulfil a personal value: that of being a responsible and loving dog owner. This example illustrates that the laddering technique furthers the capture and recording of personal values as expressed by respondents in their own words, thereby facilitating inductive analysis (Prentice *et al.*, 1998). When employing the laddering technique, follow-up probing questions (laddering) are used to encourage respondents to think on a more emotional level and in terms of what they value by asking them, 'Why is that important to you?' It is argued that this allows for in-depth experiences to be determined and allows researchers to sense the layering of meanings associated with tourists' cultural experiences (Pearce, 1990). Thus, through follow-up questions, researchers can delve even deeper into the subjective nature of experiences tourists give in their own words (Botterill, 2001). For the current study, only the principles of the means–end chain, using the laddering technique, were followed, as means–end chain theory was originally based on a quantitative model of consumers' cognitive structures and involves structural examination of the relationship between attributes, benefits and values (Klenosky *et al.*, 1998; McIntosh and Thyne, 2005). Through following the principles only of means–end chain theory, the current authors could maximize the benefits of a qualitative approach to exploring tourists' experiences.

Within the current study, key interview questions that utilized the laddering technique included: 'What have the heritage buildings added to your experience of the region?' ('Why was that important to you'?) and 'Have you got any stories or experiences that you can share with me about the buildings in particular?' ('Why was that important to you?'). Through the use of probing questions, rich narratives were reported, as tourists were able to give personal meaning and content to the experiences that they had gained. For example, one respondent used the heritage buildings to 'transport' herself back to her childhood and to reminisce fondly:

> (*Have you got any stories or experiences that you can share with me about the buildings in particular?*) Napier reminds us of England when we were young – and the 1920s' theme reminds me of my parents. They used to wear these funny hats and would have grown up in a place just like this. (*Why is that important to you?*) I think the presence of these buildings brings back memories that are nice to think about.

The laddering technique provided rich insight into the personal meaning tourists attributed to their experiences and worked in synergy with the photographs to reveal personal narratives. Specifically, on a number of occasions, the photographs unearthed experiential elements that would probably not have been revealed without further probing; through the laddering technique, these experiential elements could then be explored in detail and added significant richness to the data. To illustrate, one respondent noted that, for her, a photograph of a heritage building that was once a fire station (Fig. 12.6) held personal meaning. When prompted: 'What is it about this photograph that is meaningful to you?' the respondent noted that 'My brother is a firefighter and I haven't seen him for a while. This building just made me think about him and sometimes we've had together'. Without the use of laddering, this depth of experience would not have been yielded; specifically, through laddering, which requires people to think more critically, the personal meaning of this particular building to the respondent came to the fore.

The laddering technique requires careful ethical consideration and a high degree of researcher skill. For instance, in certain situations, researchers must determine whether it is ethical to continue probing respondents if they are drawing out particularly emotional or personal information. The current researchers encountered this dilemma when one respondent cried from the grief of having lost her father, prompted by the memory of a particular style of building; rich information was being yielded but the researchers did not want to unnecessarily upset the respondent. Certainly, for the laddering technique to be effective, a strong rapport is required between researcher and respondent: generally respondents will not share their innermost experiences and feelings with a researcher if they do not trust them (Li, 2000; Sandoval and Adams, 2001). For effective laddering to occur, respondents must feel relaxed, that they are not being judged and, ideally, a researcher will tell them that there are no right or wrong answers (Reynolds and Gutman, 1988). Researchers need to be particularly skilled in the art of active listening and know when to interject or to allow respondents to continue. Often the current authors felt that the richest insight into tourists' experiences came after a significant pause, during which respondents had time to think deeply about the question being asked. Inexperienced researchers could feel uncomfortable during times of silence and might seek to fill this with interjection; potentially then, key insight could be lost.

The laddering technique presents further challenges to the researcher because often, owing to the abstract nature of discussion, the researcher may feel they are losing control of the interview (Reynolds and Gutman, 1988). Using the question 'why?' may also be viewed as judgemental by some in the context of personal probing, and thus it is imperative that the researcher creates an empathetic environment and allows the respondent to believe that responses are simply being recorded and not judged (Reynolds and Gutman, 1988). The laddering technique also will not work in every situation or with every tourist. Reynolds and Gutman (1988) noted that there are two common difficulties associated with the laddering technique. First, even with probing, respondents may not 'know the answer', and thus a ladder cannot be effectively formed. Secondly, owing to the sensitive nature of certain discussions, respondents may act with aggression towards the interviewer, go 'into their shell' or start to 'waffle'; some people will simply not 'open up' to researchers. The current authors did encounter this on a few occasions, where respondents showed they were guarded by simply repeating their answers or responding in very short sentences. To counter this, Reynolds and Gutman (1988) suggest that researchers may turn the situation into a third-person role-play, tell the respondent something personal about themselves in order to make the respondent feel less inhibited by comparison and/or approach the question at a later time.

Critics of the laddering technique argue that the approach may force connections between values and behaviour that may hold no meaning to the respondent or suggest that underlying knowledge may not have a hierarchical structure (McIntosh and Thyne, 2005). The effectiveness of laddering theory has also not been sufficiently explored from a non-Western perspective; however, McIntosh and Thyne (2005) argue that as personal values associated with tourism are grounded in the words of tourists themselves, laddering may present a more suitable method for cross-cultural application than, for example, culturally predetermined value scales.

Conclusion

This chapter supports a growing body of literature which advocates that photographs have much to offer experiential researchers, particularly so because they can yield rich insight into the personal meaning of tourists' experiences (Albers and James, 1988; Groves and Timothy, 2001; Fairweather and Swaffield, 2002; Garlick, 2002; Denzin and Lincoln, 2003). Specifically, this study demonstrates that photographs can provide support for the preservation of buildings within a townscape as the important ways they contribute to tourists' experiences are recorded. They are able to help elicit rich and personal narratives, can act as a novelty for respondents, thus potentially increasing response rate and respondent interest, and can act as a trigger in helping tourists to remember aspects of their life or the consumption experience. We argue that the potential of photographs in exploring tourists' experiences is particularly enhanced when combined with the laddering probing technique, which encourages respondents to think critically and to provide 'thick' descriptions of experience.

Conceptually, tourists' experiences have developed from being seen as holding largely peripheral significance to one's life (Lowenthal, 1962; Boorstin, 1964) to now constituting an integral, central and deeply meaningful part of many people's lives (Cohen, 1979; Noy, 2004; Uriely, 2005; Zahra, 2006). Specifically, tourists' experiences are now viewed as being personal, subjective, heterogeneous and inseparable from tourists' wider lives (Munt, 1994; Crouch, 2000; Uriely, 2005). However, it is argued that within tourism research there remains a need to delve deeper into the personal meaning tourism holds for individuals and situate this within the wider context of tourists' lives (Cohen, 1979; Larsen *et al.*, 2007). From a cultural tourism perspective, Timothy (1997) argues that there remains a significant gap in the literature looking at the more individualized, personal meanings that tourists place on their cultural and heritage experiences. The current authors argue that it is within this context that creative research methods such as photograph-based interviews using the laddering technique have much to offer cultural tourism research. In particular, photographs are central to many tourists' lives: this can be seen through the fact that many people take photographs to record and symbolize meaningful events, experiences and interactions. As such, they are able to take researchers into the everyday world of respondents and help researchers to explore the personal meaning of the experience to tourists' wider lives (Denzin and Lincoln, 2003). It is perhaps here that the true potential of photographs and the laddering technique lies.

References

Albers, P.C. and James, W.R. (1988) Travel photography: a methodological approach. *Annals of Tourism Research* 15(1), 134–158.

Art Deco Trust (2005) Art Deco Napier: New Zealand. Available at: www.artdeconapier.com (accessed 5 August 2005).

Ateljevic, I., Harris, C., Wilson, E. and Collins, F. (2005) Getting 'entangled': reflexivity and the 'critical turn' in tourism studies. *Tourism Recreation Research* 30(2), 9–21.

Ayikoru, M. and Tribe, J. (2005) Enhancing the interpretive and critical approaches to tourism inquiry through discursive semiotic analysis. *International Conference on Critical Tourism Studies, on Embodying Tourism Research: Advancing Critical Approaches*. Dubrovnik, Croatia.

Beeho, A.J. and Prentice, R.C. (1997) Conceptualizing the experiences of heritage tourists: a case study of New Lanark World Heritage Village. *Tourism Management* 18(2), 75–87.

Beyer, J.M. (1992) Researchers are not cats – they can survive and succeed by being curious. In: Stablein, P.F.R. (ed.) *Doing Exemplary Research*. Sage Publications, London, pp. 65–72.

Bharath, B.M., Josiam, M., Mattson, M. and Sullivan, P. (2004) The histronaut: heritage tourism of Mickey's Dining Car. *Tourism Management* 25(4), 453–461.

Bigne, J.E. and Andreu, L. (2004) Emotions in segmentation: an empirical study. *Annals of Tourism Research* 31(3), 682–696.

Boorstin, D. (1964) *The Image: a Guide to Pseudo Events in American Society*. Harper, New York.

Botterill, D. (2001) The epistemology of a set of tourism studies. *Leisure Studies* 20(3), 199–214.

Botterill, D. and Crompton, J.L. (1996) Two case studies exploring the nature of tourists' experiences. *Journal of Leisure Research* 28(1), 57–82.

Cohen, E. (1979) A phenomenology of tourist experiences. *Sociology* 13(2), 179–201.

Colmar Brunton Social Research Agency (2003) Demand for cultural tourism: summary of research findings. Available at: www.creativenz.govt.nz (accessed 10 November 2004).

Crouch, D. (2000) Places around us: embodied lay geographies in leisure and tourism. *Leisure Studies* 19(2), 63–76.

Denzin, N.K. and Lincoln, Y.S. (1994) *Handbook of Qualitative Research*. Sage Publications, Thousand Oaks, California.

Denzin, N.K. and Lincoln, Y.S. (2003) *Collecting and Interpreting Qualitative Materials*. Sage Publications, Thousand Oaks, California.

Fairweather, J.R. and Swaffield, S.R. (2001) Visitor experiences of Kaikoura, New Zealand: an interpretative study using photographs of landscapes and Q method. *Tourism Management* 22(3), 219–228.

Fairweather, J.R. and Swaffield, S.R. (2002) Visitors and locals experiences of Rotorua, New Zealand: an interpretative study using photographs of landscapes and Q method. *International Journal of Tourism Research* 4(4), 283–297.

Feighy, W. (2003) Negative image? Developing the visual in tourism research. *Current Issues in Tourism* 6(1), 76–85.

Garlick, S. (2002) Revealing the unseen: tourism art and photography. *Cultural Studies* 16(2), 289–305.

Gengler, C.E. and Reynolds, T.J. (1995) Consumer understanding and advertising strategy: analysis and strategic translation of laddering data. *Journal of Advertising Research* 35(4), 19–33.

Gordon, A. (2004) Heritage and authenticity: the case of Ontario's Sainte-Marie-among-the-Hurons. *Canadian Historical Review* 85(3), 507–532.

Groves, D.L. and Timothy, D.J. (2001) Photographic techniques and the measurement of impact and importance attributes on trip design: a case study. *Loisir et Société* 24(1), 311–317.

Gutman, J. (1982) A means–end chain model based on consumer categorization processes. *Journal of Marketing* 46(2), 60–72.

Jennings, G. (2001) *Tourism Research*. Milton, UK, and Wiley, Australia.

Klenosky, D.B., Frauman, E., Norman, W.C. and Gengler, C.E. (1998) Nature-based tourists' use of interpretive services: a means–end investigation. *The Journal of Tourism Studies* 9(2), 26–37.

Larsen, J., Urry, J. and Axhausen, K.W. (2007) Networks and tourism. Mobile social life. *Annals of Tourism Research* 34(1), 244–262.

Lau, A.L.S. and McKercher, B. (2004) Exploration versus acquisition: a comparison of first time and repeat visitors. *Journal of Travel Research* 42(3), 279–285.

Li, Y. (2000) Geographical consciousness and tourism experience. *Annals of Tourism Research* 27(4), 863–883.

Lowenthal, D. (1962) Tourists and thermalists. *Geographical Review* 52(1), 124–127.

MacKay, K. and Fesenmaier, D. (1997) Pictorial element of destination in image formation. *Annals of Tourism Management* 24(3), 537–565.

Markwell, K.W. (1997) Dimensions of photography in a nature-based tour. *Annals of Tourism Management* 24(1), 131–155.

Masberg, B.A. and Silverman, C.H. (1996) Visitor experiences at heritage sites: a phenomenological approach. *Journal of Travel Research* 34(4), 20–25.

McIntosh, A. (1998) Mixing methods: putting the tourist at the forefront of tourism research. *Tourism Analysis* 3(2), 121–127.

McIntosh, A.J. and Prentice, R.C. (1999) Affirming authenticity: consuming cultural heritage. *Annals of Tourism Management* 26(3), 589–612.

McIntosh, A. and Siggs, A. (2005) An exploration of the experiential nature of boutique accommodation. *Journal of Travel Research* 44(1), 74–81.

McIntosh, A.J. and Thyne, M.A. (2005) Understanding tourist behaviour using means–end chain theory. *Annals of Tourism Research* 32(1), 259–262.

Miller, J. and Glassner. B. (2004) The 'inside' and the 'outside': finding realities in interviews. In: Silverman, D. (ed.) *Qualitative Research: Theory, Method, and Practice*. Sage, London, pp. 99–112.

Morgan, D., Moore, K. and Mansell, R. (2005) Adventure tourists on water. Linking expectations, affect, achievement and enjoyment to the sports tourism adventure. *Journal of Sports Tourism* 10(1), 73–88.

Munt, I. (1994) The 'other' postmodern tourism: culture, travel and the new middle class. *Theory, Culture and Society* 11(3), 101–123.

Noy, C. (2004) This trip really changed me: backpackers' narratives of self-change. *Annals of Tourism Research* 31(1), 78–102.

O'Dell, T. (2005) Experiencescapes: blurring borders and testing connections. In: O'Dell, T. and Billing, P. (eds) *Experiencescapes: Tourism, Culture and Economy*. Copenhagen Business School, Copenhagen, pp. 1–14.

Otto, J.E. and Ritchie, J.R.B. (1996) The service experience in tourism. *Tourism Management* 17(3), 165–174.

Palmer, C. (1999) Tourism and the symbols of identity. *Tourism Management* 20(3), 313–321.

Pearce, P.L. (1990) Farm tourism in New Zealand. A social situation analysis. *Annals of Tourism Research* 17(3), 337–352.

Pearce, P.L. (2005) *Tourist Behaviour, Themes and Conceptual Schemes*. ChannelView Publications, Clevedon, UK.

Pine, B.J. and Gilmore, J.H. (1999) *The Experience Economy*. Harvard University Press, Cambridge, Massachusetts.

Powe, N.A. and Willis, K.G. (1996) Benefits received by visitors to heritage sites: a case study of Warkworth Castle. *Leisure Studies* 15(4), 259–275.

Prentice, R.C., Witt, S.F. and Hamer, C. (1993) The experience of industrial heritage: the case of Black Gold. *Built Environment* 19(2), 137–146.

Prentice, R.C., Witt, S.F. and Hamer, C. (1998) Tourism as experience: the case of heritage parks. *Annals of Tourism Research* 25(1), 1–24.

Prosser, J. (1992) Personal reflections on the use of photography in an ethnographic case study. *British Education Research Journal* 18(4), 397–412.

Reynolds, T.J. and Gutman, J. (1988) Laddering theory, method, analysis and interpretation. *Journal of Advertising Research* 28(1), 13–32.

Richins, M. (1997) Measuring emotions in the consumption experience. *Journal of Consumer Research* 24(2), 127–146.

Sandoval, V.A. and Adams, S.H. (2001) Subtle skills for building rapport. *The Law Enforcement Bulletin* 70(8), 1–9.

Schanzel, H.A. and McIntosh, A.J. (2000) An insight into the personal and emotive context of wildlife viewing at the Penguin Place, Otago Peninsula. *New Zealand Journal of Sustainable Tourism* 8(1), 36–52.

Silberberg, T. (1995) Cultural tourism and business opportunities for museums and heritage sites. *Tourism Management* 16(5), 361–365.

Simonson, I., Carmon, Z., Dahr, R., Drolet, A. and Nowlis, S.M. (2001) Consumer research: in search of identity. *Annual Review of Psychology* 52(1), 249–275.

Sontag, S. (1977) *On Photography*. Penguin Books, London.

Statistics New Zealand (2006) 2006 Census of Population and Dwellings. Available at: www.stats.govt.nz (accessed 9 January 2007).

Timothy, D.J. (1997) Tourism and the personal heritage experience. *Annals of Tourism Research* 34(3), 751–754.

Tourism Research Council New Zealand (2005) Hawke's Bay RTO. Available at: www.trcnz.govt.nz (accessed 16 September 2005).

Trapp-Fallon, J.M. (2003) Searching for rich narratives of tourism and leisure experiences: how oral history could provide an answer. *Tourism and Hospitality Research* 4(4), 297–306.

Tribe, J. (2005) New tourism research. *Tourism Recreation Research* 30(2), 5–8.

Turley, S.K. (2001) Children and the demand for recreational experiences: the case of zoos. *Leisure Studies* 20(1), 73–88.

Uriely, N. (2005) The tourist experience: conceptual developments. *Annals of Tourism Research* 32(1), 199–216.

Van Manen, M. (1990) *Researching Lived Experience*. State University of New York Press, Albany, New York.

Walle, A.H. (1997) Quantitative versus qualitative tourism research. *Annals of Tourism Research* 24(3), 524–536.

Willson, G. and McIntosh, A. (2007) Heritage buildings and tourism: an experiential view. *Journal of Heritage Tourism* 2(2), 75–93.

Zahra, A. (2006) The unexpected road to spirituality via volunteer tourism. *Tourism: an Interdisciplinary Journal* 54(2), 173–185.

Ziller, R.C. (1990) *Photographing the Self*. Sage Publications, Thousand Oaks, California.

13 Measuring the Image of a Cultural Tourism Destination through the Collage Technique

Ana M. González Fernández, María Carmen Rodríguez Santos
and Miguel Cervantes Blanco

Introduction

Image is becoming an increasingly important element in the competitive struggle to attract cultural tourists. In particular, 'new' tourism destinations, such as inland cities and towns, often start out at a disadvantage compared with traditional coastal destinations, which often have a stronger image among potential tourists. As a result, destinations strive to offer an image that is unique and clearly recognizable, in order to increase their attractiveness for tourists (Hunt, 1975; Goodrich, 1978; Britton, 1979; Mayo and Jarvis, 1981; Mathieson and Wall, 1982; Pearce, 1982; Woodside and Lysonsky, 1989; Ahmed, 1991; Ross, 1993; Milman and Pizam, 1995; Chen and Kerstetter, 1999; Andreu et al., 2000; Bigné et al., 2001; Beerli Palacio and Martín Santana, 2002). The search for a more effective image has been an issue for the inland areas of Spain for many years. In this chapter we apply the method of collage to the analysis of the image of León, a city in the inland region of Castilla y León.

Cultural Tourism in Spain and Castilla y León

Spain has for several years been vying for one of the top two positions in global tourism rankings, and it received over 57 million foreign visitors in 2008. These visitors came from a wide range of countries, primarily in Europe. However, domestic tourists are increasingly accounting for a greater portion of tourism income, and in fact more than 168 million journeys per year arise from this source (IET, 2009a,b).

Despite the fact that Spain offers a wide variety of forms of tourism (cultural tourism, rural tourism, health tourism, religious tourism, beaches and so forth), it is sun and beaches that Spain has specialized in for a good few decades. Nevertheless, changes in tourist behaviour that have taken place recently, particularly in the 1990s, have led Spain to start developing other potential destinations associated with cultural and natural resources and, at a local level, encouraging these locations to see the development of tourism as a new source of income. The interior regions of a country must explore ways of providing a distinctive appeal to tourists, promoting elements of their identity that mark them off from other, more conventional, 'sun, sea and sand' destinations. In this way, cultural characteristics acquire greater weight for inland destinations because they can be used as unique selling propositions.

Castilla y León is an inland region, located in the north of Spain, with a total area of 94,224 km² and 2,500,000 residents. This region is visited for a range of cultural reasons: it has heritage cities (Ávila, Salamanca, Segovia), cathedrals, monuments, castles, monasteries, historic routes (the Camino de Santiago, the Ruta de la Plata or Roman road to the south), archaeological sites (Atapuerca, Las Médulas), religious festivals (especially during Holy Week), food and drink, folklore and customs.

Since the early 2000s, tourism in Castilla y León has steadily grown, although not as fast as tourism in Spain as a whole. There has been a much greater increase in the number of foreign tourists visiting the region, which has risen at practically double the overall Spanish rate. This is significant, since it may mean that the region is becoming recognized at an international level as a cultural destination. As for Spanish tourists visiting this autonomous community, although there was also major growth in percentage terms, it was considerably smaller than the rise in the number of local tourists travelling to other parts of Spain.

In 2008, Castilla y León received more than 6.2 million staying tourists; including 1 million from outside S[...] source of domestic touri[...] mous community of M[...] lowed by the Castilla y [...] community itself (16%), [...] Galicia (7%). The main s[...] foreign tourists are in Eu[...]pe, principally from nearby countries, including France (21.4%), the UK, Germany and Portugal (with approximately 12% each), the Benelux countries (9.3%) and Italy (6.4%).

The main activities in which tourists engage when they visit the autonomous community of Castilla y León are linked to learning about the culture of the region (Fig. 13.1). This is because their main interests are visiting its monuments, becoming acquainted with its art and history, sightseeing in cities or towns and enjoying local foods and drinks, along with the landscape and nature.

Within the autonomous community, cities constitute the main destinations for domestic cultural tourism. In 2008, the city being studied here, León, received a total of 353,553 tourists, mostly from within Spain, although the number of foreigners coming to the city is growing year by year. Those visiting León do so principally between the

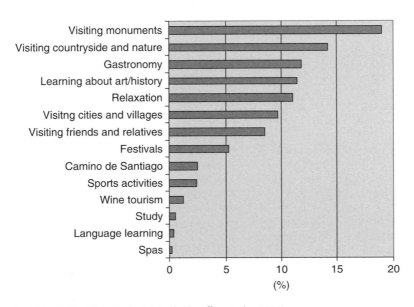

Fig. 13.1. Activities in Castilla y León (Junta de Castilla y León, 2009).

onths of May and October, with the peak flow being in summer. However, in recent years there has also been an increase in length of stay for those tourists coming to the city in winter.

Projecting the Image of Cities by Means of Collage Techniques

Each destination offers a variety of products and services to attract tourists. However, each visitor also has the opportunity and freedom to choose from a set of destinations (Crompton, 1992). Research findings indicate that different factors may have an influence on destination choice or on the attractiveness of one particular destination (Mayo and Jarvis, 1981; Sirakaya et al., 1996). Indeed, on many occasions human behaviour depends more on the image we have of a reality than of the reality itself, as all individuals have a psychological representation of the reality around them (Bergier, 1981; Gitelson and Kerstetter, 1990; Baloglu and McCleary, 1999a).

A number of image studies have been carried out to explore positive and negative perspectives of destinations in terms of several attributes (Pearce, 1982; McLellan and Fousher, 1983; Richardson and Crompton, 1988; Embacher and Buttle, 1989; Echtner and Ritchie, 1991). This research suggests that tourists' behaviour is influenced by the images they have of the destination (Hunt, 1975; Pearce, 1982).

Emphasizing the importance of images for tourists, Hunt (1975) argues that the images, beliefs and perceptions that people have about a destination can influence the growth of a tourist area as much as, or even more than, tangible resources. Destination image studies play a key role in the marketing and promotion of destinations, particularly for those who have never been to the destination before (Baloglu and McCleary, 1999b). Various authors agree that the theoretical framework is still insufficiently clear (Mazanec and Schweiger, 1981; Fayeke and Crompton, 1991) and that there are various different definitions of the

image of the destination, but no consensus has emerged. In many cases these definitions concern the factors influencing the way this image is formed, and this is also one area where research is lacking (MacKay and Fesenmaier, 1997; Baloglu and McCleary, 1999a; Beerli Palacio and Martín Santana, 2004).

There are three main factors that impact on the formation of the image of a destination in an individual's mind. The first is the cognitive image, which relates to the individual's knowledge and beliefs about the destination and is measured in terms of the resources that are attractive for tourists and which may lead them to visit the destination. Second is the affective image, which relates to the emotional responses generated by the destination and by its overall image. Third and final is perception, or the positive or negative assessment of the destination (Lew, 1987; Moutinho, 1987; Stabler, 1990; Gartner, 1993; Stern and Krakover, 1993; Alhemoud and Armstrong, 1996; Baloglu and Brinberg, 1997; Walmsley and Young, 1998; Baloglu and McCleary, 1999a,b). This latter aspect is directly determined by the cognitive and affective evaluations, with the cognitive evaluation in turn being shaped by the affective or emotional evaluation (Holbrook, 1978; Russell and Pratt, 1980; Anand et al., 1988; Stern and Krakover, 1993; Baloglu and McCleary, 1999a,b).

A review of the literature on the image of destinations reveals the existence of a series of factors influencing the formation of this image and, as a result, the fact that certain destinations are viewed by tourists as a good place to visit (Moutinho, 1987; Woodside and Lysonsky, 1989; Um and Crompton, 1990; Fakeye and Crompton, 1991; Mansfeld, 1992; Gartner, 1993). Among these factors are the sources of information tourists consult before visiting the destination (preexperience), also known as driving factors or agents in image formation, and the characteristics of the tourists themselves (Gartner, 1993; Stern and Krakover, 1993; Baloglu and McCleary, 1999a). The image of the destination may also be affected by the actual experience during the tourist's visit, although little empirical work has been done on this aspect (Beerli Palacio and Martín Santana, 2002, 2004).

The Collage Technique

Collage (Schlackman, 1989; Solomon *et al.*, 1999; Schiffman and Kanuk, 2000; Moisander and Valtonen, 2006) is a projective technique that can be described as 'a method in which participants are asked to represent a topic or phenomenon visually by composing and gluing together a collage of images, drawings and texts on a piece of cardboard or paper' (Moisander and Valtonen, 2006: 96). From this representation, an interpretation is made using a perceptual diagram that differentiates three perceptual levels: observation level, evaluative level and level of values and feelings. The observation level considers the most objective image about the resources of the city, including tangible resources, such as infrastructure, urban development and buildings, and intangible resources, such as traditions, customs and personality traits associated with the residents (Kotler *et al.*, 1993). The evaluative level reveals their attitudes towards each one of the issues identified in the preceding level and, finally, the last level reflects the subjective perception of the city, linked with the values and feelings that it transmits (Laaksonen *et al.*, 2006).

The current study uses the qualitative technique of collage to analyse the perceived image of León among residents and tourists. As a projection technique, collage allows responses to be obtained which individuals might be unwilling or unable to provide if they knew the purpose of the study. Moreover, it is very well suited to describing motivations, beliefs and attitudes operating at a subconscious level (Malhotra, 2008). Furthermore, collage in particular has certain advantages relative to other projection techniques. For instance, it permits initial stimulation of non-verbal activity, making it easier to gain verbal responses thereafter through descriptions of why certain images were selected and what they signify. Such responses would not be obtainable

through verbalization. In addition, visual stimuli activate the right-hand side of the brain and bypass more rational evaluation procedures, going deeper into the subconscious of individuals. The use of visual imagery allows access to the creative parts of the brain (Boddy, 2007). Further advantages of collage are that the use of illustrations as a stimulus to collaboration and the association of images and messages facilitate free expression by participants, reduce the influence of the interviewer relative to quantitative techniques such as surveys, trigger synergic effects in the contributions made by individuals and reduce potential losses of important components of the image.

Collage nevertheless also has certain disadvantages, like other qualitative techniques. It does not involve a structured direct approach; there may be bias due to interpretation; it requires the assistance of specialists in the technique; and it allows only limited statistical analysis of results (Malhotra, 2008). Other disadvantages specific to this method are that it is a time-consuming technique (Boddy, 2007); it can generate dimensions and attributes for images and levels of detail that are not comparable; and also subjective interpretation by the researcher may affect the perceptual map.

Visual and metaphorical research underlies the collage technique. This visual method has been justified by Zaltman (1996), who argued that thoughts develop as images, without which it is impossible to exchange social meanings in a verbal way. Thoughts are not word-based but image-based (Zaltman and Coulter, 1995; Zaltman, 1996, 1997). Moreover, metaphors, as 'the representation of one thing in terms of another' (Zaltman, 1996: 14), contribute to the expression of thoughts and phenomena (Goatly, 1997).

The collage technique has been applied empirically in other studies, for example those by Havlena and Holak (1996), Sijtsema *et al.* (2002), Belk *et al.* (2003) or Costa *et al.* (2003). Laaksonen *et al.* (2006) first applied the collage technique to measuring the image of a city. They developed visual collages through 20 focus groups representing different interests, 15 with local groups and five groups from outside the city. In these collages, pictures as well as adjectives describing the city were used. First, participants developed their own collages, which were discussed in a second stage within the group, raising the issues that were particularly important for individuals. Moreover, innovatively, in order to understand the interaction between the city and the individual, they used cartoon balloon questions: 'What do I think about Vaasa?', 'What does Vaasa think about me?'.

Analysing the Perception of a City's Image

Collage is a new technique based on visual methods that permit thought to be stimulated by showing images, attitudes and feelings in a wall display. These displays can be constructed in two ways, both of which are illustrated here. The first involves handing over to participants a selection of magazines, not in this instance linked to the city under study. The participants then choose photographs, words or phrases from them which for various reasons are linked to their image of the city in question. The second method is based on working with a large number of pictures and descriptive words preselected by the researchers. These are offered to the participants so they can freely pick those they linked, for any reason, with the city being considered, with the sole condition that there has to be a consensus among the group when it comes to including these pictures and words in the collage. Additionally, in both cases in this project, participants were given marker pens so that they could add other opinions that they could not find amongst the material initially provided. This technique was enriched by the different profiles of the people related to each of the various collages produced. Both techniques were applied to residents of the city and to tourists, these being the second grouping targeted by the city.

A detailed explanation will now be given of the process of gathering information, and how this was interpreted and processed, for each of the methods used for producing all of the collages.

Analysis of residents' perceptions of the image of León through collage techniques

Group dynamic sessions were held, using the qualitative technique of collage, with residents of León. The groups were selected on the basis of age and employment status.

Collage by young residents: technique – preselected attributes

This collage was produced by eight people aged between 22 and 24 years who had studied at tertiary level and were skilled workers (Fig. 13.2). In preparing this collage, the participants separated negative from positive points. They also specified those attributes that were not currently present in the city and which they felt should not be present either. With reference to the negative aspects of the city, they highlighted the scarcity of young people, contrasting with an ageing population, and the fact that this population tended to be very stubborn or aloof, and conservative. They believed that León lacks employment opportunities; there is little industry and few factories; and there is not much choice of leisure activities.

However, as positive factors, they stated that it is a small city, crossable on foot, where everything seems close by. Moreover, from an environmental point of view, it has no pollution and there are no traffic jams. They also emphasized late-night partying and eating typical local small bar snacks or 'tapas', which they related to food and drink. They felt that the food in this city is very good and added that the accommodation and catering trade is a way of life here. With reference to tourism, they linked this to the natural surroundings and believed that the climate was favourable for it. They considered this a good city for tourism, with many places to visit and welcoming for tourists. Finally, they described the city as tranquil, inexpensive, safe, clean and small: 'it's no bigger than a pocket handkerchief: everyone knows everyone'. They also set a positive value on the fact that it is a city surrounded by nature.

In order to interpret the collages, a qualitative factorial analysis was performed in two phases. During the first phase, tangible attributes were extracted and resources, both for tourism and for other purposes, were identified: human, historical, artistic and similar infrastructures. On a second level, subjective valuations were picked out that were linked to the previous aspects and the values with which the city is associated. The information derived from this interpretation served to shape a perceptual map based on two main factor axes, on which the significance of each piece of information was determined and placed on three levels:

observation level, evaluative level and the level of values and feelings. Figure 13.3 shows the perceptual map derived from the information gathered in collage 1.

Collage by residents: technique – free choice

The second collage was produced by eight people aged between 21 and 26 years, students who were not in work (Fig. 13.4). While the collage was being built up, the participants mentioned history and art in the city, quoting the cathedral, the churches,

(a)

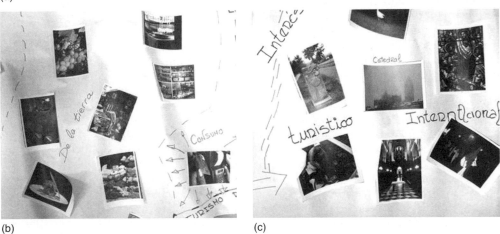

(b)

(c)

Fig. 13.2. (a) Overview of collage 1; (b) extract from collage 1 – consumption and tourism; (c) extract from collage 1 – international tourism.

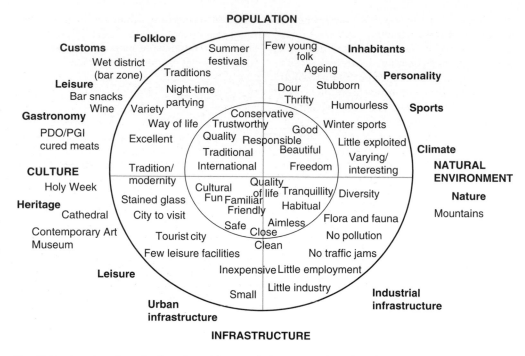

Fig. 13.3. Interpretation of collage by residents: technique – preselected attributes.

the Camino de Santiago, the state-owned luxury hotel with its ornate 16th-century façade, Holy Week and the more recent appearance of the Museum of Contemporary Art. With respect to history, they referred to the city's major role in the historical development of Spain. However, they wondered about adding a map of Spain: 'you have to look hard for it', as it is difficult to find and is not really recognized.

A considerable part of the collage was occupied with food and drink, since they felt that food and festivities are very typical of the city. They related this concept to the zone where bars offering snacks are concentrated, adding 'a small drink and a bite of something, the best thing in this city are the bar snacks', 'the wine is the best thing, wherever you get it'. Nevertheless, despite the good features that they pointed out in respect of the wet district (bar zone), they also mentioned its poor image and the dirt that there is in some places. They added that some bars do not pay much attention to hygiene.

With regard to shopping, they pointed out the significant role of the city's shopping centres. This is particularly because they attract many people in from outlying villages to the city on weekends, to go shopping and spend some time in the provincial capital. They highlighted the need to create new leisure facilities, but without cutting back in any way on those already in existence. They perceived the city as having the characteristics of being small, quiet, unpolluted and a place to 'recharge your batteries' and rest. However, they also pointed out that the traffic can be heavy and that there are too many vehicles on the roads. They also stressed the city's hinterland, considering it 'second to none', with rivers, mountains, snow, wild animals, caves and other features. They felt it had a zone of natural surroundings, suggesting tranquillity and restfulness.

They saw the general image of the city as 'beautiful as well as classical', saying that it is comfortable with the passage of time and that as it ages it remains beautiful. Their view was that it is a city that is cultured, but not modern or much fun. They believed it has numerous places to get to know, and added descriptions such as 'mature but beautiful', 'attractive and calm', and other similar phrases. With reference to the population, all the participants agreed that it was characterized by ageing, although a growing number of emigrants are coming to the city.

Another aspect they highlighted was the university. They pointed out that there are a large number of students, so that there are also young people in the city. They noted that although the city has its university, it is not a 'university city, on the lines of Salamanca'. In relation to this aspect they added that it is a city of contrasts between 'students and the elderly', 'modern and ancient'. They stressed how deep-rooted certain traditional customs are, although not mentioning any specific one, and also spoke of the mining and cattle-farming tradition.

Finally, they referred to cinema, making a comment on the 2006 film *Alatriste*, which according to them is identified with the province of León. Its leading actor, Viggo Mortensen, who is internationally known, was said to 'represent the area and he's even bought a house in a village in the province'.

Once a number of collages had been completed, it became clear that a certain level of saturation had been achieved (in principle when information started to be repeated). At this point a complete analysis was made of the resident collages in order to interpret the overall perception of the image of León (Figs 13.5 and 13.6).

Analysis of tourists' perceptions of the image of León through collage techniques

The same process of collage development was repeated for groups of tourists visiting the city.

Collage by Spanish tourists: technique – preselected attributes

The qualitative technique of collage was used with a group of nine young people (25–35 years) from various regions of Spain who had completed the first stages of tertiary education (Fig. 13.7). Participants first emphasized that the city evokes an image of tranquillity and calm, that it offers a great quality of life and is one of the few where one can eat 'marvellously well' (Fig.13.4). In relation to this topic, they noted that the culture of food and drink experienced in this city is very prominent ('all the food is delicious') and that it is a source of pride for the inhabitants. They stressed that in the wet district (bar zone) the small snacks are given free with each glass of wine bought, so that 'if you've had five drinks, you've had your dinner as well'. They also underlined the fact that the restaurants were good and the meat of high quality, in particular the giant grilled chops. With reference to tourism, their attention was drawn to the fact that there are many tourists, 'forever taking photographs with their cameras, whether they're Japanese or Spanish'.

People resident in the city seemed to them very traditional, with a culture strongly centred on the family. They stressed the contrast between the elderly population and the population of young people attracted by the university, with their 'night-time revels'. They felt that they were hospitable, friendly and amusing people.

When speaking of the city's heritage, they emphasized the gothic cathedral, 'the most attractive cathedral in Spain', and also other monuments, from the early medieval Romanesque and 15th- and 16th-century Plateresque periods and those built by Gaudí. They pointed out that it also has several important museums, such as the Museum of Contemporary Art, as well as other more traditional museums. People are extremely strongly committed to celebrating Holy Week. They also stressed nature, mountains and rivers, the sports that can be practised and the presence nearby of the Picos de Europa mountain range.

They felt that this is a city 'that oozes peacefulness and the good life', where you are always made to feel welcome, since the people are very hospitable. It is a very clean place, where attention is paid to ensuring mobility for the disabled by removing architectural obstacles. However, the climate is somewhat

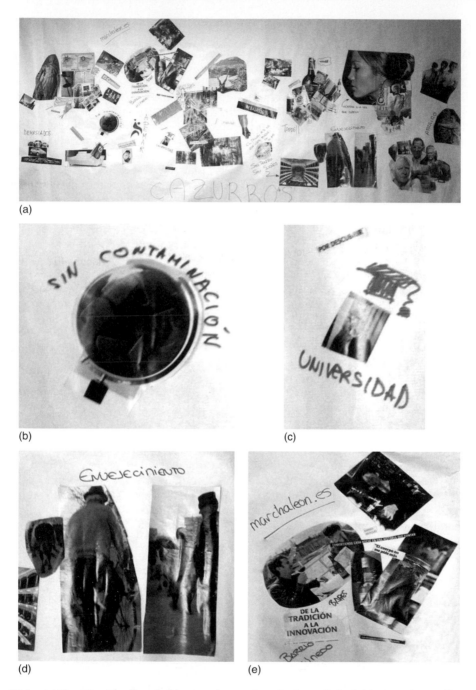

Fig. 13.4. (a) Overview of collage 2; (b) extract from collage 2 – 'no pollution'; (c) extract from collage 2 – 'university'; (d) extract from collage 2 – 'ageing'; (e) extract from collage 2 – 'old and new'.

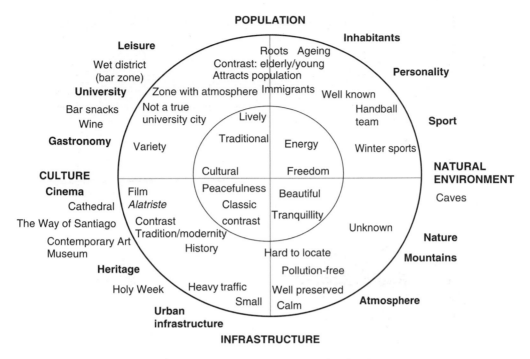

Fig. 13.5. Interpretation of collage by residents: technique – free choice.

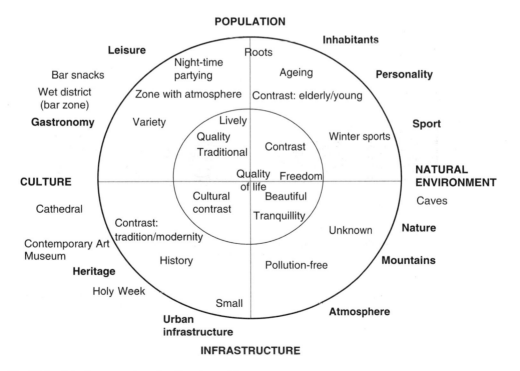

Fig. 13.6. Joint interpretation of collage by residents.

(a)

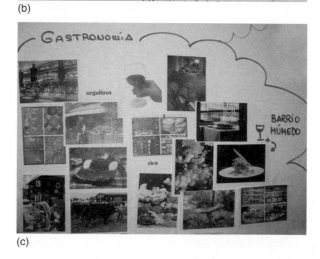

(b)

(c)

Fig. 13.7.   (a) Overview of collage 3; (b) extract from collage 3 – people; (c) extract from collage 3 – gastronomy.

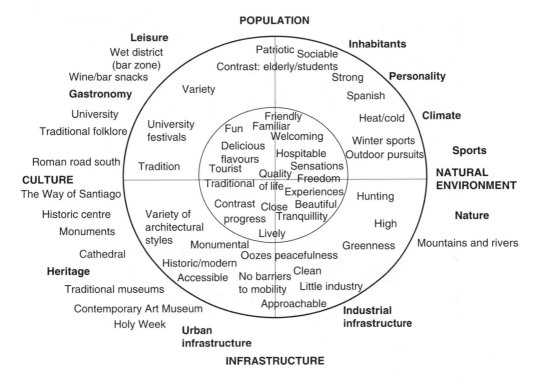

Fig. 13.8. Interpretation of collage by Spanish tourists: technique – preselected attributes.

extreme, since it is either very cold or very hot. They added that the university is well known, especially for some of its courses.

The perceptual map obtained from the information highlighted in the collage is presented in Fig. 13.8.

*Collage by foreign tourists:
technique – free choice*

The fourth collage was carried out with a group of six young people (20–25 years) from outside Spain who had a high level of education (Fig. 13.9). They came from a variety of countries, including Mexico, the USA, France and Germany.

A mural was constructed by selecting photographs taken from various publications, catalogues, magazines and so forth, as well as using texts, phrases, words and even drawings, with the aim of showing their perception of the image of the city being studied. While they were leafing through these materials, spontaneous comments

arose, such as: 'This is a place where nobody ever seems to sleep', 'For every child there must be at least 60 elderly folk', 'It's hard to leave', 'Every street always has something new' (this referring to building work). They loved the bar snacks, but felt that the bars are very dirty and could not understand the way that rubbish is thrown on the floor in such places. However, they agreed that the streets in the city are very clean and they were greatly impressed that the streets were hosed down every night.

Once the photographs and texts to be used in the collage had been cut out, the process of deciding which to use and how to place them began. This group placed the cathedral in the centre and around it the various aspects they wished to emphasize. On the left they placed several photographs of children and on the other side pictures of the elderly, since they felt that there was a large retired or elderly population that passed the time playing cards and walking dogs, which they saw as very striking.

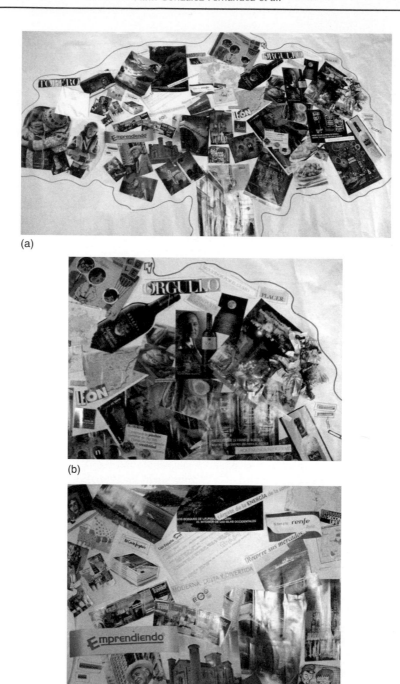

Fig. 13.9.   (a) Overview of collage 4; (b) extract from collage 4 – pride and pleasure; (c) extract from collage 4 – attractions and character.

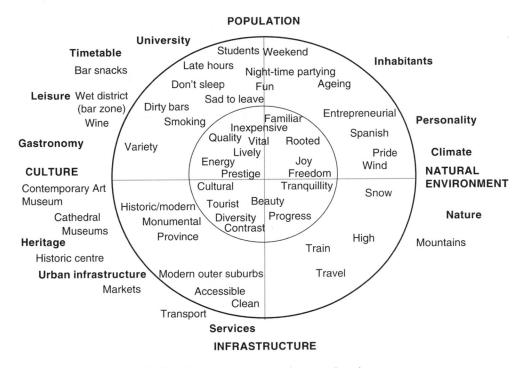

Fig. 13.10. Interpretation of collage by foreign tourists: technique – free choice.

On the right they grouped photographs that they wished to link with food and drink and with nightlife, especially student nightlife. They thought that people smoke too much, that wine is extremely cheap and insisted that the city's bars are very dirty, since rubbish is just thrown on the floor. This detail was reflected in the collage by sticking up a piece of heavily crumpled paper in contrast to a smooth blank sheet of paper at the other end, alluding to how clean they considered the city of León itself to be.

They felt that there was a great wealth of culture and major museums like the Museum of Contemporary Art. To encapsulate that idea they stuck on several photographs of monuments. They defined the city as ancient in the centre and very modern on the outskirts. They considered this contrast to be quite attractive. Another aspect that drew their attention was the daily timetable in Spain, and specifically in this city. Everything stops from two till five in the afternoon, but then life restarts and goes on until very late at night, as they saw it. At a couple of

points, brief mention was made of the province, but not much stress was laid upon this.

Once the collage had been produced, with data being gathered as it was built up, a perceptual map was again constructed. Figure 13.10 presents the overall interpretation of the image of Leon as it is perceived by tourists.

Once again, after the collages produced with each group of tourists had been interpreted, a perceptual map was drawn up to include all the relevant pieces of information (Fig. 13.11). The aim of this was to interpret the overall perception of the image of León by tourists.

Conclusions

The use of the collage technique illustrated here shows how such qualitative projective techniques can be useful in eliciting the image of cultural destinations from groups of residents and tourists. The intensive and interactive nature of the data gathering

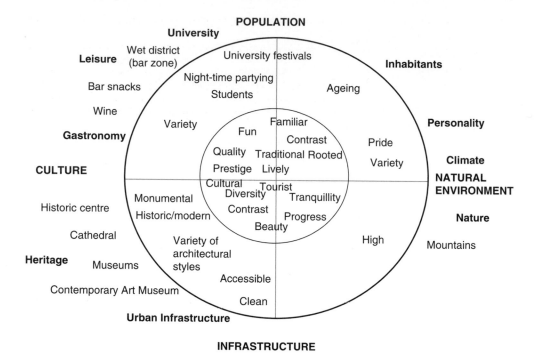

Fig. 13.11. Joint interpretation of collage by tourists.

generates information that would be difficult to obtain from surveys or even standard in-depth interviews. The use of visual material also allows participants to express themselves in different ways and to generate non-verbal information about the destination image. Given the importance of image in the marketing of cultural destinations, this is a potentially useful technique for exploring the perceptions of different target groups for a destination. It may be of particular value for those destinations, such as 'new' or 'non-traditional' destinations, which do not have a clear image in the minds of tourists.

References

Ahmed, Z.U. (1991) The influence of the components of a state's tourist image on product positioning strategy. *Tourism Management* 12(4), 331–340.

Alhemoud, A.M. and Armstrong, E.G. (1996) Image of tourism attractions in Kuwait. *Journal of Travel Research* 34(4), 76–80.

Anand, P., Holbrook, M.B. and Stephens, D. (1988) The formation of affective judgments: the cognitive–affective model versus the independence hypothesis. *Journal of Consumer Research* 15, 386–391.

Andreu, L., Bigné, E. and Cooper, C. (2000) Projected and perceived image of Spain as a tourist destination for British travellers. *Journal of Travel and Tourism Marketing* 9(4), 47–67.

Baloglu, S. and Brinberg, D. (1997) Affective images of tourism destinations. *Journal of Travel Research* 35(4), 11–15.

Baloglu, S. and McCleary, K.W. (1999a) A model of destination image formation. *Annals of Tourism Research* 26(4), 11–15.

Baloglu, S. and McCleary, K.W. (1999b) US international pleasure travelers' images of four Mediterranean destinations: a comparison of visitors and nonvisitors. *Journal of Travel Research* 38, 144–152.

Beerli Palacio, A. and Martín Santana, J.D. (2002) El proceso de formación de la imagen de los destinos turísticos: una revisión teórica. *Estudios Turísticos* 154, 5–32.

Beerli Palacio, A. and Martín Santana, J.D. (2004) Factores que influyen en la imagen de los destinos. *Annals of Tourism Research* 6(2), 357–384 [in Spanish].

Belk, R.W., Ger, G. and Askegaard, S. (2003) The fire of desire: a multisited inquiry into consumer passion. *Journal of Consumer Research* 30, 326–349.

Bergier, M.J. (1981) A conceptual model of leisure-time choice. *Journal of Leisure Research* 13(2), 139–158.

Bigné, J.E., Sánchez, M.I. and Sánchez, J. (2001) Tourism image, evaluation variables and after purchase behaviour: inter-relationship. *Tourism Management* 22(6), 607–616.

Boddy, T. (2007) Aberdeen Centre – Richmond, British Columbia, Canada (Bing Thom Architects). *Architectural Record* 195(2), 132–134.

Britton, R.A. (1979) The image of the third world in tourism marketing. *Annals of Tourism Research* 6(3), 318–329.

Chen, P.J. and Kerstetter, D.L. (1999) International student image of rural Pennsylvania as a travel destination. *Journal of Travel Research* 37(3), 256–266.

Costa, A.I.A., Schoolmeester, D., Dekker, M. and Jongen, W.M.F. (2003) Exploring the use of consumer collages in product design. *Trends in Food Science and Technology* 14(1/2), 1–15.

Crompton, J.L. (1992) Structure of vacation destination choice sets. *Annals of Tourism Research* 19, 420–434.

Echtner, C.M. and Ritchie, J.R.B. (1991) The meaning and measurement of destination image. *The Journal of Tourism Studies* 2(2), 2–12.

Embacher, J. and Buttle, F. (1989) A repertory grid analysis of Austria's image as a summer vacation destination. *Journal of Travel Research*, Winter, 3–7.

Fakeye, P.C. and Crompton, J.L. (1991) Image differences between prospective, first time, and repeat visitors to the Lower Rio Grande Valley. *Journal of Travel Research* 30(3), 10–16.

Gartner, W. (1993) Image formation process. *Journal of Travel and Tourism Marketing* 2(2/3), 191–216.

Gitelson, R.J. and Kerstetter, D.L. (1990) The relationship between sociodemographic variables, benefits sought and subsequent vacation behaviour: a case study. *Journal of Travel Research* 28, 24–29.

Goatly, A. (1997) *The Language of Metaphors*. Routledge, London.

Goodrich, J.N. (1978) The relationship between preferences for and perceptions of vacation destinations: application of a choice model. *Journal of Travel Research*, Fall, 8–13.

Havlena, W.J. and Holak, S.L. (1996) Exploring nostalgia imagery through the use of consumer collages. In: Kardes, F. and Sujan, M. (eds) *Advances in Consumer Research* 23. Association for Consumer Research, Provo, Utah, pp. 35–42.

Holbrook, M. (1978) Beyond attitude structure: toward the informational determinants of attitude. *Journal of Marketing Research* 15, 545–556.

Hunt, J.D. (1975) Image as a factor in tourism development. *Journal of Travel Research* 13(3), 1–7.

IET (2009a) *Movimientos turísticos en fronteras (FRONTUR)*. Informe Anual 2008. iet.tourspain.es.

IET (2009b) *Movimientos turísticos de los españoles (FAMILITUR)*. Informe Anual 2008. iet.tourspain.es.

Junta de Castilla y León (2009) *Boletín de Coyuntura Turística de Castilla y León. Resultados 2008*. Consejería de Cultura y Turismo. Dirección General de Turismo, Valladolid, Spain.

Kotler, P., Haider, D.H. and Rein, I (1993) *Marketing Places – Attracting Investment, Industry and Tourism to Cities, States and Nations*. The Free Press, New York.

Laaksonen, P., Laaksonen, M., Borisov, P. and Halkoaho, J. (2006) Measuring image of a city: a qualitative approach with case study. *Place Branding* 2(3), 210–219.

Lew, A.A. (1987) A framework of tourist attraction research. *Annals of Tourism Research* 14, 553–575.

MacKay, K.J. and Fesenmaier, D.R. (1997) Pictorial element of destination in image formation. *Annals of Tourism Research* 24, 537–565.

Malhotra, N.K. (2008) *Investigación de Mercados*, 5th edn. Pearson Prentice Hall, Naucalpan de Juárez, Estado de México, Mexico.

Mansfeld, Y. (1992) From motivation to actual travel. *Annals of Tourism Research* 19, 399–419.

Mathieson, A. and Wall, G. (1982) *Tourism: Economic, Physical and Social Impacts*. Longman, New York.

Mayo, E.J. and Jarvis, L.P. (1981) *The Psychology of Leisure Travel: Effective Marketing and Selling of Travel Services*. CBI Publishing Company, Boston, Massachusetts.

Mazanec, J. and Schweiger, G. (1981) Improved marketing efficiency through multiproduct brand names? An empirical investigation of image transfer. *European Research* 9, 32–44.

McLellan, R.W. and Fousher, K.D. (1983) Negative images of the United States as expressed by tour operators from other countries. *Journal of Travel Research* 22, 2–5.

Milman, A. and Pizam, A. (1995) The role of awareness and familiarity with a destination: the central Florida case. *Journal of Travel Research* 33(3), 21–27.

Moisander, J. and Valtonen, A. (2006) *Qualitative Marketing Research*. Sage Publications Ltd, London.

Moutinho, L. (1987) Consumer behaviour in tourism. *European Journal of Marketing* 21(10), 5–44.

Pearce, P.L. (1982) Perceived changes in holiday destinations. *Annals of Tourism Research* 9, 145–164.

Richardson, S.L. and Crompton, J. (1988) Vacation patterns of French and English Canadians. *Annals of Tourism Research* 15(4), 430–448.

Ross, G.E. (1993) Resident perceptions of the impact of tourism on an Australian city. *Journal of Travel Research* 30, 13–17.

Russell, J.A. and Pratt, G. (1980) A description of affective quality attributed to environment. *Journal of Personality and Social Psychology* 38(2), 311–322.

Schiffman, L.G. and Kanuk, L.L. (2000) *Consumer Behavior*, 7th edn. Prentice-Hall International, Upper Saddle River, New Jersey.

Schlackman, B. (1989) Projective tests and enabling techniques for use in market research. In: Robson, S. and Foster, A. (eds) *Qualitative Research in Action*. Edward Arnold, London, pp. 58–75.

Sijtsema, S., Linneman, A., Backus, G., Jongen, W.M.F., van Gaastive, T. and Dagevos, H. (2002) Consumers' perception of cognitive and affective health promoting food characteristics. In: *Proceedings of the Xth Food Choice Conference*. 30 June–3 July 2002, Wageningen, the Netherlands.

Sirakaya, E., McLellan, R.W. and Uysal, M. (1996) Modelling vacation destination decisions: a behavioural approach. *Journal of Travel and Tourism Marketing* 5(1/2), 57–75.

Solomon, M., Bamossy, G. and Askegaard, S. (1999) *Consumer Behavior: a European Perspective*. Prentice Hall, Barcelona, Spain, pp. 27–30.

Stabler, M.J. (1990) The image of destination regions: theoretical and empirical aspects. In: Goodall, B. and Ashworth, G. (eds) *Marketing in the Tourism Industry: the Promotion of Destination Regions*. Routledge, London, pp. 133–159.

Stern, E. and Krakover, S. (1993) The formation of a composite urban image. *Geographical Analysis* 25(2), 130–146.

Um, S. and Crompton, J.L. (1990) Attitude determinants in tourism destination choice. *Annals of Tourism Research* 17(3), 432–448.

Walmsley, D.J. and Young, M. (1998) Evaluative images and tourism: the use of perceptual constructs to describe the structure of destination images. *Journal of Travel Research* 36(3), 65–69.

Woodside, A. and Lysonsky, S. (1989) A general model of traveller destination choice. *Journal of Travel Research* 27(4), 8–14.

Zaltman, G. (1996) Metaphorically speaking. *Marketing Research* 8(2), 13–20.

Zaltman, G. (1997). Rethinking market: putting people back. *Journal of Marketing Research* 34, 424–437.

Zaltman, G. and Coulter, R.H. (1995) Seeing the voice of the customer: metaphor-based advertising research. *Journal of Advertising Research* 35, 35–51.

14 Ethnographic Research on Cultural Tourism: an Anthropological View

Xerardo Pereiro

Methods of Anthropological Research

The epistemological bases of anthropological research methods

A research project in anthropology must begin on the basis of specific epistemological, methodological and technical considerations. The epistemological framework of a project defines questions relevant to the paradigms that will be used and the research problem itself, as is common in scientific research in general. Overall, it theoretically frames the conceptualization of the research subject. It is on this epistemological basis that the design of the problem being researched is built.

Regarding the methodological considerations that must precede the initiation of a project, we must be clear about why certain social research techniques will be used, their meaning and significance, their underlying principles and their connection with the epistemological framework and the problem under study. In reference to the general area of technique, we must consider the specific social research tools that are most adequate to the problem and to the field being investigated. If the methods may be considered to be the way of organizing the research process to achieve our aims, the techniques are the specific procedures used in applying this organization.

The articulation of these three levels will allow a better design and development of a research project. Regarding the epistemological levels, in the social sciences there are two dominant approaches: quantitative and qualitative. For both of them, there are two possible perspectives:

- The perspective of viewing these approaches as oppositional and distinctive.
- The perspective of seeing these approaches as interrelated, which implies a mixed focus, supporting the idea of a continuum between both approaches and the combined use of both, depending on the specific research problems, contexts and situations being examined.

From the first perspective, we can establish a dichotomy originating in the historical beginnings of the modern social sciences (Table 14.1):

Positivism stresses the natural sciences as the model for the social sciences through the measurement of quantitative and manipulated variables in order to study their relationship, resulting in data which are used to verify specific theories. Researchers using a positivist approach look for evidence of the operation of universal laws through statistics, surveys, sampling and the generalization of results, appealing to

Table 14.1. Quantitative and qualitative foci in the social sciences.

	Quantitative focus	Qualitative focus
Spiritual fathers	August Comte, Émile Durkheim (positivism)	Max Weber
Principle	'Scientific' research connected to the natural sciences (e.g. physics)	Social phenomena are different from physical phenomena. Human behaviour is not mechanical
Objective	To measure things or phenomena, looks for facts and causes	To look for understanding ('verstehen'), subjective meanings and an understanding of the context
Methodology	Statistical methods, surveys and experimentation	'Ideal types', description of the concrete experience, its rules, social patterns and social meanings
Analysis of social reality	To look for universal laws through explanation, deduction, sampling, generalization of results, use of variables and verification of the answers and hypotheses	To try to understand the frameworks of the social actors To analyse the way people understand the world; inductive rather than hypothetical–deductive

Adapted from Hammersley and Atkinson (1994: 17); Taylor and Bodgan (1998: 15–30); Hernández Sampieri *et al.*, (2006: 3–30).

universal laws that are thought to remain constant and establish regular relationships between variables. Positivism differentiates between science and common sense and observes reality based on the senses according to the principles of traditional empiricism (Mauss, 1988; Durkheim, 1982).

The opposite stream represented by phenomenology and hermeneutics (Gadamer, 1978; Lisón Tolosana, 1983) defends a different type of research, arguing that the main objective of the social researcher should be to find out what happens in a place, the meaning of the actions for those involved and their representation. Social phenomena and social relationships, being different from natural and physical phenomena, cannot be understood in terms of cause and effect or on the basis of universal laws. Social actions obey intentions, motivations, attitudes, beliefs, values, meanings, senses, feelings and emotions, none of which can be reduced to a quantitative law.

From another perspective, the quantitative and qualitative approaches intersect in a mixed perspective (see Part II of this volume); even though one may dominate the other, they are both employed together in many research projects. This eclecticism justifies the idea that these two approaches are complementary and meets the need to provide complex answers to complex problems. At

the core of anthropological research, with its preference for qualitative techniques, are the units of meaning specific to particular contexts and the interpretation of their significance.

Anthropology acknowledges that there are other ways of accessing knowledge besides the scientific one – for example, art, poetry and literature, and photography. For anthropology, reality is socially and culturally constructed through historical processes. Humans are significant beings, who place a meaning on everything they do, think and say. The research topics are known through the mediation of the subject and his or her language. This does not mean that the subjectivity and inter-subjectivity characteristic of the human and social sciences cannot be scientifically controlled through objectification processes and mechanisms used to understand interpreted reality.

From a critical anthropological perspective, any social reality cannot be understood only through mathematical quantification. Issues such as happiness, sadness, pain and other feelings cannot be reduced to numbers. The whole production of scientific knowledge is exposed to ethical principles and values. The results of a scholarly research project should answer two questions: Whom does it serve? And for what purpose(s)? The research of a scientist who works on the creation of an atomic bomb and another who works to find a cure for cancer do not share the same ethical values. Therefore, knowledge production should be ethically controlled in its applications and social functions.

The Theoretical and Methodological Approaches of Anthropological Fieldwork

The methods of anthropological research differentiate anthropology from other fields. Methodology is not just a set of research techniques; rather, it is the set of principles that guide research. In anthropology, there are two fundamental methodological principles:

1. The importance of ethnography and of making observations in specific field sites, immersing oneself in the lives of 'Others' with the purpose of understanding them.
2. The comparison one can make between different human groups, time periods, genders and other social and cultural features.

Anthropological knowledge comes from human cultures and groups, rather than from laboratories (Burgess, 1997: 11), and therefore the anthropologist does research on what is most profoundly human: people's daily lives and the meanings associated with these lives. Yet we must recognize that knowledge produced by anthropology is linked to personal and social interests, not only academic and scientific ones, and thus it is important to reflect upon those factors.

The methods of anthropological research are known within the discipline as 'fieldwork' or 'ethnography'. At the same time, ethnography can be considered as a research technique guided by a theory or a discipline of social sciences. Anthropological fieldwork is what differentiates anthropology from other fields, and according to Velasco and Díaz de Rada (1997: 18) we can define this as:

- A methodological situation, which implies 'to be surprised, to have curiosity, to densely describe, to translate and to interpret' the social–cultural reality. In

this situation of meeting others, the researcher deals with their problems, their perceptions, their behaviour and their ways of life in their own terms.
- A process of knowledge based on a period in the field, through which the social–cultural meanings are studied in their own context.
- An experience of inter-cultural contact with the purpose of knowing 'Otherness' and on the basis of the assumption that there are different ways of doing fieldwork.

Therefore, anthropological fieldwork is not just a research technique or an instrument of primary data collection; it is something more. It is a way of inquiring and writing that produces descriptions and records on the ways of life of the studied subjects and of the anthropologist (Kenzin, 1997). Fieldwork is a way of producing knowledge based on the researcher's experience, i.e. a direct contact with reality, a knowledge obtained by repeated observations and/or by proof of ideas or hypotheses (Hessen, 1961).

Fieldwork is also a rite of passage for entering the anthropological tribe, which has its heroes and its myths. One of them was Bronislaw Malinowski (1973), who in the 1920s systematized the ethnographic method of fieldwork, in his work on The Argonauts of the West Pacific:

> It must be taken into account that natives, by seeing me constantly everyday, are no longer interested, alarmed or self-controlled because of my presence, since I stopped being a disturbing element of the tribal life I intended to study, which had been changed by my first approach, as it always happens in the primitive communities when someone new arrives.
> (Malinowski, 1973: 25)

> I had to learn to behave and, to a certain extent, I acquired the 'sense' of the good and bad native manners. And it was thanks to this, by knowing how to enjoy their company and to participate in some of their games and amusements, that I started to truly be in contact with the natives; and this is certainly the previous condition to be able to successfully carry out any fieldwork.
> (Malinowski, 1973: 26)

Malinowski turned into a sort of founding myth of anthropological fieldwork. His fieldwork was carried out in New Guinea in the 1910s, specifically in the Trobriand Islands (currently the Kiriwina Islands, part of Papua New Guinea), where he lived with the natives for 2 years, learning to coexist with them, their language and their habits. We can extract from Malinowski's work some guiding principles for fieldwork:

- Participate in the social life of the subjects being studied.
- Regard ethnographic data as capable of shaping a theory. The anthropologist knows that the persons about whose lives he or she does research produce 'native theories'.
- Provide a clear and coherent scheme of the social structure.
- Highlight the cultural rules.
- Study the daily phenomena, as well as the extraordinary ones.
- An anthropologist should clarify which data were obtained from his or her direct observations and which data were obtained indirectly (e.g. from others' reports of events).
- The anthropologist should collect reports from the informants, documents and data from his or her own observations of behaviour (this combination of methods sometimes being referred to as triangulation).
- The field diary is a necessary tool, in which must be reported: social agents, actions, spaces, peculiarities, repeated behaviours, etc. The following aspects of the social–cultural life should be taken into consideration: the mentality of the people being studied, native concepts, forms of expression, ideas, feelings, motives, the acts influenced by 'tradition', people's vision of the world. But above all what they feel and think as members of a given community (it is necessary to quote the native statements and to learn the native language).

Malinowski is considered to have invented the ethnographic method (Álvarez Roldán, 1994), thus breaking the former separation between data collection and theory elaborated by others and turning the anthropologist into a research instrument (Velasco and Díaz de Rada, 1997: 21). Other anthropologists who have decisively contributed to the invention of the ethnographic method were the Americans Franz Boas, Margaret Mead and Ruth Benedict.

As a methodological process, fieldwork makes the researcher describe, translate, explain and interpret the culture and the studied social relationships, what people say, what people do, what people think should be done, and the confrontation between what people claim they do and what they really do. Ethnographic description should be dense (Geertz, 1987), comprehensive and microscopic (Velasco and Díaz de Rada, 1997: 48), in order to differentiate between several behaviours, spaces and cultural rules, and to better interpret cultural meanings. To interpret is to discover the structural order of the society; it is to capture the – plural – meanings of the social–cultural reality.

Fieldwork follows a dynamic of spatial and cultural displacement in the search for Otherness. Therefore, first the researcher observes others from close by and with a certain intimacy, then does so from a further distance, and therefore builds up an interpretative frame with another lens and another focal length (Velasco and Díaz de Rada, 1997). Obviously there may be different ways of carrying out fieldwork (Velasco and Díaz de Rada, 1997), and hence there is a need to explain the conditions in which the fieldwork and the knowledge production are carried out. This is one of the major contributions of reflexive anthropology: a good way of addressing the theoretical and the practical problems of the research methodology is to walk those paths of the interaction between the researcher and the researched. Those interactions reveal power relationships, spaces where identity roles were negotiated and, in some cases, empowerment of the studied subjects themselves.

Fieldwork is a methodological requirement which consists of going from a distant relationship to the subjects to being in proximity with them, soon returning from this proximity to the distance, in order to build an interpretation and a comparison between the researcher and the others. Fieldwork can sometimes have a psychological status close to courtship (Buxó Rey, 1995), but it can also cause intensely human anguish, anxieties and fatigues, as reflected in Malinowski's field diary (1989).

Moreover, fieldwork may be considered to be a rite of passage for entering the anthropological tribe, a self-transforming experience, an initiation ritual and a double cultural shock: to become native and to re-become native (Peacock, 1989: 95). As a passing ritual, those who do not perform fieldwork are not, for many anthropologists, considered to be anthropologists, since fieldwork is part of the construction of the anthropologist's professional identity. Fieldwork is conditioned by the position that the anthropologist holds in political, social and economic systems. These agendas, often hidden, should be studied and made conscious in order to better understand the experience of fieldwork. This will help us to better understand the 'Rashomon effect' (Cardín, 1988; Heider, 1988) in anthropology, i.e. during our fieldwork the researcher does not select all the natives' voices but chooses some of them within the complex social reality. To reflect upon the causes of hearing some voices over others forces us to adopt a position of reflection and self-awareness.

Fieldwork is the basis for making comparisons between cultures, and its aim is to arrive at a good representation of the culture being studied. We may state that ethnography today is a 'fusion of horizons', an intercultural conversation without impositions (Gadamer, 1978). Ethnography is 'dialogical', a conversation with the Other, with the aim of increasing one's awareness rather than arriving at unanimity or truth. Ethnography is a way of negotiating differences; it is a 'trans-valuation', a way of learning to see ourselves anew after having looked at the others; it is to turn upon ourselves the view previously informed by contact with the 'Other'. It is also a bridge across which information goes from one human group to another; it is a kind of inter-cultural translation (Todorov, 1988: 9–31).

In order for ethnography to be good, it must necessarily be comparative. We may establish four aims as part of the goal of undertaking comparisons:

1. Comparisons between cultures: Us and the Others.
2. Comparisons across time periods, between the past and the present, or also between two historical times.
3. Comparison between two or more theories.
4. Comparison between the ideas held prior to fieldwork and the final ideas developed after the fieldwork is completed.

Comparison is born from diversity and from the need to analyse that diversity. The comparative method implies a search for similarities and differences, and, likewise, something more important: to question ethnocentrisms and rationalities that are unique to particular cultures.

Participant Observation as a Technique of Ethnographic Research

Ethnographic observation is a fundamental research technique in anthropology, along with others such as collecting censuses, genealogies, life reports, interviews or audiovisual ethnography. Additionally, ethnographic observation is a research attitude on the part of the anthropologist in the field. It is neither a merely qualitative nor merely quantitative methodology, as it may integrate both approaches. Its methodological principle is cultural relativism: observe others according to their own cultural logics and confront these observations with anthropological theories, categories, concepts, ideas and hypotheses about the problem being studied.

Ethnographic observation may be of two kinds according to Roigé i Ventura *et al.* (1999):

• With non-participant or external observation, the observer is not part of the actions that occur in the scenario, and the observed facts are easier to objectify owing to the distance that is maintained. But this kind of observation has the disadvantage of having little control over the information and limitations in accessing it.

- In participant observation or internal observation, the observer shares the life of the studied community, institution, organization or human group; he or she participates in their daily lives. In this second kind of observation, the anthropologist assumes a role in the field and apprehends the individuals' rules, values and perceptions, as well as the meanings of the observed behaviours, even though he or she risks inhibiting the studied subjects with his or her presence (the way the researcher's presence conditions the reactions of the subjects being observed is a factor that should systematically be taken into consideration).

The advantages of this technique are the richness and depth of social–cultural information produced in its own context. Data reliability is ensured with valid observation techniques, which will test what people say and think, by comparing these with what they do. Participant observation depends on the researcher's training and experience, but also on his or her rigour and commitment to an involvement with the subjects being studied.

The anthropologist should be accepted in order to be able to interpret the vision of the world from within the group. He or she must also be able to receive a normal and everyday treatment, which is often achieved only by investing a lot of time, inspiring trust and creating social networks of informants. The anthropologist is generally catalogued as a stranger or intruder (e.g. different ways of dressing), because of which the fear of the locals may be great at the beginning. At other times, due to his or her youth, the researcher may experience protectionism and paternalism by those being studied.

Classic fieldwork involves a stay and observation time that lasts for at least 1 year (description of ritual, agricultural and urban life cycles, etc.). Prolonged research produces richer and more reliable data, but applied anthropology has already taken into consideration techniques of 'quick valuation', which include spending less time in the field.

The big advantage of participant observation is that the researcher creates a text in its context, in its spontaneity. At other times, our presence somehow endangers and makes vulnerable people's spontaneity, by leading them to say what we want to hear. However, participant observation allows for researchers not to force the data; it allows them to develop a better understanding of culture through the awareness of coexistence among cultures. It thus enables access to restricted information. The researcher is the main collection instrument; he or she looks and observes with previously built categories but also with imagination and creativity. It is an exercise of empathy, of putting oneself in the other's shoes in order to better understand what is said (and what is not said), what is done and what is thought.

And although there is not a single model for conducting participant observation, according to Burgess (1997: 21) there are three types of observation:

1. To 'become a native', i.e. when the researcher learns to behave as a 'native' in the situation under study.
2. 'Hidden agent', in which the researcher tries to assume a largely unnoticed behaviour and frequently involves a dissimulated participation.
3. 'Lawyer', which is a situation in which researchers intervene in helping and improving the position of the studied individuals.

A problem with ethnographic observation arises when we apply it to our own social–cultural context. In this case, the objective will be to make strange what is familiar, similar to when we work on another culture, subculture or social group we have to turn the strange into the familiar. Presently, visual anthropology (El Guindi, 2004) allows us to study and re-study the text and the context of a research project. Therefore, it is a critical observation tool, but it is also a way of reporting and interpreting the field and the research problem.

Other kinds of observation are the following (Roigé i Ventura *et al.*, 1999):

- panoramic observation (global): deals with identifying problems and characteristics of the life of a social group:
- selective observation (focused): implies the delimitation of a specific scope, aiming at knowing it more in-depth;
- transversal observation: for example, the observation of organizations in all their complexity; and
- longitudinal observation: to follow a person or a group during a given period of time.

Ethnographic observation is definitely a research technique created by anthropologists and potentially usable by other social researchers. However, the anthropologist uses this technique in a distinctive way, as he or she follows the methodological and theoretical principles that are peculiar to anthropology.

Anthropological Research on Tourism

In this section we will question the relationship between anthropology and tourism. Even though we share the idea that the study of tourism is interdisciplinary (Tribe, 1997) and also comprises a distinctive field of work or arena (Ritchie and Goeldner, 1994; Smith, 1995; Callejo Gallego *et al.*, 2003; Phillmore and Goodson, 2004), we recognize that tourism also may have a monodisciplinary anthropological approach, which presents a coherent integration of specific theoretical, conceptual and methodological approaches (Graburn and Moore, 1994).

Following this line of thought, many anthropologists have reflected upon the relationship between anthropology and tourism. Some, such as Claude Lévi Strauss, who in his famous work *Tristes Tropiques*, confessed that he hated travel and travellers (Crick, 1995). The history of anthropology underlines the importance of missionaries, travellers and adventurers in the ethnographic description of the Otherness. Over time, the anthropologists themselves turned into travellers and became instruments for producing anthropological knowledge. Anthropology was built as a science of

social–cultural diversity based on these travels, which created encounters among people of different backgrounds. However, in this progression, the anthropologist rejected and avoided tourism and tourists (Crick, 1985, 1995), and only later did tourism turn into a legitimated anthropological object of study.

According to Edward Bruner (1989), colonialism, classic ethnography and tourism are phenomena that belong to different historical periods but have their origin in the same social formation and are variants of the expansion of the dominating powers. Criticizing the attitude of anthropologists that has led them to leave tourism out of their ethnographic studies, Crick (1995) stated that 'at the present time, in order to understand the world political economy, one cannot leave out the analysis of international tourism'. In anthropology, tourism, as research object and problem, is increasingly ceasing to be considered as something banal and shallow. It is therefore being less underestimated by academia. The interest of anthropology for the study of tourism is related to four main factors:

- The growth of the tourism industry is a fact that is impossible to ignore (Wallace, 2005). We live in a tourism world, which cannot be neglected as a social–cultural phenomenon. Anthropologists stumble, in their fields, into tourists and locals who produce tourism.
- When analysing cultural contact and its flows, it is difficult to explain culture as a process without considering tourism, as it is more and more present everywhere. We can say that tourism is an activity that consumes cultures (Santana, 2003: 121) and that the tourist is a kind of nomad (Urbain, 1993), carrying culture and causing its circulation.
- Tourism has turned into a producer of new cultural forms (MacCannell, 1992), which means that, in order to understand those new forms, it is necessary to study tourism, which is a good window for observing culture production.
- Tourism and anthropology are two forms of pilgrimage in the search for lost

meaning, wanting to demonstrate that one 'has been there'; both are practised with a round-trip ticket and involve a certain incommodity (Delgado Ruíz, 2002: 52).

And what is anthropology's role in the study of tourism? From our point of view, the contributions of anthropology to the study of tourism have been very positive and are of three specific kinds:

- Methodological: anthropology is distinguished from other disciplines by its focus on fieldwork and the holistic and comparative method (Hammersley and Atkinson, 1994; Gmelch, 2004). Anthropological fieldwork is based on participant observation and intensive coexistence with the human groups studied, in order to try to interpret empathically and understand the social–cultural problems addressed.
- Theoretical–conceptual: in order to understand tourism, an objective and functional definition is not enough; rather, it is necessary to ask social agents involved in tourism about the meaning it has for them. Anthropology has predominantly an integrated and subject-oriented approach to the study of tourism (e.g. holism, comparison and cultural relativism).
- The whole set of ethnographies that have helped us to understand such a complex phenomenon now comprise an important reference: the objective of these ethnographies is to interpret the role of tourism (e.g. the role of tourism in the re-invention and production of culture) and to help us better deal with the impacts of tourism, exercising, thus, the applicability of anthropology. These ethnographies are useful for creating guides for responsible tourism and may also turn tourists into better travellers (Chambers, 2005).

One of the most important journals of scientific research on tourism, the *Annals of Tourism Research*, was established by an anthropologist, Jafar Jafari, and approximately 15% of the published articles are authored by anthropologists (Wallace, 2005). This gives an idea of the weight of anthropology in research on tourism.

Methods of Anthropological Research Applied to Tourism

In the course of the study of tourism, the use of quantitative methods has been predominant (Dann *et al.*, 1988; Walle, 1997: 524). In a way, research has been dehumanized on behalf of a false 'rigour', which has produced, in some cases, sterile and superficial research. In recent decades, and since quantitative methods were alone unable to approach the key problems of the tourism field, qualitative methods have earned increased prestige and legitimacy (Walle, 1997: 526).

The value of both methodological focuses and also their limitations are recognized today, and hence some tourism researchers use mixed methodological approaches according to the research problems they are addressing (see Part II). On this point, Walle (1997: 535) is perfectly right when he states that the field of tourism must recognize the legitimacy of the diversity of research methods.

As previously mentioned, one of the disciplinary contributions of anthropology to the study of tourism is a methodological one. Since tourism is a complex human activity, the theoretical and methodological instruments of anthropology are critical for its holistic understanding. The anthropological methods and techniques are relevant for the following fields of tourism research:

- the study of the resources potentially convertible into tourism products;
- the interpretation of cultural and natural heritage as potential tourism resources and products;
- the analysis of the impacts of tourism on the host communities but also on tourists themselves;
- the role of tourism politics;
- the role of tourism marketing;
- the understanding of mediation in tourism (e.g. images, guides, agency);
- the analysis of tourist visitors;

- the study of tourist memories; and
- the study of tourism as a system that causes the mobilization of persons and the circulation of cultural meanings at a planetary level.

Anthropology is especially useful in the conceptualization and analysis of the social and cultural changes caused by tourism, of the effects and adaptations it leads to. Anthropological methods thus focus better and are more appropriate for investigating the meanings associated with social and cultural processes, the experiences and voices of the participants (Simpson, 1993).

Thanks to their ability to allow researchers to understand complex realities empathically, anthropological methods help especially to enter social universes such as native communities and institutional organizations such as hotels, companies, administrations and so forth. Therefore anthropologists are able to perform readings of proximity and intimacy, allowing us to see the plurality of perspectives and the complexity of tourism activities instead of reducing them to expressions of exoticism and folklore.

An Ethnographic Research Project: Kuna Tourism in Panama

Reflexive ethnography of the project on Kuna tourism

Anthropological research is connected with intellectual and personal concerns but also concrete biographical trajectories. My interest in tourism arose in 1997, soon after having concluded my PhD thesis in anthropology (Pereiro, 2005), when I was working in the Ethnographic Park of Allariz (Galicia, Spain). There I had to deal with tourists who visited the eco-museum and explored its cultural heritage. It was due to them that I was forced to re-read cultural heritage from the point of view of the tourists.

Previously, I had taken a doctoral course, in Santiago de Compostela, with Agustín Santana, a Spanish anthropologist who is an expert in the anthropology of tourism, and who had alerted me to the importance of tourism as a new mechanism of cultural change and production. In 1998, I started working in the Applied Anthropology Programme of the Universidade de Trás-os-Montes e Alto Douro (UTAD), then delivered on the Miranda do Douro campus, and in 2000 I started to teach the discipline of Cultural Tourism in the Tourism Programme of the UTAD campus in Chaves. The latter activity strongly motivated me to undertake theoretical reflection about tourism and to begin research projects within this area of specialization (see www.utad.pt/~xperez/).

In 2000, I met the Kuna anthropologist Cebaldo de León Inawinapi, and later encouraged him to prepare a research project about ethnic tourism among the Panama Kuna. This was a theme that, in that field, had not been approached in depth since the 1970s.

The initial questions that guided the research project were to investigate the role of tourism as a lever for social and cultural change among an ethnic group that seemed to control its process of tourism development politically. The Kuna from the Republic of Panama are a human group of approximately 60,000 people who live on the Atlantic coast of the country (2500 km² of rainforest), on the 365 islands of the Kuna Yala archipelago and in the urban centres of Panama. The Kuna have been much studied by anthropologists, due to their strong political autonomy and to their resistance to political domination (Pereiro and Inawinapi, 2007). So Cebaldo de León Inawinapi opened up the possibility of starting a project from Europe and of personally experiencing the similarities and the differences between a 'home anthropology' and an 'anthropology out of home', by performing ethnography of the tourism system in the context of the geo-political periphery. Another reason to start the project was the fact that Cebaldo de León Inawinapi was our 'gatekeeper' in the field. This factor would be a determinant during the project, as in the mediation with the Kuna, he mediated in getting the permission to research, in facilitating the contacts with people, in lodging, etc. Therefore, the integration period was shortened and a better communication with the Kunas was facilitated

In 2003, the research team, with the addition of Ana Rita Lopes, started work on Kuna tourism, in what may be considered as teamwork and a collaborative research with the Kuna (Greenwood, 2000, 2002).

The study developed in several stages. After a brief bibliographical review and the resolution of practical issues, in September 2003 the team started an exploratory field visit, with the purpose of designing a research project to be carried out. In that exploratory visit we visited the city of Panama and the Gardi region, the most touristic area of Kuna Yala (San Blas). Soon we made our first contacts in the field and asked for permission to develop our project from the highest Kuna authorities, represented in the Kuna General Congress (KGC). In the spring of 2004, Ana Rita Lopes went back to the field in order to perform anthropological fieldwork on the impacts of cruise boat tourism on the island of Gardi Suitupu (Lopes, 2004). In the summer of 2004, I made another field visit, with the specific purpose of studying the images that the tourism system had created of the Kuna and their political habits. During that stay, the team developed an intense bibliographical and documental collection, visited tourism projects and conducted exploratory interviews and debates with Kuna tourism business people.

During the summer of 2005, Cebaldo de León Inawinapi made a new field stay, working and analysing the environmental impacts of tourism in Kuna Yala, establishing contacts with the communities and researching their perception of tourism. In 2006, Cebaldo de León Inawinapi and I carried out a thorough study about the supply of tourism products and services in Kuna Yala. We conducted extensive participant observation in all the hotel projects (over 20) and interviewed their promoters, the workers at the hotel projects, the tourists and the sailas (or chiefs) of each community developing tourism. We also built live reports and censuses of tourism projects and of the tourists. Besides that, and still on this stage, we participated in debate groups

with the Kuna Tourist Business Association and the Tourism Commission of the Kuna General Congress; we consulted Kuna specialists and collected documental and statistical material, mainly in the city of Panama.

In 2007, the research team incorporated the Catalan anthropologist Mónica Martinez Mauri, who had already carried out intensive fieldwork in Kuna Yala (Martínez Mauri, 2007). In that year we undertook a field stay that allowed us to enlarge the units of analysis and the areas being explored. We investigated the new tourism supply projects in Kuna Yala, observed and informally interviewed tourists, explored cruise boat tourism, sailboat tourism and travel agencies. Additionally, we organized debate groups with Kuna tourism business owners and conducted interviews with politicians and tourism guides. The project is taking place between 2008 and 2011, thanks to support from the National Office of Science and Technology (SENACYT) of the government of the Republic of Panama. In 2008, the biologist Jorge Ventocilla Cuadros joined the research team; he has already conducted a significant amount of fieldwork among the Kunas (through the Smithsonian Institute of Tropical Investigations). The Kuna scholar Yadixa del Valle has also joined the team, which will enable the training of Kuna students in the area of anthropology and tourism. These two new elements will undoubtedly reinforce the interdisciplinary synergy of the research.

For an Ethnography of the Tourism System

Tourism may be regarded as a system. The present research project has always been thought of as an ethnography of the tourism system that focuses on the relationships between the local and global, even though it is contextualized in the case of a native group, the Kuna, that politically controls its own tourism development. According to this presupposition, we have developed a multi-sited ethnography (Marcus, 1995), which entailed the collection of about 35 h of audio-visual records.

This ethnography followed a mixed and eclectic research approach, yet qualitative predominated over quantitative methods. The adoption of this mixed approach has allowed us to carry out a more in-depth and more historical ethnography of tourism.

This methodological approach was fundamentally a mix of three research strategies (Pujadas Muñoz, 1992; Velasco and Díaz de Rada, 1997; Quivi and Van Campenhoudt, 1998; Roigé i Ventura *et al.*, 1999; Da Silva Ribeiro, 2003; Hernández Sampieri *et al.*, 2006):

- anthropological fieldwork, based on participant observation and audio-visual ethnography;
- oral interviews, debate groups and life history reports; and
- bibliographical and documentary research.

Through this triangulation we were able to understand in ethnographic detail the relevant local–global relationships and also the plurality of perspectives, interpretations and meanings regarding this case of ethnic tourism. In addition, this ethnography is an open work, since the data collected may be studied by other researchers, according to other theoretical and analytical frameworks. Similarly, but not of lesser importance, the Kuna themselves may also analyse and re-interpret the data. In the autumn of 2006, the first ethnographic research report was presented to the Kuna General Congress and to the Kuna Tourism Business Association, and eventually contributed to the redefinition of the politics of Kuna tourism. The methodological strategies adopted in these kinds of projects are useful in medium- to long-range projects, in which there is time to engage in extensive collaborative work in the field.

The advantages of participant observation have already been defended above, but in the present case, it has also allowed us to better understand tourism as an interactive social practice. By articulating intensive observation of specific places with multi-sited observation in an extended area, we were able to create a basis of comparative information between tourism projects (relating to the local tourism supply), types of tourism, types of host communities and types of tourists. This approach makes it possible to illustrate the diversity existing in tourism to Kuna Yala, to question ethnocentric viewpoints and to build up a basis for comparisons.

The use of audio-visual records enables better subsequent interpretation and analysis, as well as facilitating debate about the research problem with other researchers. A documentary in production will allow us to return the knowledge produced to the subjects studied.

The recorded interviews were a means of objectifying and ethnographically documenting the supply side of tourism and understanding the perspectives and voices about Kuna tourism. They were especially useful for analysing the different points of view in the conflicts between the Kuna and the state of Panama or between the Kuna and foreign researchers.

It is also worth stressing the application of life history reports about the business people involved in Kuna tourism. This technique made it possible to better study the history of Kuna tourism from the perspectives of the protagonists, who are the promoters of this industry. This technique also allowed us to improve the assessment of the origin of tourism projects and the reasons that have led the Kuna to become producers of tourism. The analysis of documents is required in these kinds of research projects: for example, the analysis of newspapers has contributed to the production of a historical ethnography, which has helped to analyse diachronically tourism processes and to contextualize the problems being examined better. Notwithstanding this, the research faced a number of constraints:

- Financial limitations. The project started with no financial support whatsoever and required a strong personal investment by the research team. Over time, we managed to get recognition and support for the presentation of partial research outcomes.

- Permission to undertake the research. To research in Kuna Yala implies asking for permission from the Kuna General Congress, which generally operates relatively slowly, made easier in our case by the role of Cebaldo de León Inawinapi, highly accredited among the Kuna authorities. Besides that, each one of the 44 Kuna communities that inhabit the Kuna Yala may, and have the right, to refuse to accept the permissions granted by the Kuna General Congress, and thus to research in this context means to negotiate and to renegotiate. Audio-visual records cannot be made without permission, and this demands much ethical care and collaborative attention.
- Learning the Kuna language. For research of this kind, it is necessary to know the indigenous language, which allows access to the social and cultural universes of the communities from the inside. Spanish represents, in many Kuna communities, a kind of foreign language.
- Adaptation to the local culture and climate. The adaptation to the local food and the physical and mental adaptation to the islands and to the jungle are some of the accommodation processes needed in this kind of research.
- Mistrust. The researcher's social identities are a very important subjective factor in the process of knowledge production. In our case, to be male, European and 'white' has conditioned the entrance into the field and the winning of the Kunas' trust, as well as that of the tourists. The author's ethnic identity helped in this case, as the fact of being a 'Galician' (from Galicia, a differential ethnic community of the Spanish state) helped to establish bonds with the Kunas, who distrust the 'Spanish', to whom the stereotype of imperialist is attributed. On the other hand, while carrying out fieldwork in the city of Panama among politicians, travel agents and other public institutions, 'the magic of the white man' (perception of the superiority of the European) worked towards doors opening more quickly.

Applications of the Anthropology of Tourism

In the field of tourism, the distance between theoretical anthropology and applied anthropology may become very small, and thus there is space for research that may have a strong, sometimes immediate, social impact. This reflection causes unrest in anthropologists who think of their work as an exclusively theoretical exercise separated from anthropological practice and praxis. However, theory and practice, theory and application (applicability), and theory and implication are closer than anthropologists sometimes admit. Whatever the role the anthropologist adopts — researcher, consultant, advisor, mediator, guide, tourist, professor, student, manager, tourist promoter, etc. — the problem of the relationship between theory and practice will always be present.

In fact, during our work, it was interesting and gratifying to observe how our research project started from the beginning to interest the Kuna communities themselves. The Kuna Tourism Business Association, the Panama Institute of Tourism (IPAT), the Usdup School of Agro-ecotourism and some travel agencies all saw the benefits the project could bring them in terms of training, advisory, recommendations, tourism publicity, strategic consultancy, etc. In any case, the research purpose was to know, investigate and produce knowledge. Obviously, the same knowledge production is achieved within the framework of social and political relations, in the face of which we tried to establish a critical lens, allowing a better understanding of the research problem.

The research was a guide for Kuna authorities and business people involved in tourism to better rethink and redefine the future of tourism in Kuna Yala. Therefore our first report was used by the Kuna in community-wide conferences on tourism and in their internal debates. Although it is not the only source of change, tourism is one of motors for the social–cultural change that may cause positive and negative effects on the local communities and tourists. Therefore anthropological research on tourism systems may help to identify and to correct possible negative effects and it may likewise contribute to the building up of responsible tourism from the social and environmental point of view (Gascón and Cañada, 2005).

We also wish to highlight how the results of our scientific research project had a reciprocal impact, i.e. our work did not just work as a mirror for the Kunas but also for the Europeans and other Westerners. The reception on the part of academia in the West was very positive, and this project was awarded the first prize in tourism research by the International Tourism Fair in Madrid (FITUR) in 2007 (Pereiro and Inawinapi, 2007), as well as another award by the National Geographic Society. In 2008, SEN-ACYT granted us specific funding to carry out a strategic study of tourism in Kuna Yala, and thus guaranteed the continuity of the project. This recognition allows for several readings, but one of them is that the post-Fordist tourism system itself is interested in fragmenting the market and in finding new alternative destinations for the new niches of tourism demand. Even though this was not previously foreseen, our research work meets those interests.

Erve Chambers (2005: 27) asked whether an anthropology of tourism might help us become better travellers. Obviously, this kind of research, if built upon the participation of the communities involved in tourism and in following specific ethical principles, may help tourists to become better and more responsible travellers, to unveil the interests and strategies of many tourism systems and to plan more efficient tourism strategies. We believe, therefore, from our experience, that the work of the anthropologist who does research on tourism may play an important mediating role with the actors involved in processes associated with tourism development.

Acknowledgements

We are grateful to the anthropologist Sharon Roseman (Memorial University of Newfoundland) and Santiago Prado Conde (Ethnological Museum of Ribadavia-Galiza), for their critical comments and review of the text presented here.

The findings of the project were presented at the 4th Congress of the Portuguese Association of Anthropology, which took place in Lisbon in April 2006; in the CETRAD (UTAD) Seminars in July 2006; in the Americanists World Congress, which took place in Seville, also in July 2006; in the Master on Tourism of the Vigo University (Galicia), in 2006–2007; and in the International Tourism Fair (FITUR) in Madrid, in January 2007.

References

Alvarez Roldán, A. (1994) La invención del método etnográfico. Reflexiones sobre el trabajo de campo de Malinowski en Melanesia. *Antropologia* 7, 83–100.

Bruner, E.M. (1989) Of cannibals, tourists and ethnographers. *Cultural Anthropology* 4, 438–445.

Burgess, R.G. (1997) *A Pesquisa de Terreno. Uma Introdução.* Celta Editora, Oeiras, Portugal.

Buxó Rey, M.J. (1995) El arte en la ciencia etnográfica. In: Aguirre Baztán, A. (ed.) *Etnografía. Metodología Cualitativa en la Investigación Sociocultural.* Boixareu, Barcelona, Spain, pp. 64–72.

Callejo Gallego, J., Gutiérrez Brito, J. and Viedma Rojas, A. (2003) *Análisis Empírico de la Demanda Turística.* Ramón Areces, Madrid.

Cardin, A. (1988) *Tientos Etnológicos.* Ediciones Jucar, Madrid.

Chambers, E. (2005) Can the anthropology of tourism make us better travelers? In: Wallace, T. (ed.) *Tourism and Applied Anthropologists: Linking Theory and Practice.* NAPA Bulletin 23, Arlington, Virginia, pp. 27–44.

Crick, M. (1985) Tracing the anthropological self: quizzical reflections on fieldwork, tourism and the Ludic. *Social Analyses* 17, 71–92.

Crick, M. (1995) The anthropologist as tourist: an identity in question. In: Lanfant, M.-F., Allcock, J.B. and Bruner, E.M. (eds) *International Tourism. Identity and Change.* Sage, London, pp. 205–223.

Da Silva Ribeiro, J. (2003) *Métodos e Técnicas de Investigação em Aantropologia*. Universidade Aberta, Lisbon, Portugal.

Dann, G., Nash, D. and Pearce, P. (1988) Methodology in tourism research. *Annals of Tourism Research* 15(1), 1–28.

Delgado Ruíz, M. (2002) *Disoluciones Urbanas*. Universidad de Antioquia, Medellín, Colombia.

Durkheim, E. (1982) *The Rules of Sociological Method*. Macmillan, London.

El Guindi, F. (2004) *Visual Anthropology: Essential Method and Theory*. AltaMira Press, Walnut Creek, California.

Gadamer, H. (1978) *Verdad y Método I*. Sígueme, Salamanca, Spain.

Gascón, J. and Cañada, E. (2005) *Viajar a Todo Tren. Turismo, Desarrollo y Sostenibilidad*. Icaria, Barcelona, Spain.

Geertz, C. (1987) *La Interpretación de las Culturas*. Gedisa, Barcelona, Spain.

Gmelch, S.B. (ed.) (2004) *Tourists and Tourism. A Reader*. Waveland Press, Long Grave, California.

Graburn, N.H. and Moore, R.S. (1994) Anthropological research on tourism. In: Ritchie, J.R. and Goeldner, C.R. (eds) (1994) *Travel, Tourism and Hospitality Research: a Handbook for Managers and Researchers*. John Wiley and Sons, New York, pp. 233–242.

Greenwood, D.J. (2000) De la observación a la investigación-acción participativa: una visión crítica de las prácticas antropológicas. *Revista de Antropología Social* 9, 27–49.

Greenwood, D.J. (2002) Aplicar o no aplicar: per què l'antropologia i les ciències socials no poden existir sense l'acció. *Revista d'Etnologia de Catalunya* 20, 6–11.

Hammersley, M. and Atkinson, P. (1994) *Etnografía: Métodos de Investigación*, 2nd edn. Paidós, Barcelona, Spain.

Heider, K.G. (1988) The Rashomon effect: when ethnographers disagree. *American Anthropologist* 90, 73–81.

Hernández Sampieri, R., Fernández-Collado, C. and Baptista Lucio, P. (2006) *Metodología de la Investigación*. McGraw-Hill, Mexico City, Mexico.

Hessen, J. (1961) *Teoría del Conocimiento*. Espasa-Calpe, Madrid.

Kenzin, N.K. (1997) *Interpretative Ethnography. Ethnographic Practices for the 21st Century*. Sage, London.

Lisón Tolosana, C. (1983) *Antropología Social y Hermenéutica*. Fondo de Cultura Económica, Madrid.

Lopes, A.R. (2004) O turismo e os seus impactos numa comunidade de índios kuna do Panamá. MSc thesis. The University of Trás-os-Montes and Alto Douro, Miranda do Douro, Portugal.

MacCannell, D. (1992) *Empty Meeting Grounds*. Routledge, New York.

Malinowski, B. (1973) *Los Argonautas del Pacífico Occidental*. Península, Barcelona, Spain.

Malinowski, B. (1989) *Diario de Campo en Melanesia*. Júcar, Madrid.

Marcus, G.S. (1995) Ethnography in/of the world system: the emergence of multi-sited ethnography. *Annual Review of Anthropology* 24, 95–117.

Martínez Mauri, M. (2007) De Tule Nega a Kuna Yala. Mediación, territorio y ecología en Panamá, 1903–2004. PhD thesis, The Autonomous University of Barcelona, Barcelona, Spain.

Mauss, M. (1988) *Ensaio Sobre a Dádiva*. Edições 70, Lisbon, Portugal.

Peacock, J.L. (1989): *El Enfoque de la Antropología*. Herder, Barcelona, Spain.

Pereiro, X. (2005) *Galegos de Vila: Antropoloxía dun Espazo Rurbano*. Editorial Sotelo Blanco, Santiago de Compostela, Spain.

Pereiro, X. and de León Inawinapi, C. (2007) *Los Impactos del Turismo en Kuna Yala. Turismo y Cultura entre los Kuna de Panamá*. Editorial Ramón Areces, Madrid.

Phillmore, J. and Goodson, L. (eds) (2004) *Qualitative Research in Tourism. Ontologies, Epistemologies and Methodologies*. Routlege, London.

Pujadas Muñoz, J.J. (1992) *El Método Biográfico: el Uso de las Historias de Vida en Ciencias Ssociales*. CIS, Madrid.

Quivi, R. and Van Campenhoudt, L. (1998) *Manual de Investigação em Ciências Sociais*. Gradiva, Lisbon, Portugal.

Ritchie, J.R. and Goeldner, C.R. (eds) (1994) *Travel, Tourism, and Hospitality Research: a Handbook for Managers and Researchers*. John Wiley and Sons, New York

Roigé i Ventura, X., Estrada i Bonell, F. and Beltrán Costa, O. (1999) *Tècniques d'Investigació en Antropologia Social*. Universitat de Barcelona, Barcelona, Spain.

Santana, A. (2003) Mirando culturas: la antropología del turismo. In: Rubio Gil, A. (ed.) *Sociología del Turismo*. Ariel, Barcelona, Spain, pp. 103–125.

Simpson, R. (1993) Tourism and tradition: from healing to heritage. *Annals of Tourism Research* 20, 164–181.

Smith, S.L.J. (1995) *Tourism Analysis. A Handbook*, 2nd edn. Longman, Harlow, UK.

Taylor, S.J. and Bodgan, R. (1998) *Introducción a los Métodos Cualitativos de Investigación*. Paidós, Barcelona, Spain.

Todorov, T. (1988) El cruzamiento entre culturas. In: Todorov, T. (ed.) *Cruce de Culturas y Mestizaje Cultural*. Júcar, Madrid, pp. 9–31.

Tribe, J. (1997) The indiscipline of tourism. *Annals of Tourism Research* 24, 638–657.

Urbain, J.D. (1993) *El Idiota que Viaja. Relatos de Turistas*. Endimión, Madrid.

Velasco, H. and Díaz de Rada, A. (1997) *La Lógica de la Investigación Etnográfica. Un Modelo de Trabajo para Etnógrafos de la Escuela*. Trotta, Madrid.

Wallace, T. (ed.) (2005) *Tourism and Applied Anthropologists. Linking Theory and Ppractice*. NAPA, Arlington, Virginia.

Walle, A.F. (1997) Quantitative versus qualitative tourism research. *Annals of Tourism Research* 3, 524–536.

15 From Local to Global (and Back): Towards Glocal Ethnographies of Cultural Tourism

Noel B. Salazar

The Local-to-global Nexus

Tourism, the multifaceted global phenomenon of travel for leisure, offers many fascinating research topics across disciplines. Ethnographic research on cultural tourism has come a long way, from ethnographers ignoring tourists during their fieldwork and disregarding the seriousness of tourism research (Lévi-Strauss, 1955) to cultural anthropologists taking active roles in tourism planning and development (Wallace, 2005). Nowadays, tourism is seen as one of the exemplary manifestations of global flows that blur traditional territorial, social and cultural boundaries and create hybrid forms. Perhaps more than any other practice, tourism demonstrates (in the absence of a clearly identifiable hegemonic power) the importance of multiple centres from which people, ideas and capital circulate across the globe and interact dialectically with local circumstances.

Travel destinations worldwide are adapting themselves to rapidly changing global trends and markets while trying to maintain, or even increase, their local distinctiveness. This competitive struggle to obtain a piece of the lucrative tourism pie becomes a question of how 'the local' is (re)presented. On the one hand, global marketing companies and national as well as local authorities play a crucial role in manufacturing and selling destination images and imaginaries. On the other hand, tourism stimulates localization, a dynamic process characterized by the resurgence of competing socio-culturally defined local identities (Cawley *et al.*, 2002). There are many weaknesses associated with stressing local, national, regional or global processes separately. Apart from acknowledging the fact that power relations in tourism operate on different levels, it is necessary to link those levels theoretically and methodologically.

In my own research, I explore the discourse, politics and practices of tour guiding, by way of a multi-sited and multi-temporal ethnography of local tour guides in Yogyakarta, Indonesia and Arusha, Tanzania (Salazar, 2005, 2006b, 2007, 2008, 2010). This chapter deals solely with the Asian part of my study. I chose to focus on tour guides because they are key vehicles through which local-to-global flows are articulated. Understanding how and why these cultural mediators create, negotiate and transform the meanings of cultural heritage for tourists and local people reveals new insights about how processes of worldwide interdependence and convergence and local differentiation intersect, overlap and conflict. In what follows, I describe a novel ethnographic methodology to capture the intricacies of the local-to-global nexus. I discuss how it is distinct from other approaches and why it is particularly useful when researching cultural tourism. I then present the challenges I faced with this methodology during my own research in Yogyakarta. I end with a critical reflection on the use of glocal ethnography in cultural tourism studies.

Glocal Ethnography

What's in a name?

The holistic mixed-methods contribution of socio-cultural anthropology to tourism studies is widely acknowledged (Nash, 2000; Palmer, 2001; Smith and Brent, 2001; Graburn, 2002; Wallace, 2005; Leite and Graburn, 2009). The interpretive approach characterizing this discipline is ethnography, a methodology that has been applied successfully to the study of tourism, especially in developing countries (Moon, 1989; Crick, 1994; Van den Berghe, 1994; Picard, 1996; Bras, 2000; Dahles, 2001; Causey, 2003; Ness, 2003; Yamashita, 2003; Bruner, 2005; Adams, 2006; Wynn, 2007; Cole, 2008). In the strict etymological sense of the term, ethnography refers to something that is written about a particular group of people. The basis for this descriptive writing is an extended period of fieldwork, which traditionally involves participant observation but very often includes other methods such as interviews, surveys and questionnaires (Bernard, 2006). More broadly, ethnography is used to describe a kind of research methodology whose characteristics include sharing in the lives of those under study, gaining an emic understanding of things, a holistic approach and the observation of everyday life. Because theory has tended to lag behind mere ethnographic description, academics now stress the need to link fieldwork with theoretical development (Snow *et al.*, 2003).

Twenty years after the so-called 'crisis of representation', much of which was centred on the question of ethnographic authority, ethnography as a research methodology is facing a new challenge: What do detailed studies of the local tell us about the global and globalization, the complex process of growing worldwide interdependence and convergence? Critics have pointed out that much ethnographic writing invokes notions of the global or globalization, rather than empirically analysing them. The result is ethnography situated within an imagined, if not imaginary, global context or studies of globalized processes that lack ethnographic detail. Underpinning such criticisms is a perfectly understandable intellectual tension. On the one hand, there is the persistent question as to whether ethnographic research of the global is possible. On the other hand, there is a clear recognition that this question does not make much sense since it is not feasible to fully separate the local from the global (Marcus, 1998). Scholars still have a long way to go in understanding exactly how local-to-global scales are connected, disconnected and reconnected. The fact that such linkages exist is indisputable; the major problem is how to operationalize them so that they can be studied and analysed.

Contemporary anthropological theorizing acknowledges that 'the local' refers not solely to a spatially limited locality (Gupta and Ferguson, 1997); above all, it is a socio-cultural metaphor for a collectively imagined space inhabited by people who have a particular sense of place, a specific shared way of life and a certain ethos and worldview. It is the site where supralocal processes and flows fragment and are localized, transformed into something place-bound and peculiar. The local is constructed in contradictory ways and has always been, at least in part, the product of outside influences (Appadurai, 1996: 178–199). The global and the local should certainly not be treated as binary oppositions. The local–global dichotomy is artificial; it arose as a heuristic necessity to meet the shortcomings of a model that tied group and socio-cultural characteristics to territory and simply saw the global as a metaphor for all that the model cannot account for. Globalization theories too easily encourage the equation of an abstract global with capital and change versus a concrete local (or national) with labour and tradition. In reality, processes of globalization and localization assume numerous forms connected by highly unequal power relations. It is therefore more accurate to employ a relational understanding to globalization than a territorial one. Globalization always takes place in some locality, while the local is (re)produced in the global circulation of products, discourses and imaginaries. In other words, the local does not oppose but constitutes the global, and vice versa (Tsing, 2005). Tourism nicely illustrates how the processes of all place making and force making are both local and global, i.e. both socially and culturally particular and productive of widely circulating interactions.

The conundrum of scale

Because globalizing processes operate across time and space, traditional ethnographic methods, which tend to be place-bound, must be supplemented with information linking the particular research moment to the broader context, and the research site(s) to the broader translocal forces, connections and imaginations that constitute the global (Robbins and Bamford, 1997). The fundamental methodological challenge that the condition of localities in current interconnected conditions poses is one of scale. How well can we encompass increasingly wider and complex contexts of analysis? Scale is not the same as size; it has to do with the presence or absence, and relative efficacy, of overarching institutions, not geographic or demographic extent.

Robertson (1995) develops the notion glocalization to better grasp the many interconnections of the local–global nexus. He argues against the tendency to perceive globalization as involving only large-scale macro-sociological processes, neglecting the way in which globalization is always localized. In other words, the local contains much that is global, while the global is increasingly penetrated and reshaped by many locals. The term glocalization captures the dynamic, contingent and two-way dialectic between the two realms. Glocalization invites us to rethink ethnography's

conventional scale, treating the local as a space contained or encompassed by larger spaces. The main ethnographic advantage of rethinking the local is the possibility of reclaiming some of the questions that the conventions of scale ordinarily preclude.

There are two major ways to address the conundrum of scale. First, one can scale vertically ('scale up'), by providing close-grained analyses of how a single site is connected locally, nationally, regionally and globally. Traditional fieldwork, however, may be just the beginning if the goal is deep understanding. Instead of cherishing a fetishistic obsession with participant observation, therefore, we need to reinforce this traditional technique with other methods. Gupta and Ferguson (1997: 38), for instance, call for bringing in a multitude of other forms of representation besides fieldwork: archival research, the analysis of public discourse, interviewing, journalism, fiction or statistical representations of collectivities. Using the extended case study method, Burawoy (2000) describes a set of strategies for combining abstract, theoretical insights about globalization with concrete, historically contextualized, geographically situated practices, an approach he and his team of researchers term 'global ethnography'. Vertical scaling can also include a multi-temporal (longitudinal or historical) dimension. The presence of these new types of material may require, and also provide openings for, new skills of composition and synthesis (Hannerz, 2003: 35).

The second strategy is to scale horizontally ('scale out'), by including more than one site in the analysis. For many ethnographers, the global is an emergent dimension for exploring the connections among sites. This latitudinal approach is better known in anthropology as 'multi-sited ethnography' (Marcus, 1998). Such a research strategy maintains the local focus of ethnography while at the same time it complicates the definition and construction of the larger system. Multi-local or multi-sited research might actually not be an adequate description, as many places are somehow linked or networked to each other – what Hannerz (2003: 21) calls a 'network of localities' or 'several fields in one'. A single site within a complex society may be conceptualized as a multiple site, whereas multiple localities can be seen as 'a single geographically discontinuous site' (Hage, 2005). Hannerz (2003: 21) therefore advocates 'translocal' research, clarifying the nature of relations between localities. While the analytical entity is translocal or glocal, the fieldwork is multi-local, because the ethnographer is always somewhere. Merry (2000: 130), on the other hand, proposes a 'deterritorialized ethnography', not restricted to predefined sites but following patterns of circulation.

Building on Robertson's (1995) conceptual framework, I propose the neologism glocal ethnography to describe my own research in Yogyakarta, Indonesia (see Table 15.1). I define glocal ethnography as a fieldwork methodology to describe and interpret the complex connections, disconnections and reconnections between local-to-global phenomena and processes. This is achieved by firmly embedding and historically situating the in-depth study of a particular socio-cultural group, organization or setting within a larger (and ultimately global) context. This happens figuratively by putting the G of global in front of the concept local: g-local. This implies that the focus is still on the local but that local is now embedded in a larger context. Contrary to Burawoy's (2000) global ethnography approach, the stress is not on the global but on the intricate ways the local is linked to national, regional and global scales (scaling up). Glocal ethnography enriches Marcus's (1998) multi-sited ethnography approach by combining his method of scaling out with methods of scaling up.

Table 15.1. General characteristics of glocal ethnography.

Aim	Describe and interpret the characteristics, structures and interactions of a particular socio-cultural group or organization in a naturally occurring setting, with all its diversity and multiplicity of voices and situated within a larger (and ultimately global) framework. Find the local in the global and vice versa, by revealing local-to-global meaning and thus glocal complexity
Research questions	Why do people think and act the way they do and how are these thoughts and behaviours shaped by local-to-global influences? How are people positioned in glocal settings and networks, and how do they interact with each other, especially with significant others? What are the power relationships within and between those various settings and what kind of agency do people have to bring about change on different levels?
Data gathering	Extensive fieldwork, characterized by observation (direct or participant) and various types of interviews with key informants and other significant actors. Sustained presence in the research site(s), combined with an intensive engagement with the everyday life of the people that form the focus of the study. Ancillary data include secondary sources, audio-visual data, news media, documents, archives, the Internet, etc. Given the in-depth approach, one study is usually limited to investigating a small number of cases. Use of exhaustive notes and personal diary entries to record the findings
Data analysis	Working initially with unstructured data rather than a closed set of externally imposed analytic categories. Systematic coding and building patterns demand certain procedures, but the choice and development of theoretical frameworks depend on the individual researcher, who adds an etic (outsider) view to the emic (insider) perspectives of the participants. Interpretation of data is usually in the form of elaborate verbal descriptions rather than statistical analysis (but quantification is not excluded)
End product	The primary result takes the form of a coherent descriptive narrative, representing the multiplicity of voices and perceptions of the participants as well as the researcher's own views and interpretations. The final product is a detailed ethnographic account – in words, spoken or written, a lecture, article or monograph. Conveying the sense of 'being there', producing unexpected details and conclusions, reflecting the multiple modes of ordering and offering explanations wrapped in 'thick descriptions'
Knowledge claim	Knowledge and understanding about the complex connections, disconnections and reconnections between glocal phenomena and processes

A Glocal Study of Tourism

Cultural tourism offers many possibilities for glocal ethnography, especially where international tourists meet local manufac- turers, retailers and service providers in the production, representation and consump- tion of glocalized tourism goods and serv- ices (Yamashita, 2003). As Bruner (2005: 17) elucidates, the 'touristic borderzone' is about the local, but what is performed there takes account of global cross-currents. Most of the local-to-global connections in tour- ism are marked by inequalities and power struggles (Alneng, 2002). Without using the conceptual framework of glocalization, geographers studying tourism have repeat- edly stressed the importance of the global– local nexus. Chang et al. (1996: 285), for instance, argue that 'the global and the local should be enmeshed in any future theoreti- cal frameworks that are developed to help understand the processes and outcomes of … tourism'. Similarly, Teo and Li (2003: 302) state that 'for tourism, the global and the local form a dyad acting as a dialectical process'. In what follows, I briefly sketch how I have used glocal ethnography to study tourism-related processes in Yogyakarta, Indonesia.

Yogyakarta is the name of one of Indo- nesia's 33 provinces and its capital city, situated on the island of Java. The region has been participating in international tour- ism for over 30 years. Since the early stages, it has been promoted by the Indonesian government as 'the cultural heart of Java' (or even Indonesia) and an ideal cultural tourism destination for both domestic and international markets. The most important attractions include the 8th-century Buddhist monument of Borobudur and the 9th-cen- tury Hindu temple complex of Prambanan (both recognized in 1991 as UNESCO world heritage sites). The city, with its Kraton, the 18th-century walled palace where the Sultan resides, cherishes its Javanese roots, attract- ing a large number of painters, dancers and writers. Jogja, as the city is affectionately called by Indonesians, is famous for tradi- tional crafts such as batik (intricate wax- resist dyed textiles), silverware, pottery,

clothing, woodcarving and wayang kulit (shadow puppets). Although Jogja is a small provincial capital, its population reaching half a million, the city's vibrant communi- ties of artists and students ensure that it is well connected nationally as well as inter- nationally. Interestingly, the current tour- ism discourses about Jogja, as uttered by the government, by travel agencies, tour opera- tors, marketers and by tour guides, only focus on the renowned heritage sites men- tioned above and on the traditional arts and crafts performed or produced in the city itself or in its vicinity (Salazar, 2005).

The core of my research centred on analysing the discourses and practices of local tour guides. More particularly, I wanted to understand how guides in Jogja rely on supralocal networks and resources to better glocalize their tour commentaries about local culture for a varied international audience of tourists. I started my year of fieldwork in December 2005. The fact that I had been in Jogja before on two different occasions seriously reduced the expected cultural shock. Proficiency in Indonesian and other languages proved to be of great value when observing the interactions between tourists and guides and when inter- viewing people. As is usual for ethnographic fieldwork, I spent considerable time inter- viewing guides (using various interview for- mats) and directly observing them while guiding. However, in order to capture how the guides are influenced by global cross- currents of information and imaginaries promoted by tourism, my research had to include many other facets as well.

Collecting data

Because tour guides are often the only local people with whom tourists interact for a considerable amount of time, it is in the interest of the authorities to streamline their narratives and practices. In the case of Jogja, guiding is controlled by guidelines and reg- ulations imposed by organizations and insti- tutions at various levels: local (Yogyakarta City Department of Tourism, Arts, and

Culture), provincial (Yogyakarta Provincial Tourism Office), national (Ministry of Culture and Tourism, Indonesian Guide Association), regional (ASEAN Common Competency Standards for Tourism Professionals Framework, APEC Tourism Occupational Skill Standards) and global (UNWTO, UNESCO, World Federation of Tourist Guide Associations). One of my first fieldwork tasks consisted of contacting these regulatory bodies, interviewing some of their key personnel and obtaining copies of the various laws, directives and guidelines. This is a good example of scaling up.

In addition, I interviewed local tour operators who employ guides (most of whom work on a freelance basis). Although it is Indonesia's second most important destination, Jogja's tourism growth is highly dependent on the development of tourism on the neighbouring island of Bali. This power hierarchy translates on many levels. At the time of my research, for example, the Minister of Culture and Tourism was Balinese. A considerable number of Jogja's tour operators are branch offices from Balinese travel agencies. In other words, it is in Bali that tour packages for Jogja are constructed and sold. Obviously, these larger structural characteristics of tourism are beyond the control of local guides in Jogja.

One way the narratives and practices of guides can be shaped and controlled is through education and licensing. The second step in my research therefore involved investigating how guides are professionally schooled and informally trained. I collected information from tourism academies providing guiding courses, and since many guides in Jogja are autodidacts who did not receive much formal training, I also sent a questionnaire to guides to collect basic demographic information and data on education, guiding, tour preparation and information resources, travel, hobbies and the use of new information and communication technologies. The addresses were provided by the Yogyakarta chapter of the Indonesian Guide Association. Based on the usefulness of the information returned, I contacted 25 respondents to conduct in-depth interviews on the same theme. The licensing of tour

guides is in the hands of the Institution of Certification for Tourism Professions, currently outsourced by the local authorities to the semi-private Jogja Tourism Training Centre. The licensing process is controlled by the Yogyakarta City Department of Tourism, Arts, and Culture as well as the Indonesian Guide Association and the Association of Indonesian Tour and Travel Agencies. Untangling this web of interrelated organizations involved interviewing officials working for each one of them.

A major part of the actual fieldwork consisted of extensive observation. As a participant, I joined tourists on 28 tours through central Java. As an observer, I spent countless hours socializing with local tour guides and informally interviewing them. These different types of observation led to hundreds of pages of field notes. The second-most important source of data was interviews. I conducted and recorded in-depth interviews with 25 guides and semi-structured interviews with six people involved in guide training, five local tour operators and 11 tourism officials at local, national and regional levels. Because I also wanted to find out what local people think about tour guiding, I decided to train my two local research assistants to conduct short, semi-structured interviews and sent them out to converse with people in the respective cities and the surrounding villages. They conducted 35 additional short, structured street interviews. My assistants and I transcribed most interviews shortly after conducting them.

In order to grasp the complexity of tour guiding in Jogja, it is necessary to place the contemporary local tourism scene in a wider historical, politico-economic and socio-cultural context (again, an example of scaling up). During my fieldwork, I undertook background literature research in academic libraries. I frequently consulted secondary media sources such as Indonesian newspapers (*Kedaulatan Rakyat*, *Kompas* and *The Jakarta Post*), magazines (*Tempo*, *Kabare* and *Inside Indonesia*) and websites. Regular discussions with Indonesian anthropologists, tourism scholars and students in Jogja were useful to test some of my preliminary hypotheses and explanations.

I started collecting data long before I embarked on my fieldwork. I systematically kept track of information appearing on the World Wide Web concerning tourism in Jogja. My research assistants and some local contacts kept me informed about what was happening in Jogja through e-mail and short text messages (SMS).

Flexible fieldwork

I had planned to spend most time during the high season observing guide–guest interactions and talking to both parties before and after the tours. However, a series of natural disasters – repeated volcanic eruptions, a major earthquake and a minor tsunami – seriously altered the course of my research. Many of the guides I was working with lost not only their houses or relatives but their income too, since many tourists cancelled their trip to Jogja. One of the advantages of glocal ethnography is its flexibility to adapt research agendas to such rapidly changing field conditions. Ironically, the calamities provided me with extra data on how closely local-to-global scales are interconnected. I was invited to help as a volunteer with Java Tourism Care, an initiative of a variety of local tourism stakeholders aimed at assisting in the relief, rehabilitation and recovery of the province's tourism sector. I systematically gathered national as well as international news media reports about the disasters in order to compare these with the actual situation on the ground. Because there were so many disparities, I felt the need to start my own anthropological blog (Salazar, 2006a). This offered me an extra opportunity to reflect on the current situation and receive feedback from readers. In addition, I collected the travel warnings issued by the governments of Jogja's largest inbound Western markets (France, the Netherlands and Germany). These could be considered examples of scaling out, because I was researching how other sites were relating to what was happening in Jogja. Finally, I was asked to be a consultant for the Jogja Tourism Information Centre, recently founded by the Yogyakarta Public Relations Association in collaboration with the Yogyakarta Provincial Tourism Office. While helping the local tourism sector, these new involvements gave me easier access to some of its key players.

The severe 27 May 2006 earthquake revealed many hitherto hidden facets of local tour guiding in Jogja. It stressed how for most people guiding is only a temporary job. After the golden years of tourism (1980s to mid-1990s), few people on Java are able to make a living from guiding alone. Most freelance guides now have second jobs as teachers or owners of small businesses (often tourism-related). In the aftermath of the quake, many of them earned extra income by working as translators and scouts for international NGOs, medical teams and government delegations. The never-ending sequence of catastrophes also disclosed the politics and poetics of the local tourism industry. The local-to-global nexus and the low position guides occupy in the hierarchy of tourism became particularly relevant in the case of the Prambanan temple complex. It took almost a month before international experts from UNESCO came to measure the damage to the world heritage site. During all that time, the monument was closed to visitors. After the assessment, a newly built viewing platform (very similar to the ones erected after 9/11 around Ground Zero, New York) allowed tourists to see the temples from a safe distance, without being allowed to enter them. However, PT Taman Wisata, the Indonesian government enterprise managing the park, decided not to lower the entrance fees (US$10 for foreigners). Anticipating tourist complaints, many local travel agencies decided to suspend tours to Prambanan. The few tourists who still visited the temple complex did not want the service of a local guide (approximately US$5) because they knew that they could not get near the temples anyway. This left the Prambanan guides in a very precarious situation.

This volatile state of affairs shifted my original research design in the direction of an exploration of the extremely fragile position of guides within a glocal tourism context. Although most of them are well networked, they do not seem to be able to capitalize on their translocal connectedness, at least not for their work as guides. Furthermore, the local chapter of the Indonesian Guide Association is not in a bargaining position to give its members more job security. I ended my period of fieldwork with a long series of in-depth interviews with guides about their work, the current situation, tourism in general, tourists and globalization. These meetings gave me an excellent opportunity to test my interpretations of the preliminary findings. I also talked to tour operators, trying to find out how they value the service of local guides.

Bringing it all together

My fieldwork revealed the Janus-faced role and liminal positionality of local guides. On the one hand, they act as 'mechanics of glocalization', performing partially as actors of hegemonic forces well beyond their reach. They are part of an expansive but loosely structured global tourism system that represents peoples and places in predefined and scripted ways. Guides are instrumental in tourism because they give the system not only a 'local' but also a human face, giving them an advantage over technological competitors like virtual or mobile tour guides. I call them mechanics because they are usually well skilled and have to labour hard to mirror globally fashionable tourism imaginaries, while selling and telling a message that is clearly not their own and performing under conditions they cannot completely determine. Their project is one of glocalization rather than globalization, because localizing the global and globalizing the local is what international tourism is all about. Local guides are not primary producers of cultural tourism discourse, but in the service encounter with tourists they maintain the tourism system of provisioning as it is, by assuring the continuity and perpetuation of the global chain of imaginaries and giving it a 'local' flavour. This role can be machine-like because at times it appears automatic or even involuntary.

Yet, guiding involves more than simply rehashing memorized screenplays, learned formally or informally. The interactive nature of the enacted guide–guest encounter can lead to results unanticipated by those crafting tourism (marketers, governments, etc.). Various meanings are communicated and negotiated, and personal responses, commitments and rules have to be accepted. On tour, guides are mediating not only cultural differences but also the interests and imaginations of various stakeholders. Guiding, like ethnographic fieldwork, is always, to some extent, improvised, creative and spontaneous, defying complete standardization. While guides perform scripted roles, having various dalang (puppeteers) manipulating their moves (e.g. tour operators, authorities at various levels, law enforcement), they are not like wayang kulit (shadow puppets) with little or no control over their own performances. A glocal ethnographic analysis of guiding practices shows how the content (tourism fantasies) can become detached from the container (the guide). This is most evident in the small talk that takes place in between stretches of guiding narrative and in the metadiscursive comments that guides transmit while guiding.

My findings also illustrated the importance of studying the scales in between the local and the global. The national is certainly not disappearing in the context of cultural tourism. In the international tourism market, dream destinations are still sold as countries: 'Amazing Thailand, dreams for all seasons', 'Croatia, the Mediterranean as it once was', 'Ireland, the island of memories', 'Colombia, the only risk is wanting to stay', 'The hidden charm: Vietnam', 'Live your myths in Greece', etc. Local guides are expected to play the role of unofficial ambassadors of national ideologies, even if countries like Indonesia have little means to enforce and control this. Something tourism scholars should pay increasing attention to is the growing power of regional blocs and associations over national as well as global processes. The increasingly important role of the Association of Southeast Asian Nations (ASEAN) and the Asia-Pacific Economic Cooperation (APEC) in shaping Indonesia's tourism is an illustration of this. It remains to be seen whether regionalism indicates the erosion of individual states or if it is a way by which nation states may secure their future by pooling sovereignty and resources.

Understanding the Glocal Aspects of Tourism

Cultural tourism research can, and does, cover the gamut from global standards of hospitality to dyadic host–guest interactions. For those scholars wanting to conduct in-depth studies, glocal ethnography offers a valuable methodology. Glocal ethnographies draw attention to the multiplicity, specificity and mobility of the tourism structures, discourses and imaginaries that sustain real communities and ways of life. In the context of international tourism, such orientation recommends increased analytical attention to the role of brokers or mediators – guides, interpreters, travel agents, accommodation providers, government at all levels and international agencies – prominent in cultural tourism development.

As Yamashita (2003: 148) states, 'what cultural anthropology today should illuminate is the realm which lies between the global and the local'. In a similar vein, Tsing (2005) calls for ethnographies with greater humility, listening skills and attentiveness to local processes, with full analytical scrutiny of every complexity and connection. The potential of this methodology lies not in a reduction of complexity, not in the construction of models, but in what Geertz (1973) called 'thick description'. Ethnographies of cultural tourism only gain in significance when placed in larger geographic and historic frameworks, in complex macro-processes, since combining understanding at the level of experience with the abstractions of impersonal processes is bound to reveal hitherto invisible processes and contingencies. At the same time, we have to pay attention that ethnographies sensitive to translocal dynamics do not resort to potentially misleading assumptions of ethereal global forces.

Ideally, a holistic approach like the one glocal ethnography proposes takes into account the local-to-global nexus. This attention to various scales – spanning from the local, over the national and the regional, to the global – should not imply a trade-off between depth and time. Unfortunately, structural limitations frequently force ethnographers to work in less than ideal circumstances. There is no methodological reason why only one individual should carry out ethnographic research. Ethnography only gains in depth by being a joint enterprise and allowing multivocality. We live in a complex world and understanding it – let alone trying to change it for the better – is a challenging task. Our research should not be determined by theoretical frameworks and methodologies, but rather creatively tack back and forth between theory and method to find answers to pressing questions. All ethnographies of cultural tourism should be analytically glocal, paying attention to the circulation of people, objects or ideas as well as to the institutional and personal domains that standardize but also glocalize them.

As described above, my own experiments with glocal ethnography were not without challenges. While the methodology I propose might help making case studies of 'the local' more relevant by increasing our understanding of the local-to-global nexus, it is not a magical tool that automatically answers all questions. As with other methodologies, much depends on the personal qualities and qualifications of the ethnographer. Take the ethics of the current study, for instance. It is the responsibility of the researcher to resolve moral dilemmas encountered whilst in the field. The degree to which an ethnographer is accountable towards the people he or she is working with depends largely on the researcher's positionality and the context of the study. Under all circumstances, it is important to remain honest and humble and to ensure that the study does not harm or exploit those among whom the research is done. Ethnographers do not possess the truth; neither do the people under study. Ultimately, the receptiveness for multiple points of view gives ethnography a great advantage over other methodologies. Echoing Tsing (2005), I would like to call for cultural tourism ethnographies that are grounded (in the glocal), critical and analytical. Tourism scholars have a great opportunity to take the lead, thereby demystifying the common stereotype that all they are able to do is applied research.

Acknowledgements

This material is based on work supported by the National Science Foundation under Grant No. BCS-0514129 and additional funding from the School of Arts and Sciences, University of Pennsylvania (USA). The research in Indonesia was conducted under the auspices of the Indonesian Institute of Sciences (LIPI Research Permit No. 8093/SU/KS/2005) and kindly sponsored by Gadjah Mada University. An earlier version of this chapter was presented at the Asia Research Institute's Fifth Graduate Workshop on 'Questions of Methodology: Researching Tourism in Asia', National University of Singapore, 5–6 December 2006. The author is most grateful to his colleagues of the Tourism Studies Centre at Gadjah Mada University in Yogyakarta for their useful comments and support. My greatest debt is to the dozens of Indonesians who welcomed me into their homes and lives.

References

Adams, K.M. (2006) *Art as Politics: Re-crafting Identities, Tourism, and Power in Tana Toraja, Indonesia.* University of Hawai'i Press, Honolulu, Hawaii.

Alneng, V. (2002) The modern does not cater for natives: travel ethnography and the conventions of form. *Tourist Studies* 2, 119–142.

Appadurai, A. (1996) *Modernity at Large: Cultural Dimensions of Globalization.* University of Minnesota Press, Minneapolis, Minnesota.

Bernard, H.R. (2006*) Research Methods in Anthropology: Qualitative and Quantitative Approaches,* 4th edn. AltaMira, Lanham, Maryland.

Bras, K. (2000) *Image-building and Guiding on Lombok: the Social Construction of a Tourist Destination.* ATLAS, Arnhem, the Netherlands.

Bruner, E.M. (2005) *Culture on Tour: Ethnographies of Travel.* University of Chicago Press, Chicago, Illinois.

Burawoy, M. (ed.) (2000) *Global Ethnography: Forces, Connections, and Imaginations in a Postmodern World.* University of California Press, Berkeley, California.

Causey, A. (2003) *Hard Bargaining in Sumatra: Western Travelers and Toba Bataks in the Marketplace of Souvenirs.* University of Hawai'i Press, Honolulu, Hawaii.

Cawley, M., Gaffey, S. and Gillmor, D.A. (2002) Localization and global reach in rural tourism: Irish evidence. *Tourist Studies* 2, 63–86.

Chang, T.C., Milne, S., Fallon, D. and Pohlmann, C. (1996) Urban heritage tourism: the global–local nexus. *Annals of Tourism Research* 23, 284–305.

Cole, S. (2008) *Tourism, Culture and Development: Hopes, Dreams and Realities in East Indonesia.* Channel View Publications, Clevedon, UK.

Crick, M. (1994) *Resplendent Sites, Discordant Voices: Sri Lankans and International Tourism.* Harwood Academic Publishers, Langhorne, Pennsylvania.

Dahles, H. (2001) *Tourism, Heritage and National Culture in Java: Dilemmas of a Local Community.* Curzon Press, Richmond, UK.

Geertz, C. (1973) *The Interpretation of Cultures: Selected Essays.* Basic Books, New York.

Graburn, N.H.H. (2002) The ethnographic tourist. In: Dann, G.M.S. (ed.) *The Tourist as a Metaphor of the Social World.* CAB International, Wallingford, UK, pp. 19–39.

Gupta, A. and Ferguson, J. (eds) (1997) *Anthropological Locations: Boundaries and Grounds of a Field Science.* University of California Press, Berkeley, California.

Hage, G. (2005) A not so multi-sited ethnography of a not so imagined community. *Anthropological Theory* 5, 463–475.

Hannerz, U. (2003) Several sites in one. In: Eriksen, T.H. (ed.) *Globalisation: Studies in Anthropology.* Pluto Press, London, pp. 18–38.

Leite, N. and Graburn, N.H.H. (2009) Anthropological interventions in tourism studies. In: Jamal, T. and Robinson, M. (eds) *The Sage Handbook of Tourism Studies*. See, London, pp. 35–64.

Lévi-Strauss, C. (1955) *Tristes Tropiques*. Plon, Paris.

Marcus, G.E. (1998) *Ethnography through Thick and Thin*. Princeton University Press, Princeton, Massachusetts.

Merry, S.E. (2000) Crossing boundaries: methodological challenges for ethnography in the twenty-first century. *Political and Legal Anthropology Review* 23, 127–134.

Moon, O. (1989) *From Paddy Field to Ski Slope: the Revitalisation of Tradition in Japanese Village Life*. Manchester University Press, Manchester, UK.

Nash, D. (2000) Ethnographic windows on tourism. *Tourism Recreation Research* 25, 29–35.

Ness, S.A. (2003) *Where Asia Smiles: an Ethnography of Philippine Tourism*. University of Pennsylvania Press, Philadelphia, Pennsylvania.

Palmer, C. (2001) Ethnography: a research method in practice. *International Journal of Tourism Research* 3, 301–312.

Picard, M. (1996) *Bali: Cultural Tourism and Touristic Culture*. Archipelago Press, Singapore.

Robbins, J. and Bamford, S. (eds) (1997) Fieldwork revisited: changing contexts of ethnographic practice in the era of globalization. Theme issue, *Anthropology and Humanism* 22(1).

Robertson, R. (1995) Glocalization: time–space and homogeneity–heterogeneity. In: Featherstone, M., Lash, S. and Robertson, R. (eds) *Global Modernities*. Sage, London, pp. 25–44.

Salazar, N.B. (2005) Tourism and glocalization: 'local' tour guiding. *Annals of Tourism Research* 32, 628–646.

Salazar, N.B. (2006a) Earthquake disaster: an anthropologist's report from Yogyakarta, Indonesia. Available at: http://web.archive.org/web/*/http://www.museum.upenn.edu/new/research/blogs/earthquake_blog.shtml (accessed 1 March 2010).

Salazar, N.B. (2006b) Touristifying Tanzania: global discourse, local guides. *Annals of Tourism Research* 33, 833–852.

Salazar, N.B. (2007) Towards a global culture of heritage interpretation? Evidence from Indonesia and Tanzania. *Tourism Recreation Research* 32, 23–30.

Salazar, N.B. (2008) "Enough Stories!" Asian tourism redefining the role of Asian tour guides. *Civilisations* 57, 207–222.

Smith, V.L. and Brent, M.A. (eds) (2001) *Hosts and Guests Revisited: Tourism Issues of the 21st Century*. Cognizant Communication Corporation, New York.

Snow, D.A., Morrill, C. and Anderson, L. (2003) Elaborating analytic ethnography: linking fieldwork and theory. *Ethnography* 4, 181–200.

Teo, P. and Li, L.H. (2003) Global and local interactions in tourism. *Annals of Tourism Research* 30, 287–306.

Tsing, A.L. (2005) *Friction: an Ethnography of Global Connection*. Princeton University Press, Princeton, New Jersey.

Van Den Berghe, P.L. (1994) *The Quest for the Other: Ethnic tourism in San Cristóbal, Mexico*. University of Washington Press, Seattle, Washington.

Wallace, T. (ed.) (2005) Tourism and applied anthropologists: linking theory and practice. Theme issue, *NAPA Bulletin* 23.

Wynn, L.L. (2007) *Pyramids and Nightclubs: a Travel Ethnography of Arab and Western Imaginations of Egypt*. University of Texas Press, Austin, Texas.

Yamashita, S. (2003) *Bali and Beyond: Explorations in the Anthropology of Tourism*. Berghahn Books, New York.

16 Assembling the Socio-material Destination: an Actor–Network Approach to Cultural Tourism Studies

Carina Ren

Here is a paradox. Tourism abounds with things, tourist things, and tourists are tied up in a world of tourist things for a considerable period of their time. And yet, if you read all the past and current textbooks on tourism ... you will discover that these things are not held to be very significant ... tourist things tend to be significant only in what they represent; as a meaningful set of signs and metaphors.

(Franklin, 2003: 97)

Introduction

To claim that tourism is full of things is hardly a startling statement – or a controversial one, for that matter. However, elements of tourism covered by the term 'things' are often seen as backdrops or accessories to what is conceived of as more relevant, strictly social matters of study within tourism research. Tourism materiality is seen as a tool, a product to be sold, a means to an(other) end: the development, marketing, branding, management or selling of products, sites and destinations. The socio-material approach propagated in this chapter challenges both the primary status of the social in the investigation of tourism and the clear separation between the social world and things 'surrounding it' (Haldrup and Larsen, 2006). The socio-material approach calls into question the notion of culture as an autonomous and pure category of study (Michael, 1996), as well as the prioritization of culture within cultural tourism studies. As an alternative, it is somewhat radically asserted here that the social cannot be empirically or analytically disentangled from the material (Law, 1999), but rather that it should be included on equal terms into the study of phenomena or notions which we claim to be social – such as tourism.

A socio-material perspective affects the way we study and analyse tourism as a phenomenon by describing how the material interacts with, shapes and works within and upon the social. In the following section it is proposed that integrating the material side of tourism in our interrogations and analysis provides us with a new perspective on how tourism is organized and performed. Starting from this claim, this chapter focuses on how to study the relations and workings of the socio-material aspects of tourism, which, it is argued, heavily contribute to its shaping. It is argued that artefacts, technologies, discourses, practices and spaces supplement or even defy 'traditional' fields of study (and explanatory constructs) such as culture, socio-economic structures or human agency. To support these claims, examples are provided from the Polish tourist destination of Zakopane. As a field method, socio-material descriptions of how the destination is organized and constructed go hand in hand with a methodology more sensitive to tourism materiality, together challenging how we perceive tourism and undertake its study.

In relation to cultural tourism research, the socio-material approach breaks down preconceptions of what culture – or other categories under investigation – is, does, consists of or how it is delimited when studied. Instead, a broad variety of components termed as 'non-social' or non-human' are included in what is mostly seen and described as purely cultural, in order to demonstrate the complexities of tourism.

Actor–Network Theory and Tourism

Before unfolding my argument for a socio-material tourism methodology, I will begin by briefly introducing the socio-material approach of actor–network theory. First devised by French anthropologist and philosopher Bruno Latour (Latour and Woolgar, 1979; Callon and Latour, 1981; Latour, 1981), this approach should – despite its denomination as a theory – be seen as a methodology, a tool offering a new understanding of and insight into the entangled relations between things and categories that are often treated as separate: subject and object, nature and culture, materiality and sociality, humans and non-humans (Law, 1999). Applying an actor–network approach to the field of 'cultural tourism' as such becomes a rather messy research undertaking, in which a variety of social and natural entities are constantly intermingled (Callon, 1986). As a consequence, tourism phenomena and places emerge as heterogeneous networks or tourismscapes (van der Duim, 2007) mediating between the synchronic locality and globality in emphasizing their embeddedness in both.

By applying a principle of so-called general symmetry between heterogeneous entities, an analytical levelling is set in place by the 'bracketing of common-sense categorization of the entities under investigation' (Jensen, 2003: 226). This first, important step of symmetry evens out established dualities with which we as social and cultural researchers usually orientate ourselves. A socio-material approach focuses on both the social and material character of reality and on the relational character of their association. It demonstrates the social–constructive aspects of the world at the same time as stressing its physicality. The social and the material entangle and affect each other in a constant and not clearly distinguishable process of mutual creation (Law, 1999). In this relational perspective, separating the social and material parts, both in the collecting process and in the analysis, is pointless (Emirbayer, 1999).

Instead of offering new dualities with which to operate, actor–network theory provides us with a relational approach to our field of study in seeing 'stable sets of relations and associations as the means by which the world is both built and stratified' (Murdoch, 1998: 359). The relations between a variety of materials take place within networks in which these materials help frame social interaction by making it possible and durable (Callon and Latour, 1981). Hence, in both an ontological and analytical sense, the social is not separable from the material in human society. In that respect, the actor–network approach is an attempt to bypass the ongoing debate of realism versus constructivism by focusing on the relational effects of concepts – not on whether they might be constructed or not (Law, 1992; Murdoch, 1997; Jóhannesson, 2005). In actor–network theory, sociological dichotomies such as nature/culture, agency/structure or social/material are seen and analysed as effects or outcomes of the relations in which they stand or are put – not as a natural underlying basis of our analysis.

A central aim in actor–network theory is to unwrap the 'black boxes' of cultural and social matters by showing how these were created by the complex and intricate linking and ordering of heterogeneous entities (Latour, 1999). This ordering takes place as 'Foucauldian mini-discourses' (Law, 2001), through which certain ideas and practices are processed and integrated (van der Duim, 2007). The actor–network approach also elucidates how relational-gone-solid categories or entities are stabilized and become durable (or are questioned and vanish/transform) through their performance 'in, by and through those relations' (Law, 1999: 4).

The elucidation and description of modes and processes of ordering, as well as the tracing of which 'links hold and which fall apart' (Murdoch, 1998: 367), constitute objects of study for the actor–network researcher. Only in tracing ongoing processes of ordering and assembling are we able to determine how things came to be in a successful and seemingly natural way. As a consequence, tourism phenomena must not be taken for granted as natural starting points for the investigation. Neither may empirical or analytical importance or precedence of certain categories, phenomena, people or actions be established or assumed prior to the examination. Instead, the researcher's job is to 'trace and describe the network (relational practices) underlying these effects or categories' (Jóhannesson, 2005: 139). As we must not assume some categories as relevant prior to the investigation, neither must we exclude others in advance, as 'we can not know or establish beforehand what actors are significant or most important in certain networks' (Jóhannesson, 2005).

If someone or something acts within a network in some way, it must be part of the description. However, we must also seek to address the questions of why some things, groups, people or other entities have come to define, sell, illustrate, talk on behalf of or otherwise represent the tourism product or place instead of others. This may be done by 'describing the way in which actors are defined, associated and simultaneously obliged to remain faithful to their alliances' (Callon, 1986: 19). The actor–network approach not only provides 'a symmetrical and tolerant description of a complex process which constantly mixes together a variety of social and natural entities. It also permits an explanation of how a few obtain the right to express and to represent the many silent actors of the social and natural worlds they have mobilized' (Callon, 1986).

The socio-material direction of investigation entails a sensibility towards radically new actors, detectable through their effects, modes of ordering and workings within heterogeneous networks of tourism: 'Material resources, objects, spaces and technologies are much more than simply the outcrops of human intention and action. They also structure, define and configure interaction' (van der Duim, 2007: 151). These actor–networks are characterized by their heterogeneity and capacity of constant relational transformation between the entities of which they are comprised. Latour (1999: 15) stresses how the actor–network is a connection and mutual transformation/translation of actors and not, as often (mis)understood, 'an instantaneous, unmediated access to every piece of information'. In the actor–network, material entities have the capacity to act just as well as humans. The actor–networks relational and transformative capacity may hence be seen as a tool to overcome the agency/structure contradiction (Latour, 1999), as 'the actor–network is reducible neither to an actor alone nor to a network' (van der Duim, 2007: 150). The power to act, to create an effect, is derived from the capability to work upon our surroundings, not from being human. Action is accorded through the actors' possibility to affect and perform upon and within the network. The actor–network is characterized and necessitated by its constant activity: 'Networks require a "performance" on the part of all enrolled elements' (Murdoch, 1998: 366). If there is no performance, there is no network effect. Entities are no longer actors, no longer enrolled in the network. The network changes or even ceases to work – and hence to exist. In the relation between a given tourism network and actor, performance takes part in enabling composites of the network, at the same time as network agents make tourism spaces 'performable' (Haldrup and Larsen, 2006). The actor–networks are constantly produced, constructed and negotiated through the networking and seamless intertwining of their actors, uncovering the entangled and relational character of categories otherwise conceived as pure (Barnes, 2005). The actors' inclusion in the network is not based on a certain ontological status (such as being human), on strength and mobility or intentionality acting, but rather on the capacity and capability of linking, associating and ordering within the network. Still, as noted above, the researcher must strive not only to describe what is linked, ordered and associated in the network assemblage but also what is not.

In an actor–network perspective, order exists not in spite of, but partly because of, the non-human materiality and technologies (Callon and Latour, 1981). The 'ordering of order' takes place within the networks and is established through processes of translation, referring to 'the work through which actors modify, displace, and translate their various and contradictory interest' (Latour, 1999: 311). It is a process of 'negotiation, mobilization, representation, and displacement among actors, entities, and places' (van der Duim, 2007: 966), potentially leading to the (at least temporary) stabilizing of the meaning, socio-material expression and working of the network.

Tourism networks such as the tourism destination or other (at least permanently) stable 'black boxes' are ordered and acted upon by a broad range of actors as holiday offers pop up on the computer screen, as planes land, as receptionists greet, as keys open and lock hotel doors, as sandy beaches are flooded and as local foods are consumed and digested along with experiences and impressions. In including objects and technologies as an active part in creating and mediating tourism places and experiences, actor–network theory transcends the traditional social and analytical division between the individual and the collective, humans and non-humans, action and structure, micro and macro (Callon and Latour, 1981). Although this reveals a more chaotic and messy picture of the field of tourism, it also discloses a complex, embodied materiality (Ren, 2009).

A Socio-material Tourism Methodology

According to Sandra Harding, 'a research methodology is a theory and analysis of how research does and should proceed' (1987: 2–3). Related to a research undertaking, it helps to frame the questions, determine the methods deployed and shape the analysis (Belsky, 2004). It will be demonstrated in the following sections how a socio-material approach also alters our methodological focus within research, centring on how we may investigate, interrogate and make sense of the actor–networks of tourism spaces.

As opposed to more familiar cultural methodologies, socio-material methodology does not seek to uncover life-worlds and interpret meaning (hermeneutics) or reach an understanding of the informant through interaction and dialogue (phenomenology). In applying an actor–network approach, the researcher provides descriptions of the heterogeneity of tourism through the interweaving of multiple levels, narratives, characters and discourses into a single text (Haraway, 1989). The actor–network approach hence entails seeing and describing our object of study in a whole new way. Tourism phenomena or categories in question are not perceived as a priori givens to be analysed, counted, related or described as stable, static and dualistic (Jóhannesson, 2005). The destination, the travel package and products, tourism innovations, local culture, host–guest conflict or authenticity are instead regarded as effects of processes of ordering – and as having effects and generating ordering in themselves.

Tracing the heterogeneous networks of tourism displays and emphasizes the various ways in which materiality connects to tourism practices and performances, also challenging how we envision and study the spaces and places of tourism. Through its relational approach, actor–network theory overthrows the Euclidean notion of space as fixed and absolute while at the same time rejecting 'the Kantian conception of space as a "container" for human activities' (Murdoch 1998: 358). It challenges the status of tourism space as a demarcated recreational area and as a territorially bounded place (Jóhannes-son, 2005). Instead, tourism spaces emerge as ordered and hierarchical socio-material relations (Ek, 2006), mediating between the synchronic locality and globality of tourism, emphasizing its embeddedness in both. Concepts such as 'local' and 'global' become effects of the network, rather than preconceived social or geographic categories (see also Chapter 15). Distance becomes something to be evaluated through its network relatedness and connectivity, not something to be measured in absolute units. Places continuously become – not are – 'about relationships, about the placing of peoples, materials, images and the systems of difference and similarity that they perform' (Haldrup and Larsen, 2006: 282).

Actor–network-inspired methodology therefore explores the orderings, assemblages and workings of tourism by describing 'the steps in a process (which may collapse) whereby agents align the interests and functions of other agents together in a chain' (Fox, 2000: 861). Emphasis is put on processes rather than results, on entities-becoming-actors rather than fixed social categories.

From Socio-material Methodology to Methods

Again referring to Harding, methods are defined as a 'technique for (or way of proceeding in) gathering evidence' (1987: 2–3). As both instrument and strategy, our methods provide us with the possibility to collect data based on and informed by our methodology. In the actor–network approach, importance is placed on the close descriptions of the networks in which actors are aligned, assemblages take place and places emerge. For this purpose, close ethnographic descriptions of local actors and processes are needed.

The informants

Actor–network theory sees natural objects are being 'afforded' with the possibility to act. Owing to this and to the symmetrical perspective on the field of study employed in actor–network-inspired investigations, the researcher has the opportunity to use unorthodox informants and collect very diverse data material. Documents, physical structures, food products, clothes, discourses and nature, as well as people, all become informants in tracing the network. Not only discourse and text but also materiality, physicality and practices become informants. By focusing on the integrating connections of these informants it is possible to detect a network of interacting actors.

Field of study/field of knowledge

Delimiting the field of study constitutes a challenge in actor–network theory. According to Latham (2002), the meaning of places is constructed by actors and discourses both local and distant (cited in van der Duim, 2007: 969). This means that the content, or rather the workings of the investigated network, is not to be found in a fixed geographical spot – such as the destination – as a set of structures or a delimited unit, but is to be traced through a network, whose shape, importance and workings are not known or to be taken for granted in advance of its investigation. A one-on-one relationship between the field of study and the destination region as physical entity cannot be asserted. Instead, a multi-sited approach to fieldwork must be applied, as advocated by anthropologist George E. Marcus (1998). In his words, 'strategies of quite literally following connections, associations, and putative relationships are thus at the very heart of designing multi-sited ethnographic research' (Marcus, 1998: 81). Instead of demarcating the field prior to its description, feedback from the field must guide and point on to the following places, objects, practices or discourses suited for further description. In that way, cultural complexity reveals itself in the making and is not shaped or restricted beforehand to fit research designs drawn up at the research desk. A highly practical matter for the researcher is the fact that the network has no beginning or end. The relational approach to our field of study must urge the researcher to reflect upon how a given field of study is conceptualized, delimited and studied, also taking into account that all actors are multiple and that both actors and networks may be described from infinite angles. Although very obvious within the actor–network approach, this multiplicity of ways of description is also the case with most constructivist and interpretive endeavours.

Actor–network theory sees knowledge as created through and in the research process. Knowledge is entangled and not distinguishable from our research practices. When studying the network, we work on and perform within it; we become part of it and it becomes part of us. Hence, a discussion of the use and application of methods within actor–network theory becomes a discussion of ontology and of knowledge creation (Law, 2004; Ren *et al.*, 2010). Knowledge is accessible to us not because we as researchers adopt a privileged or external position in relation to our material, but rather because knowledge is seen as something we produce through and within the very processes we try to describe through our research by our relational interaction with this research itself. All knowledge is situated (Haraway, 1988). In that sense, special attention must be accorded to the methodology and methods applied to the field of research, since these tools are seen as performative, as they work to create knowledge about and in relation to the object under study (Law, 2004).

The Destination Network: a Socio-material Assemblage

In this section, I shall try to unfold the actor–network perspective through the description of the destination as a network in which objects, discourses, nature, architecture, culture and people are enrolled and producing effects and taking meaning. As an example of how a non-human object is to be seen as an actor within a tourism network, in this case as an active part of the

tourism destination, I shall try to follow the local regional oscypek cheese, demonstrating how during my fieldwork in the winter and summer of 2007 it was involved in a number of network alliances over time and space, constantly taking on new meaning and different 'hybrid' identities (Haraway, 1988). Far from being a traditional way to undertake research on how a destination is communicated, such as interviewing tourism stakeholders or carrying out discourse or semiotic analysis of tourism brochures, the tracing of oscypek networks helped to illustrate that discourses of culture, development and 'proper' tourism products were traceable when following this cheese.

Zakopane

Zakopane, a Polish town of 30,000 inhabitants, is a year-round destination, receiving approximately three million overnight visitors a year. The overall Polish clientele is supplemented by a growing number of Western tourists, currently making up 15% of the overall visitors. After the breakdown of socialism, and as a consequence of later European integration, the nature of Polish tourism has changed profoundly in terms of scale and compostition (Hall *et al.*, 2006). In the light of these relatively recent and ongoing changes, my aim was to investigate how the destination of Zakopane, a centennial tourist destination, was being represented by tourism actors: could ideas of change, transition, new cultural divides or social change be detected in the way the destination was constructed and represented in various and possibly conflicting processes of tourism communication?

In an actor–network investigation, tourism actors are not restricted to human actors. Neither is the destination a physically bound entity, such as the first sentences of this paragraph suggested in its initial quantitative definition of Zakopane. The destination in my research was rather seen as a network, constructed both discursively (for instance in tourism marketing) and socio-materially, based on a number of practices tying and relating the city, its local inhabitants, the tourism planners and staff, the tourists and the physical environment and material culture. This tracking of discourses and practices ended up absorbing entities that would otherwise be considered as distant or irrelevant to the description of Zakopane as a tourism destination.

Oscypek

One of these 'irrelevant' entities was the oscypek, a local, salted and smoked sheep cheese in the shape of a hand grenade, traditionally manufactured in the nearby Tatra Mountains and often sold from special cheese stands to the large numbers of tourists passing by the popular main shopping street of Krupówki. This cheese was in no way part of my original investigation of how the destination was communicated. However, tracing the ways the oscypek was ordered and connected into different networks, while simultaneously taking on different hybrid identities, serves as a good example to illustrate how a multiplicity of entities are used to create the destination and how the ordering of these entities works.

The oscypek cheese is highly visible to tourists in Zakopane, as a large number of cheese stands line the pedestrian main street of Zakopane and take up a good proportion of the stands on the local market. Here, mostly elderly women, but also younger women and the occasional male, offer different locally produced cheeses, among which the oscypek is the most prominent and well known. For Poles, a visit to Zakopane necessarily includes the purchase of oscypek for family and friends back home. In observations of local daily practices connected to the production and selling of oscypek in Zakopane, the cheese was enrolled into discourses of authenticity and hygiene ('Was the cheese really smoked or just dipped in tea to obtain its dark colour?', 'Could oscypek sold in winter be genuine in spite of the fact that sheep did not give milk at that time?', 'Was it safe to eat directly from the stand in summer?'), to places (the main street, mountain pastures, cheese-smoking huts, the highway under reconstruction, places outside Zakopane in which oscypek was rare), to documents (papers and emblems permitting sale and authenticating the place of origin of the cheese), to objects (cheese carts, lorries to transport carts and cheeses, cheese moulds, smoke – or tea!) and to people (the stand owners, the vendors, the shepherds, Polish and foreign tourists and locals). In this context, the oscypek was ordered and worked to connect certain localities (Zakopane, Tatra Mountain pastures, main street) and practices (shepherding, cheese fabrication, vending) to cultural tourism (local and regional food, host–guest interaction, product purchase). In a descriptive tracing of the cheese, it seemed to work as an agent and conveyor of traditional work practices and products in tourism communication, hence shaping the destination network as one of tradition and locality.

At the time of my arrival in January 2007, the oscypek was at the centre of special local attention for yet another reason, as it was, at the time, a contestant in the race to be included on the exclusive list of regional EU products. This was discussed in a number of articles in local, regional and even national newspapers and magazines and on the Internet. The entry of oscypek on this list was obviously a controversial matter. As written on the web page of the Polish British council under a section entitled 'Heritage', oscypek had for centuries 'been produced locally by mountaineers in fairly primitive conditions and sold in stalls and open-air markets' (http://elt.britishcouncil.org.pl/elt/r_oscypek.htm). Now, however, the cheese and its fabrication were being threatened by outside demands: 'The way oscypek is made today is a long way from the demands of Brussels. If Poland is to join the Union and if oscypek is to be offered for sale, its production process must change.' (http://elt.britishcouncil.org.pl/elt/r_oscypek.htm). A number of requirements were to be met in order to secure the approval of the EU, and this, it was claimed, put the cheese in danger of extinction, or at least threatened its authentic way of production.

In one of the many 'cheese' discourses, oscypek producers were ordered to work for an EU-friendly development and towards regional branding. This is illustrated by a statement by a European agriculture spokesperson:

> We think that it's very important that European farmers and retailers can really make use of the advantages that Europe has. We live in a globalized society where there are a lot of cheap food producers around the world that are providing a lot of competition for all people and if you've got this quality logo you can really use it as a marketing and branding tool to improve your sales and to prove to your consumers that this is a really high quality and unique product.
> (http://www.polskieradio.pl/zagranica/ news/artykul75905.html)

In this network ordering, oscypek is connected to a global society and market, to branding and to marketing, to unique products and high-quality brands.

By following the actor, in this case the local cheese, and its workings outside of its immediate and apparent 'local' field of operation on the main street, at a global level we can link the cheese to policies, to electronic and print debates, to EU circular letters and to discourses of traditional versus modern cheese manufacturing, branding and hygiene. Oscypek is enrolled into a range of modes of ordering, such as 'arrangements that recursively perform themselves through different materials – speech, subjectivities, organizations, technical artefacts' (Law, 2000: 23) and which 'run through and perform material relations, arrangements with a pattern and their own logic' (Law, 2000). Related to a number of discourses and arrangements and other entities, oscypek becomes – among other things – an agent working within a network propagating a European market and regional branding strategy through quality assurance involving laboratory testing, implementing procedures, wrapping in plastic, refrigeration and national or international distribution. The agency of the oscypek in this network is a strong contrast to a 'purely cultural' description of the cheese in a 'local' context.

This network description demonstrates how a variety of human and non-human actors act and work upon the constant production and reproduction of the destination network. It demonstrates the complexity of tourism places and their intricate linking with a long row of events, phenomena, actors and objects. Seeing the cheese as an actor in the destination network may work as a way to unfold both entities in their heterogeneity and challenge our conceptions of how we may approach them as research objects. In this example, the cheese acts as a connection between entities that would otherwise be conceived as belonging to separate spheres or categories of analysis: Poland, the European Union, hygiene, tourism, local foodstuff, shepherding, laboratory testing, branding, authenticity, development, etc. Not only is the cheese transformed in this continuous linking – the destination also continuously transforms as it is connected to new entities. Through relations to socio-material actors such as the cheese, the destination as network is constantly enabled to construct, assemble and ultimately stabilize (at least temporarily) tourism categories and phenomena.

Conclusion – Implications of a Socio-material Approach

What is striking – and admittedly a little frightening – about the actor–network is its rich material texture. The ontology of the actor–network theory is populated by a multiplicity of people, objects, materiality and technologies. In this chapter, the reader was invited to explore this rich material texture of tourism through the application of actor–network theory. This approach introduced a new methodology with which to research and describe tourism entities through a symmetric levelling of the social and material, human and non-human, natural and cultural, hence including matters typically excluded from the social or cultural field of research. Through its application, actor–network methodology transforms the space encompassing our study.

This was the case with the destination, which was no longer perceived of as a physically bound entity of study or as a strictly tourism-induced construct. Instead it emerged as a stabilized network of heterogeneous actors created through the active involvement of many, often unacknowledged, actors in their various performances on and of place. The application of an actor–network approach also altered the perspective with which we would normally approach and analyse our object, seen in the example of the oscypek cheese. Through the tracing of its network, the cheese simultaneously acted as an agent in the promotion of cultural tourism in Zakopane, afforded traditional work practices such as shepherding and cheese production (as opposed to employment in tourism) and performed as an agent for regional development through strategic branding on the European stage.

The description and tracing of these (in cultural terms) contradictory work relations make it possible to envision – and to know – the destination and its network constructors in their heterogeneity or multiplicity (Law, 2000). The close descriptive and process-oriented methodology exposes contingencies (Michael, 1996) and deconstructs taken-for-granted categories of analysis, demonstrating the complexity and entanglement of tourism places, events, phenomena, actors and objects. This offers a fuller understanding of how destinations are constantly assembled in concrete practices and performances involving human and non-human actors. A relational and materially sensitive understanding of tourism potentially provides us with richer, broader and more inclusive notions of destination cultures, not only in research but also in the communication and promotion of destinations. In relation to the marketing of tourism, the heterogeneity of the destination assemblage and of the actors participating herein challenges the common brand management strategy of 'image mainstreaming', often seeking to create and promote one 'unique' selling point (Ren and Blichfeldt, unpublished results). By applying the actor–network theory, a variety of actors emerge as part of the destination construct, showing that tourism is neither 'pure' in its categorizations nor truly controllable in its planning and coordination.

References

Barnes, T. (2005) Culture: economy. In: Cloke, P. and Johnston, R. (eds) *Spaces of Geographical Thought*. Sage, London, pp. 61–80.

Belsky, J. (2004) Contributions of qualitative research to understanding the politics of community ecotourism. In: Phillimore, J. and Goodson, L. (eds) *Qualitative Research in Tourism: Ontologies, Epistemologies and Methodologies*. Routledge, London, pp. 273–291.

Callon, M. (1986) Some elements of a sociology of translation: domestication of the scallops and the fishermen of St Brieuc Bay. In: Law, J. (ed.) *Power, Action and Belief: a New Sociology of Knowledge?* Routledge, London, pp. 196–223.

Callon, M. and Latour, B. (1981) Unscrewing the big Leviathan. In: Knorr-Certina, K.D. and Mulay, M. (eds) *Advances in Social Theory and Methodology*. Routledge and Kegan Paul, London, pp. 275–303.

Ek, R. (2006) Media studies, geographical imaginations and relational space. In: Falkheimer, J. and Jansson, A. (eds) *Geographies of Communication: the Spatial Turn in Media Studies*. Nordicom, Gothenburg, Sweden, pp. 45–66.

Emirbayer, M. (1999) Manifesto for a relational sociology. *The American Journal of Sociology* 103, 281–317.

Fox, S. (2000) Communities of practice, Foucault and ANT. *Journal of Management Studies* 37, 853–868.

Franklin, A. (2003) *Tourism: an Introduction*. Sage, London

Haldrup, M. and Larsen, J. (2006) Material cultures of tourism. *Leisure Studies* 25, 275–289.

Hall, D., Smith, M. and Marciszewska, B. (2006) *Tourism in the New Europe: the New Challenges and Opportunities of EU Enlargement*. CAB International, Wallingford, UK.

Haraway, D. (1988) Situated knowledges: the science question in feminism and the privilege of partial perspective. *Feminist Studies* 14(3) 575–599.

Haraway, D. (1989) *Primate Visions*. Routledge, New York.

Harding, S. (1987) *Feminism and Methodology*. Indiana University, Bloomington, Indiana.

Jensen, C.B. (2003) Latour and Pickering: posthuman perspectives on science, becoming and normativity. In: Ihde, D. and Selinger, E. (eds) *Chasing Technoscience: Matrix for Materiality*. University of Indiana Press, Indianapolis, Indiana, pp. 225–241.

Jóhannesson, G.T. (2005) Tourism translations. Actor–network theory and tourism research. *Tourist Studies* 5(2), 133–150.

Latham, A. (2002) Retheorizing the scale of globalization: topologies, actor–networks, and cosmopolitism. In: Herod, A. and Wright, M. (eds) *Geographies of Power: Placing Scale*. Blackwell, Oxford, UK, pp. 115–144.

Latour, B. (1981) Insiders and outsiders in the sociology of science: or, how can we foster agnosticism? *Knowledge and Society* 3, 199–216.

Latour, B. (1999) On recalling ANT. In: Law, J. and Hassard, J. (eds) *ActorNetwork Theory and After*. Blackwell, Oxford, UK, pp. 15–25.

Latour, B. and Woolgar, S. (1979) *Laboratory Life: the Social Construction of Scientific Facts*. Sage, London.

Law, J. (1992) *Notes on the Theory of the Actor Network: Ordering, Strategy and Heterogeneity*. Available at: http://www.comp.lancs.ac.uk/sociology/ soc054jl.html.

Law, J. (1999) After ANT: complexity, naming and topology. In: Law, J. and Hassard, J. (eds) *Actor Network Theory and After*. Blackwell, Oxford, UK, pp. 1–14.

Law, J. (2000) On the subject of the object: narrative, technology, and interpellation. *Configurations* 8, 1–29.

Law, J. (2001) *Ordering and Obdurancy*. Online paper published by the Centre for Science Studies, Lancaster University, UK. http://www.lancs.ac.uk/fass/sociology/papers/law-ordering-and-obduracy.pdf (accessed 5 January 2009).

Law, J. (2004) *After Method. Mess in Social Science Research*. Routledge, London.

Marcus, G.E. (1998) *Ethnography in/of the World System. The Emergence of Multi-sited Ethnography*. Princeton University Press, Princeton, New Jersey.

Michael, M. (1996) *Constructing Identities*. Sage Publications, London.

Murdoch, J. (1997) Inhuman/nonhuman/human:actor–network theory and the prospects for a nondualistic and symmetrical perspective on nature and society. *Environment and Planning D: Society and Space* 15(4), 731–756.

Murdoch, J. (1998) The spaces of actor–network theory. *Geoforum* 29, 357–374.

Ren, C. (2009) *Constructing the socio-material destination*. Unpublished PhD thesis, University of Southern Denmark.

Ren, C., Pritchard, A. and Morgan, N. (2010) Constructing tourism research: a critical enquiry. *Annals of Tourism Research* (in press)

van der Duim, R. (2007) Tourismscapes. An actor–network perspective. *Annals of Tourism Research* 34, 961–976.

17 Methods in Cultural Tourism Research: the State of the Art

Wil Munsters and Greg Richards

Introduction

This final chapter presents an analytical review of major trends in cultural tourism research methodology as illustrated by the contributions to this volume. It appears that the methodological scope of cultural tourism is increasing, embracing new approaches and techniques in order to analyse the growing complexity of cultural tourism consumption, production and 'co-creation'. In particular, the chapters of the current volume demonstrate the expansion of qualitative approaches in cultural tourism research as one of the major developments in recent years. At the same time they also underline the need for further development in terms of methodological sophistication.

Towards an Interpretative Research Paradigm and Methodological Eclecticism

The epistemological context: from positivism to hermeneutics

When situating methodological innovation in cultural tourism studies in a broader, epistemological framework, it becomes obvious that renewal has been sought in leaving the dominating positivist paradigm, which takes the natural sciences as a model, and exchanging this for contrasting research paradigms founded on phenomenology and hermeneutics. As Melkert and Vos (Chapter 3) and Rakić (Chapter 11) observe, it is the theoretical research paradigm that determines the research methodology: quantitative for the positivist research paradigm versus qualitative for the non-positivist research paradigm.

Within the positivist research paradigm, the study of reality is based on the measurement and causal explanation of objective 'facts' by means of quantitative methodology. Large amounts of data are analysed with the help of diverse statistical techniques testing the representativeness, validity and reliability of the results. The outcomes of the statistical analysis are usually extrapolated to a larger reality or population. If, after verification, the research hypotheses are accepted, these are used by deduction as stepping stones for general statements.

However, many social scientists, such as Pereiro (Chapter 14), argue that social actions and relationships, because they are driven and inspired by motivations, attitudes, beliefs, values, meanings and emotions, cannot be understood in terms of cause and effect or be reduced to universal quantitative laws. This observation has led to a paradigm shift in social studies. The emerging paradigm is characterized by a change of orientation, focusing on the interpretation of the different meanings of social phenomena and cultural behaviours and leading to a deeper understanding of these multiple socio-cultural relationships and processes in the particular and individual context in which they occur (see Fox *et al.*, Chapter 7). Quantitative methodology is not deemed appropriate for this exploration of the subject matter; arguably only qualitative methods can provide the necessary instruments. Induction on the basis of a small number of detailed observations helps to develop new general insights. Within this paradigm, small-scale research is considered as 'beautiful' (Tsartas, 2006).

The qualitative paradigm arguably offers a richer palette of methods than the quantitative approach as far as the analysis of social reality and tourist behaviour is concerned. Indeed, the quantitative methods applied in cultural tourism in this volume are relatively limited in number. The main tool is survey research by means of structured (or standardized) questionnaire–interviews with respondents, the data analysis being carried out with the help of computer-based descriptive and inferential statistics. The ATLAS Cultural Tourism Research Project rests on this research method (see Richards, Chapter 2 and Munsters, Chapter 5). Such methods have advantages in terms of comparability of research results and the possibility of subjecting the data to statistical testing, which evidently aids generalization. There are only a few signs of innovation in quantitative methods in the current volume, such as the use of global positioning systems (GPS) to track tourist movements or the geotagging of tourists' photographs to their trails (see Edwards *et al.*, Chapter 9). The main directions of innovation therefore appear to lie in the combination of qualitative and quantitative methods (see Part II) or in the application of purely qualitative techniques (see Part III).

Positivist dogmatism versus postmodern eclecticism

In contrast to the dogmatic attitude often adopted by proponents of the quantitative approach, claiming that this is the only 'scientific' one, the contributors to Part II of this volume attempt to eliminate the artificial barriers between the quantitative and the qualitative approaches and to interrelate them by using mixed methods. For example, Fox *et al.* conceive their study project on garden visiting as a quantitative survey complemented by qualitative interviews (Chapter 7). The combination of quantitative and qualitative approaches is inspired by the idea of creating a fuller understanding and profounder knowledge of the cultural tourism phenomenon, with each approach adding specific insights into the subject matter. Instead of speaking of opposite approaches, it is far more fruitful to consider them as complementary (see Melkert and Vos, Chapter 3, and Pereiro, Chapter 14) or, in other words, instead of cultivating the antithesis quantitative versus qualitative, methodologists should strive for a synthesis: quantitative plus qualitative. So Castellanos-Verdugo *et al.* (Chapter 10) combine induction with deduction when they argue that grounded theory, inductive in essence, can lead to generalizable theoretical explanations as a starting point for new research hypotheses.

Trade-offs and triangulation

Once the researcher has accepted that no sacrosanct approaches exist, he/she can begin to weigh up the particular strengths and weaknesses of each methodology. In the end, only the quality of the research result counts, so an open and critical mind should be developed and maintained in order to minimize the weaknesses of each method, to maximize their strengths and to develop synergies between different methods. The search for synergies involves methodological trade-offs, i.e. compensating for the weakness of one method through the strengths of another and vice versa (see Melkert and Vos, Chapter 3). For example, a major weak point imputed to the qualitative approach is the risk of subjectivity and of researcher bias, which render it difficult to meet the standard research requirements of validity and reliability (see Melkert and Vos, Chapter 3). Since mathematical quantification, as Pereiro argues in Chapter 14, is often impossible while interpreting social reality, other objectification tools have to be employed in order to guarantee the scientific control of the research process and results. Therefore Fox *et al.* (Chapter 7) and Castellanos-Verdugo *et al.* (Chapter 10) propagate the use of software packages with a view to making the data analysis more systematic, transparent and valid. In order to augment the validity of the research and to avoid the pitfall of subjective interpretation of reality by the researcher, Castellanos-Verdugo *et al.* (Chapter 10) also recommend triangulation techniques. The basic type of triangulation is methodological triangulation, implying the use of more than two data collection methods with the purpose of checking whether the results from one method are consistent with the findings of the other methods. For example, the cultural destination audit described by Munsters (Chapter 5) measures the tourist experience by combining three different but complementary methods of both a quantitative and a qualitative nature: personal surveys, mystery tourist visits and in-depth interviews. This methodological triangulation increases the validity as well as the reliability of the audit outcomes. The same multiple-methods approach has been adopted by Puczkó *et al.* for the analysis of visitor behaviour at the Hungarian Open Air Museum from different perspectives (Chapter 6). In order to complement, connect and validate the research data, they combine the use of quantitative instruments (visitor interview with standard questionnaire) with qualitative tools (visitor-employed photography and visitor-employed diary).

Triangulation is not necessarily limited to the combination of quantitative with qualitative methods; the approach can also imply the simultaneous application of three or more merely qualitative methods. Pereiro (Chapter 14) thus intersects three qualitative research strategies, of which the first two fall under field research and the third one under desk research:

- participant observation and audio-visual ethnography;
- oral interviews, debate groups and life history reports; and
- bibliographical and documentary research.

This triangulation of methods enables the researcher to understand in depth the relevant local–global relationships as well as the multi-vocal interpretations and meanings with regard to ethnic tourism among the Kuna.

In Chapter 10, Castelannos-Verdugo *et al.* show how methodological triangulation goes, by definition, hand-in-hand with data triangulation as a means of broadening the perspectives from which the phenomenon studied can be observed and understood. The field research on Santiponce by means of interview and observation techniques provided primary data, which were integrated and compared with the data from desk research based on secondary sources such as written (place reports, strategic and tourism plans, promotional brochures) and digital documents (web pages).

Another validity enhancer used by Castelannos-Verdugo *et al.* is investigator triangulation. This technique involves the participation of multiple researchers in an investigation, who have to play the role of 'devil's advocate'. In this case the whole process of examining residents' attitudes regarding tourism development in Santiponce was critically reviewed by a researcher from outside the team.

The objective justifies the methods

Thus it appears from the contributions to this volume that each approach is considered to be valuable in its own right and that different approaches can very well be integrated in studies of cultural tourism if the researcher is aware of the limitations of each method and of his/her own bias. As Veal (1992) argues, in the end methods are not intrinsically good or bad, but appropriate or inappropriate for the research question to be addressed. Pereiro (Chapter 14) takes the same practical and eclectic view by pleading for the combined use of quantitative and qualitative tools depending on the specificity and complexity of the research case under study. According to Puczkó *et al.* (Chapter 6) this approach implies that formulating the research questions (the what) should come first, the selection of the methods (the how) that fit the questions, second. The research object and the research objectives determine the adequacy of the research methods. Every method is good if it suits the research goal. This methodological relativism helps to find the way to a truth which, by definition, is partial and provisory, since it constantly evolves with the development of research problems and contexts. The question of *how* to research cannot therefore be seen in isolation from *what* is to be researched. Conversely, the *how*, the choice of methodology and method, will strongly determine what questions can be asked in order to analyse the data gathered and draw conclusions from the research outcomes. So the *what* and the *how* interact in a permanent process of cross-fertilization.

Interdisciplinary Sources of Methodological Renewal: Focus on Ethnography

Tourism is a multidisciplinary field of research resting on a number of scholarly pillars, including economics, geography, history, psychology, sociology and anthropology (see Melkert and Vos, Chapter 3). The methodology of tourism research is therefore highly determined by these different disciplinary roots. One of the major disciplines contributing at present to the methodological innovation of cultural tourism studies and to the focus on the qualitative approach is without doubt anthropology,

and specifically ethnography, as illustrated by the contributions to this volume by Fox *et al.* (Chapter 7), Rakić (Chapter 11), Pereiro (Chapter 14), Salazar (Chapter 15) and Ren (Chapter 16) (see also Graburn, 2002). An important reason for this lies in the expansion of anthropological research into tourism, prompted by the growing awareness by some anthropologists of the ambivalent roles of tourists and anthropologists. Anthropological methods have also been gladly grasped by tourism researchers keen to develop insights into the wider meanings of tourism and the relationship of tourism to different social groups. However, the ethnography practised by some tourism researchers does not have the disciplinary grounding of the anthropologist, nor usually the time-rich depth of *in-situ* data collection that usually accompanies it. As the contributions from Pereiro (Chapter 14) and Salazar (Chapter 15) both make clear, well-structured ethnographic research often requires years in the field. Although there are arguments to be made for the development of 'instant ethnography' as an antidote to the idea that human groups and cultures are fixed and unchanging phenomena, it is plain that the understanding generated by a quick dip into the local setting will be different from that gathered through a prolonged sojourn based on immersion in the indigenous community. In the same way that a cultural tourist who repeatedly visits the same destination in order to know better various facets of the local culture will have a broader experience than the casual day tripper, so the results of instant ethnography are likely to be different from more protracted methods of ethnographic description. However, there is little doubt that the pressure to generate and publish research results quickly will tend to lead researchers more and more in the direction of instant ethnographies. In some respect this approach to studying the socio-cultural reality mirrors the rather superficial cultural experience of the first-time tourist visitor, but the important question is whether it increases our understanding of the cultural tourists and their relationship and interaction with the local context.

Work in Progress

At first sight the degree of methodological innovation in tourism research in general, and cultural tourism research in particular, seems to be relatively low. The overall approach in the current volume remains relatively traditional, focusing largely on data collection by means of in-depth interviews and observation. However, if one goes beyond this general methodological level and considers the particular qualitative techniques applied to the cultural tourism case studies, one notes that, within the main categories of interviewing and observing, new methods have been introduced by borrowing from other disciplines. Examples are the laddering technique, which has its origins in marketing theory (see Willson and McIntosh, Chapter 12) and the mystery tourist, a tool invented within the field of service studies (see Munsters, Chapter 5). Another form of methodological renewal of the in-depth interview and participant observation is the use of audio-visual supports, for example by basing the interrogation of respondents on photos (see Willson and McIntosh, Chapter 12) and by recording of participant observation on video (see Rakić, Chapter 11). These kinds of audio-visual stimuli and records generate a wealth of additional data for exploring tourists' experiences. The innovation goes one step further when visual media are no longer used as supporting tools for researcher-conducted interviews and observations but are applied by the tourists themselves as subjects of research. This is the case of visitor-employed photography, which enables tourists to capture immediately their experiences (see Puczkó *et al.*, Chapter 6 and Edwards *et al.*, Chapter 9), and also of the collage technique applied as an instrument to analyse the image of a historic city among both visitors and locals (see González Fernández *et al.*, Chapter 13). By reducing the presence and the influence of the researcher, these subject-oriented methods contribute to enhancing the validity of the research outcomes.

The highest degree of innovation is attained in the case of new methods specifically conceived for and developed within the field of cultural tourism studies. These kinds of innovations are driven by the availability of sophisticated information and communication technology for data analysis. In combination with more quantitative approaches such as the use of GPS tracking, these methods allow detailed analysis and understanding of the tourist experience, as Edwards *et al.* show by applying the technique of geotagging (see Chapter 9). At present, much of this ICT technology is being used for the study of tourist behaviour by the researcher rather than harnessing the potential of more collaborative, co-creational approaches, described by Binkhorst *et al.* in Chapter 4. In principle, emerging developments such as Web 2.0 make it possible to generate much more interactional data about the way in which tourists perceive destinations, make travel choices, behave in and experience the destination. The problem then will be to shift towards the formulation of adequate, soluble research questions which can focus attention on issues of import within the gathering and analysis of the data cloud. Because of the dialectic relationship between the research question and the research method (the what and the how), the introduction of new methods and the framing of new research questions will often be a matter of trail and error. An iteration of research questions and the deployment of different techniques as practised by Edwards *et al.* (see Chapter 9) can lead to valuable new insights.

All contributions to this volume considered, most of them are characterized by a multi-method approach and can therefore be qualified as belonging to the stage of 'blurred genres' within Denzin and Lincoln's (2005) periodization of qualitative research (see Richards and Munsters, Chapter 1). Some chapters go beyond this phase and can be regarded as illustrations of post-experimental enquiry, such as the plea of Binkhorst *et al.* (Chapter 4) for the study of tourism experience networks and in particular the contributions clustered in Part IV. So Pereiro (Chapter 14) makes use of debate groups and life history as methods; Salazar (Chapter 15) shows how the application of glocal ethnography allows multivocality;

and Ren (Chapter 16) describes and explores the role objects can play as actors within the tourism destination network. Furthermore, answering the critics who blame the lack of paradigmatic foundations of tourism research (see Richards and Munsters, Chapter 1), many contributors to the current volume, including Melkert, Vos, Rakić, Willson, McIntosh, Pereiro and Salazar, transcend the level of practical application of methods and reach the stage of meta-reflection by placing their methodology within the framework of a research paradigm. All this justifies the final conclusion that the research experiences gathered in this book can help to point the way to further innovations of research methods in cultural tourism studies in future.

References

Denzin, N.K. and Lincoln, Y.S. (eds) (2005) *Handbook of Qualitative Research*, 3rd edn. Sage, London.

Graburn, N. (2002) The ethnographic tourist. In: Dann, G. (ed.) *The Tourist as a Metaphor of the Social World*. CAB International, Wallingford, UK, pp. 19–39.

Tsartas, P. (2006) Qualitative methodologies: in search of synergies and appropriate solutions. Keynote lecture at the *24th EuroChrie Congress In Search of Excellence for Tomorrow's Tourism, Travel and Hospitality*, Thessaloniki, Greece.

Veal, A.J. (1992) *Research Methods for Leisure and Tourism: a Practical Guide*. Longman, London.

Index